EU General Data Protection Regulation (GDPR)

An Implementation and Compliance Guide

Third edition

EU General Data Protection Regulation (GDPR)

An Implementation and Compliance Guide

Third edition

IT GOVERNANCE PRIVACY TEAM

IT Governance Publishing

IT Governance Publishing Ltd
Unit 3, Clive Court
Bartholomew's Walk
Cambridgeshire Business Park
Ely, Cambridgeshire
CB7 4EA
United Kingdom
www.itgovernancepublishing.co.uk

First published in the United Kingdom in 2016 by IT Governance Publishing:

ISBN 978-1-84928-835-4

Second edition published in the United Kingdom in 2017 by IT Governance Publishing:

ISBN: 978-1-84928-945-0

Third edition published in the United Kingdom in 2019 by IT Governance Publishing:

ISBN: 978-1-78778-191-7

ABOUT THE AUTHOR

IT Governance is a leading global provider of IT governance, risk management and compliance expertise, and we pride ourselves on our ability to deliver a broad range of integrated, high-quality solutions that meet the real-world needs of our international client base.

Our privacy team, led by Alan Calder, has substantial experience in privacy, data protection, compliance and information security. This practical experience, and our understanding of the background and drivers for the GDPR, as well as the input of our fast-growing team of consultants and trainers, are combined in this manual to provide the world's first guide to implementing the new data protection regulation.

CONTENTS

Contents

Contents

Contents

Contents

Contents

INTRODUCTION

Enforced from 25 May 2018, the European Union's General Data Protection Regulation (GDPR) requires all data controllers and processors that handle the personal information of EU residents to "implement appropriate technical and organisational measures [...] to ensure the ongoing confidentiality, integrity, availability and resilience of processing systems and services" or face fines of up to €20 million or 4% of annual global turnover – whichever is greater.

The GDPR is the latest step in the ongoing global recognition of the value and importance of personal information. Although the information economy has existed for some time, the real value of personal data has only become more recently evident. Cyber theft of personal data exposes people to significant personal risks. Big data analysis techniques enable organisations to track and predict individual behaviour, and can be deployed in automated decision-making. The combination of all these issues, together with the continuing advance of technology and concerns about the misuse of personal data by governments and corporations, has resulted in a new law passed by the EU to clarify the data rights of EU residents and to ensure an appropriate level of EU-wide protection for personal data.

The GDPR applies across all the Member States of the EU, but its reach is far wider: any organisation anywhere in the world that provides services into the EU that involve processing personal data will have to comply. This means that the GDPR is probably now the most significant data security law in the world. Although it builds on the work of the EU's Data Protection Directive (DPD), the US's HIPAA and various other data protection regimes, the GDPR can be regarded as a distillation and comprehensive update of the EU's goals in protecting the rights and freedoms of the people who live within it.

The purpose of the GDPR

The DPD was in place for 20 years and set a minimum standard for data protection law in EU Member States. Many states went significantly further in terms of legislating to protect personally identifiable information (PII), which made it increasingly difficult for EU residents to know how their rights were protected across the EU and for organisations to determine which set of laws they should comply with, particularly when trading across multiple Member States.

The European Commission therefore decided that a single, unified law would be a more effective way of achieving two key goals:

1. Protecting the rights, privacy and freedoms of natural persons in the EU.
2. Reducing barriers to business by facilitating the free movement of data throughout the EU.

In terms of EU legislation, a regulation is quite distinct from a directive, which is how data protection was previously handled under the DPD. While directives set minimum standards and then ask EU Member States to provide their own legislation to meet those standards, regulations exist as laws themselves, superseding any relevant laws passed by Member States.

Although Member States are allowed to apply directives in whatever way suits them, a regulation is applied consistently in all Member States. If there is room for local variations, it is specifically identified in the text of the Regulation. Regulations are, therefore, an effective mechanism for applying a consistent approach across 500 million people in 28 Member States – and often beyond.

Structure of the Regulation

Appendix 1 of this manual provides a breakdown of the overall structure of the Regulation. The Regulation itself can be downloaded, in all the official languages of the EU, at *https://eur-lex.europa.eu/legal-content/EN/TXT/?uri=celex%3A32016R0679*. There is also a pocket guide to the EU GDPR, available from IT Governance Publishing,[1] which gives an overview of the legislation.

The GDPR is divided into two broad sections, which is standard for EU directives and regulations. The first section comprises the recitals, which essentially provide context, direction and guidance so that the later explicit requirements can be better understood.

The second part of the Regulation comprises the articles. The articles set out the specific requirements with which those entities within the scope of the Regulation must comply. Not every article in the GDPR applies to every organisation – given that some articles are relevant only to the Commission, the European Data Protection Board (EDPB) or the

---

[1] *www.itgovernancepublishing.co.uk/product/eu-gdpr-a-pocket-guide-second-edition*.

supervisory authorities, it may actually be impossible for every article to apply to a single organisation. In many cases, only a few articles may be completely relevant.

In broad terms, Chapters VI, VII, X and XI of the GDPR talk primarily about the Commission and the supervisory authorities so, if you are using this manual to plan your GDPR compliance programme, you may not need to give extensive attention to those sections.

Impact on the EU

As an EU regulation, the GDPR operates above the level of other Member State laws. It cannot be simply overturned or repealed by a single government or nation, nor can those governments or nations modify the legislated requirements to make compliance simpler or less effective. This is because it has already been agreed by representatives from all Member States through the standard EU legislative process.

The GDPR asserts a number of rights for individuals in relation to their personal data, and these rights are set out in Chapter III of the Regulation. The protection of these rights naturally results in a number of obligations on the part of the organisations that collect, store and process that personal data. Data controllers and processors have to act in accordance with the GDPR to ensure that the fundamental data rights of individuals are protected. This is not a simple 'if A then B' law, of course, and there are various conditions that protect businesses' rights to do business, as well as protecting public authorities' ability to serve the public.

On one hand, the Regulation appears to be disruptive. Every organisation in the EU has to comply with the law and that means the Regulation has an impact on their operations; there have been significant changes to how most organisations collect, process and store personal data; and the GDPR is, of course, bolstered by the threat of punitive and 'dissuasive' administrative fines. On the other hand, the Regulation is trying to tread a fine line between protecting the rights of the individual and removing barriers to the "free movement of personal data within the internal market". In other words, although the GDPR sets out specific restrictions on the use and storage of personal data, it does so in order to preserve the interests both of the EU's residents and the organisations that do business within it.

Organisations that act to ensure compliance with the Regulation will be those that thrive in the evolving regulatory environment. Equally, some organisations will be able to make significant process improvements, as with standardised requirements for data protection, organisations can streamline their processes – particularly for pan-EU and Internet services operations – and significantly improve efficiency.

Implementing the GDPR

The prerequisites for implementing a complex compliance framework are knowledge and competence; the IBITGQ (*www.ibitgq.org*) Certified EU GDPR Foundation and Practitioner qualifications are designed so that individuals can gain the skills and competence they need.

This manual explains how to achieve compliance with the Regulation and how to do so while minimising the impact of the necessary changes. In any compliance project, there are many instances where organisational processes must be structured to meet legal or regulatory requirements, and it is important to ensure that your organisation is able to do this cost-effectively and efficiently.

It is also important to understand that the GDPR will apply in varying measures to organisations *outside* the EU. Much as you are expected to abide by the laws of any country you live in, non-EU organisations that provide services into the EU, where those services involve processing personal data, will also need to abide by the Regulation. Although compliance with the Regulation may be difficult for some organisations – typically smaller ones that have no other interest in the EU – simple supply-chain forces, and the explicit GDPR requirements around extra-territorial data processing will put compliance pressure on organisations that want to do business within the EU.

In fact, the only real way to avoid complying with the GDPR will be to avoid doing business with the EU entirely. Given that the EU is the largest trading bloc in the world, this would be impractical for any organisation that wants to take advantage of the Internet or works with modern global markets and supply chains.

This book does not lay out a one-size-fits-all framework for achieving GDPR compliance. Organisations operate in different ways, with different partners and suppliers, different business objectives and a variety of business models, and no single compliance framework is likely to work – or even be suitable as a general approach – for all organisations in all parts of Europe or the world. Rather, this book provides information about the features of a compliance framework that are known to work in many organisations and which reflect the GDPR requirements. The manual identifies the specific requirements of the GDPR and provides analysis and recommendations for pragmatically and effectively achieving compliance.

Readers should, however, note that this manual does not cover every possible situation in which the GDPR might apply, nor does it deal with the compliance requirements in every sector and industry. It instead focuses on the core activities and issues that most GDPR compliance projects have to face, and provides advice and guidance that is broadly applicable in most – but not all – circumstances.

Finally, it should be noted that this is a manual for implementing a GDPR compliance framework in an organisation; it is explicitly not a legal compliance manual and you will need specific legal advice on aspects of the GDPR, particularly in relation to contracts and other legal statements. Your legal advisers have an important role to play in your GDPR project, but most lawyers are not experts on cyber security, information assurance or business continuity, nor do they usually have expertise in organisational management. Direct their services to the maximum value of your GDPR compliance project, and remember that GDPR compliance is much bigger and more important than legal documentation; the GDPR has to become part of the fabric of the organisation in much the same way as health and safety, internal control or information security.

Key definitions

There are a number of key terms that are used throughout the manual, many of which have very specific definitions. These definitions all originate in the GDPR itself. Article 4 of the GDPR contains all the key definitions and should be thoroughly reviewed. Of these, there are five terms universally applied throughout the Regulation that need to be clearly understood from the outset.

Processing

'Processing' means any operation or set of operations which is performed on personal data or on sets of personal data, whether or not by automated means, such as collection, recording, organisation, structuring, storage, adaptation or alteration, retrieval, consultation, use, disclosure by transmission, dissemination or otherwise making available, alignment or combination, restriction, erasure or destruction.[2]

Controller

'Controller' means the natural or legal person, public authority, agency or other body which, alone or jointly with others, determines the purposes and means of the processing of personal data; where the purposes and means of such processing are determined by Union or Member State law, the controller or the specific criteria for its nomination may be provided for by Union or Member State law.[3]

The data controller is the organisation that determines the purpose for processing personal data and what processing will be done. As we have seen, 'processing', under the terms of the GDPR, includes collecting and storing information, so it is possible that an organisation may be accountable as a controller but otherwise have little involvement with the actual processing of personal data. For a consumer products

---

[2] GDPR Article 4(2).

[3] GDPR, Article 4(7).

company that hires a marketing agency to profile its customers, and which provides the marketing company with the specific data necessary to provide those profiles, it will clearly be the data controller and the marketing agency will be the data processor. If, however, the marketing agency determines what customer data it needs to see and how that data will be used, and simply provides summary information to the consumer products company, then the marketing agency will be the controller.

Processor

> 'Processor' means a natural or legal person, public authority, agency or other body which processes personal data on behalf of the controller.[4]

Data processors are organisations or entities that process personal information on behalf of a data controller. As noted above, 'processing' is essentially anything done to the data, including storage, archiving or just looking at it. It is normal for an organisation to be both a controller and a processor in respect of most personal data; it is only processing that is carried out by third parties on behalf of the controller that has to be addressed in line with the requirements on processors.

Personal data

> 'Personal data' means any information relating to an identified or identifiable natural person ('data subject'); an identifiable natural person is one who can be identified, directly or indirectly, in particular by reference to an

---

[4] GDPR, Article 4(8).

identifier such as a name, an identification number, location data, an online identifier or to one or more factors specific to the physical, physiological, genetic, mental, economic, cultural or social identity of that natural person.[5]

Personal data under the GDPR is a broad set of types of information about "an identified or identifiable natural person". This means that the information is *not* personal data if there is no way to link it to a natural person. Personal data is anything that could be linked in any way to the data subject, so organisations will need to be careful about how information is gathered and used, as it may be possible to accidentally gather sufficient information to remove the anonymity of the subject. Note that the definition specifically includes biometric, genetic and health information, as well as online identifiers, such as an IP address that can be used to identify a person. The GDPR does not extend any rights to deceased persons.

Supervisory authority

'Supervisory authority' means an independent public authority which is established by a Member State pursuant to Article 51.[6]

The supervisory authority is the governmental organisation in each Member State that is responsible for enforcement of the GDPR. Your organisation may need to interact with the

---

[5] GDPR, Article 4(1).

[6] GDPR, Article 4(21).

supervisory authority on a number of occasions, so it is worth making sure you know who that is (in the UK, for instance, it is the Information Commissioner's Office (ICO), while in France it is the Commission Nationale de l'Informatique et des Libertés, and so on). There is a full list of the current EU/EEA national supervisory authorities in Appendix 2.

If your organisation operates in more than one Member State, you may have a lead supervisory authority in whichever Member State the main establishment of your organisation is based.[7]

---

[7] GDPR, Article 56.

Part 1: Core considerations for the GDPR

CHAPTER 1: SCOPE, CONTROLLERS AND PROCESSORS

The GDPR applies widely, but it is not universal. Equally, not all personal data processing falls under its purview. Many organisations will exist in 'grey' areas where certain processing may not be governed by the GDPR while others are, or could believe themselves exempt when they are not.

Scope of the GDPR

The GDPR applies a material scope and a territorial scope. These are the uses of personal data and the geographic regions that are governed by the Regulation.

In its broadest sense, the GDPR applies to:

> the processing of personal data wholly or partly by automated means and to the processing other than by automated means of personal data which forms part of a filing system or are intended to form part of a filing system.[8]

A 'filing system' refers to personal data that is organised, presumably for ease of access and use, and could include anything from an alphabetised set of papers in a cabinet through to an enormous, searchable database. A number of papers in a box in a back room is unlikely to qualify, although emails in an inbox will.

---

[8] GDPR, Article 2(1).

There are, of course, exemptions to the material scope – for activities outside the scope of EU law, such as for national security of a non-EU state; processing by Member States pursuing activities related to the common foreign and security policy of the EU; for processing purely of a personal or household nature; and for competent authorities in Member States related to crime and security (such as police activities).

So, this is already very broad, and any organisation that makes much use of personal data at all is likely to be required to the comply with the Regulation.

The territorial scope is equally broad, and brings with it a number of additional concerns for organisations outside the EU and for those within the EU that do business with organisations outside. The Regulation applies under three territorial conditions[9]:

1. Organisations within the EU that process personal data, even if the actual processing activity is conducted outside the EU.

2. Organisations outside the EU that process the personal data of EU residents as part of offering good or services into the EU, or monitoring the behaviour of EU residents.

---

[9] GDPR, Article 3.

3. Organisations outside the EU that are otherwise governed by EU law on the basis of public international law.

The second of these is clearly problematic. In simple terms, it will apply to an organisation that provides processing services to an organisation within the EU, and it will apply to an organisation that clearly offers goods and/or services into the EU. For instance, if you sell products and your website lists prices in euros, then you are clearly selling into the EU and will need to abide by the GDPR. If you are a hotel in Australia, however, and do not market your hotel in the EU, then the personal data of any EU residents who might stay with you is exempt from the law.

The scope of the GDPR is obviously a complex topic and informs how you need to structure your compliance activities, especially where you might have a long or complicated supply chain. The scope is discussed in more detail in chapter 4 of this manual.

Controller and processor

The roles of data controller and data processor are central to the GDPR and it is crucial that you understand these roles. The basic definitions have already been set out in the introduction to this manual, but the detailed requirements around the roles need to be thoroughly understood.

Data controllers

The data controller is the party responsible for ensuring that personal data is processed in accordance with the Regulation. Article 4 of the GDPR provides the standard definition for a controller:

'controller' means the natural or legal person, public authority, agency or other body which, alone or jointly with others, determines the purposes and means of the processing of personal data; where the purposes and means of such processing are determined by Union or Member State law, the controller or the specific criteria for its nomination may be provided for by Union or Member State law.[10]

The controller is the entity that determines the purposes of processing activities. This includes determining which data will be collected, who to collect data from, whether there is a justification for not notifying the data subjects or seeking their consent, how long to retain the data, and so on.

It is also the data controller's duty to ensure that any third-party processors abide by the rules, in accordance with the Regulation's statement that:

the controller shall use only processors providing sufficient guarantees to implement appropriate technical and organisational measures in such a manner that processing will meet the requirements of this Regulation and ensure the protection of the rights of the data subject.[11]

The controller will usually be the 'public-facing' entities to which data subjects supply their information. For instance, a hospital might have an online form for entering health information; even if the online form is provided by a third

---

[10] GDPR, Article 4(7).

[11] GDPR, Article 28(1).

party, the hospital (which determines what the data is processed for) will be the data controller. If the form is managed by a third party that has some autonomy over the design of the form and the categories of data that it collects, then that third party could become a joint controller.

It is the controller's duty to protect personal data by implementing "appropriate technical and organisational measures to ensure and to be able to demonstrate that processing is performed in accordance with [the GDPR]".[12] These measures might also be called 'controls', and should be applied in response to calculated risks, be documented clearly, and be monitored and checked for effectiveness (see chapter 11 for more information).

Implementing appropriate controls is a part of the data controller's commitment to establishing data protection by design and by default. Establishing the most secure ways of processing the personal data must be done "both at the time of the determination of the means for processing and at the time of the processing itself".[13]

Data protection impact assessments (DPIAs) are a key part of data protection by design and by default (see chapter 10). Responsibility for this falls to the data controller, and should not be foisted onto a data processor. However, the controller should consult the processors that may be affected in order to ensure that the DPIA is thorough, that the resulting plans

---

[12] GDPR, Article 24(1).

[13] GDPR, Article 25(1).

can be implemented, and that the measures are and continue to be effective.

Joint controllers

It is possible for two or more controllers to jointly determine the purposes and means of processing. If your organisation needs to establish itself as a joint controller in partnership with another organisation, you will need to ensure that the "respective responsibilities for compliance with the [Regulation]" are established before performing any processing or collection of personal data.

Data processors

Data processors are those bodies contracted by the controller to perform some function on the personal data. The Regulation's definition of a processor is as follows:

> 'processor' means a natural or legal person, public authority, agency or other body which processes personal data on behalf of the controller.[14]

The processes must fall within the parameters provided by the data controller in accordance with the Regulation. Contracts between controllers and processors have a number of specific requirements, which are listed in Article 28, and the specific terms used in these contracts may, at some point, be dictated by either the Commission or your supervisory authority.

---

[14] GDPR, Article 5(8).

The controller does not have to define every single element of how the data is processed, and can rely on the processor's "sufficient guarantees" that processing will be done securely.[15] As such, the processor might still be responsible for determining some of the following elements:

- The IT systems or other methods used to collect personal data.
- How the data is stored.
- The security surrounding the personal data.
- How the personal data is transferred from one organisation to another.
- How personal data about a specific individual is retrieved.
- Methods for ensuring a retention schedule is adhered to.
- How data is deleted or disposed of.

Processors may be free to design all of these for a number of reasons. For instance, if an organisation contracts a marketing agency to do some research, the organisation might determine the purpose of the personal data processing (e.g. to establish a measure of the organisation's reputation) but defer to the marketing agency's expertise on how best to achieve this end. The marketing agency must manage the personal data securely and in accordance with the GDPR. In

---

[15] GDPR, Article 28(1).

this instance, it is likely that the marketing agency will be a joint controller.

Processors are restricted from engaging another processor "without prior specific or general written authorisation of the controller".[16] This ensures that the controller maintains oversight of the chain of custody of personal data, and so they can be assured of the security measures in place at each stage.

Controllers that are processors

In many cases, the data controller and the data processor will be the same entity (although note that the GDPR defines a processor as an entity that processes personal data "on behalf of the controller"). Given the extremely broad definition of processing, which includes the collection and disposal of personal data, it would be extremely rare for a controller to take no part in data processing itself.

It is also possible for an organisation to be a data controller for one set of personal data and a processor for another. For instance, an organisation that provides processing services will be a data processor for its clients, but will be the data controller for personal data relating to its employees.

Controllers and processors outside the EU

We previously discussed the territorial scope of the Regulation, explaining that controllers and processors based

---

[16] GDPR, Article 28(2).

outside the EU are not exempt from the Regulation. Any organisation providing services into the EU needs to comply or face tough penalties.[17]

In order to ensure that the whole supply chain involved in processing personal data can be held accountable within Europe, the Regulation requires all such organisations to have a designated representative within the Union. There are two exemptions, which apply to:

(a) processing which is occasional, does not include, on a large scale, processing of special categories of data as referred to in Article 9(1) or processing of personal data relating to criminal convictions and offences referred to in Article 10, and is unlikely to result in a risk to the rights and freedoms of natural persons, taking into account the nature, context, scope and purposes of the processing; or

(b) a public authority or body.[18]

In exemption (a), it is important to note that the organisation's processing must meet *all* of those conditions.

Any organisation that doesn't meet these conditions for exemption (in other words, the majority of organisations) must identify a representative somewhere within the European Union. The only stipulation as to the Member State

---

[17] GDPR, Article 3.

[18] GDPR, Article 27(2).

in which the representative has to be based, is that it should be "where the data subjects are and whose personal data are processed in relation to the offering of goods or services to them, or whose behaviour is monitored".[19] Many organisations thus have a range of countries to choose from.

The representative's job is to operate as the local liaison with the supervisory authority. The supervisory authority has no access to the organisation itself, so many of its interactions will be via the representative.

Because the representative can be held to some account for the controller or processor's failures to meet the requirements of the Regulation, it is in their interests to ensure that they only represent organisations that have genuinely committed to complying with the law. Having a representative, however, will not absolve a controller or processor from liability.

If you need a representative in the EU, you must ensure that you communicate this in writing to the relevant supervisory authority in the Member State where the representative is established.

Records of processing

Organisations must retain records to prove their compliance should the supervisory authority request evidence. Organisations involved in processing data typically produce a large number of records from processing and establishing compliance with the Regulation, by way of fair processing

---

[19] GDPR, Article 27(3).

notices, retention policies, evidence of consent, DPIA reports, and so on, all of which can be used as evidence of compliance. In many instances, you may need a combination of records to demonstrate your compliance. A processing policy, for example, is a single record, but evidence that it is being correctly applied will generate additional records, any of which could be requested by the supervisory authority in the event of an audit.

Supervisory authorities across Europe have defined processes for auditing organisations, and in many cases these processes have been published to ensure that audits can be completed quickly and with minimal disruption. The UK's Information Commissioner's Office (ICO), for instance, specifies the evidence it requests ahead of audits, and this should form the basis of any set of records that you use to demonstrate compliance:

> [Evidence] may include data protection policy documents; operational guidance or manuals for staff processing sensitive data; data protection training modules; risk registers; information asset registers; information governance structures and similar.[20]

You can assume that any measures you have put in place to secure personal data – both those measures explicitly mandated by the Regulation and those that you apply out of a sense of good practice – should be documented and presentable as records. This includes documentation of your

---

[20] ICO: *A guide to ICO audits*, September 2018, *https://ico.org.uk/media/for-organisations/documents/2787/guide-to-data-protection-audits.pdf*.

privacy compliance framework (see chapter 4 of this manual), risk assessments, controls, and so on. The sorts of records you might need to be able to present to the supervisory authority could include:

- Data protection or information security policy;
- Retention and disposal policies;
- Records of destruction of information assets (including personal data);
- Service-level and non-disclosure agreements with suppliers/processors;
- Fair processing notice and/or privacy policy;
- Risk management documentation (risk treatment plans (RTP), Statements of Applicability, DPIA reports, etc.);
- Monitoring and measurement of controls to manage risks;
- Training and awareness records (records of participation, test scores, etc.);
- Internal audit reports;
- Continual improvement logs; and
- Incident management policies, procedures and logs.

The Regulation also requires many data controllers and processors to maintain a specific record of their processing activities. For controllers, this includes processing carried out by third-party data processors; for processors, it should be a record of processing activities carried out on behalf of a data controller. If your organisation is based outside the EU, your representative must also have a copy of the same record.[21]

Organisations that employ fewer than 250 people are not required to retain an explicit record of their processing activities, although organisations will not be able to claim the exemption if the processing is likely to pose a risk to the rights and freedoms of data subjects, if the processing is not occasional, or the processing involves special categories of data or data relating to criminal convictions and offences.[22]

Controllers and processors have different requirements for these records, which are given below.[23]

Table 1: Different Record Requirements for Data Controllers vs Processors

Data controller's records	Data processor's records
Name and contact details of the controller, joint controller and/or controller's representative and data protection officer (DPO).	Name and contact details of the processor(s) and of each controller that the processor works on behalf of, and the controller's or processor's representative and DPO.
Purposes of the processing.	Categories of processing carried out on behalf of each controller.

---

[21] GDPR, Article 30.

[22] GDPR, Article 30(5).

[23] GDPR, Article 30(1) and (2).

Description of the categories of data subjects and categories of personal data.	Details of any transfers of personal data to a third country or international organisation, including their identity and documentation of appropriate safeguards.
Categories of recipients to whom the data is disclosed, including recipients outside the EU.	A general description of the technical and organisation security measures.
Details of any transfers of personal data to a third country or international organisation, including their identity and documentation of appropriate safeguards.	
Time limits for erasure of the different categories of personal data.	
A general description of the technical and organisational security measures.	

Records must be written and kept in a format that can be shared with the supervisory authority. The Regulation specifically permits keeping the records "in electronic form",[24] so it should be a simple matter to ensure they are kept up to date and under strict version control.

---

[24] GDPR, Article 30(3).

Demonstrating compliance

Although records will demonstrate to your supervisory authority your *claim* that processing activities are in compliance with the Regulation, records will not show that these activities are actually conducted in accordance with the law. Without submitting to an audit, there is no real way to provide conclusive evidence that you are compliant and, because of limited time and resources, supervisory authorities are unlikely to want to subject every organisation to regular audits.

An organisation can, however, partially demonstrate compliance by "adherence to an approved code of conduct […] or an approved certification mechanism".[25] These codes of conduct and certification mechanisms can be selected, developed or "encouraged" by the Regulation's defined authorities (Member States, supervisory authorities, the Board or Commission) in order to provide a standardised and formal system of assuring the security of personal data.

The Regulation also allows "associations and other bodies representing categories of controllers or processors [to] prepare codes of conduct, or amend or extend such codes, for the purpose of specifying the application of this Regulation".[26] This means that industry bodies can work together to ensure that codes of conduct reflect the realities of business within that industry. This should enable the

---

[25] GDPR, Article 32(3).

[26] GDPR, Article 40(2).

industry to assert best practice more generally and raise the standards of business across the board.

Because codes of conduct can be established by associations of controllers and processors, it is entirely possible that you will have some say in the codes of conduct that will apply to your organisation. All codes of conduct still need to be approved by the supervisory authority, so it is not carte blanche to avoid meeting the Regulation's conditions. Furthermore, the supervisory authority will be charged with monitoring the efficacy of any codes of conduct,[27] so whatever model is chosen will need to stand up to ongoing scrutiny.

Standards and established frameworks built on best practice and validated by external audit are likely to be accepted as forms of certification or codes of conduct across the majority of the EU. ISO 27001, in particular, should be considered a safe bet for assurance of information security in most jurisdictions. If no approved code of conduct has been established, and there is no formally recognised certification mechanism to prove compliance with the GDPR, ISO 27001 and similar frameworks and management systems provide a sensible starting point.

---

[27] GDPR, Article 41(1).

CHAPTER 2: SIX DATA PROCESSING PRINCIPLES

The Regulation stipulates that infringements of "the basic principles for processing, including conditions for consent" are subject to the highest possible administrative fines – up to €20,000,000 or 4% of global annual turnover, whichever is greater. If any detail can get the attention of the people who need to understand this, it is likely that potential fines of that scale will do the job.

The GDPR lays down a set of data processing principles to guide how organisations manage personal data. The principles can be seen as an overview of your most important duties in complying with the Regulation, and anyone reading the Regulation should keep them in mind when interpreting other requirements.

The first six data processing principles can be found in Article 5 of the Regulation and are as follows:

1. Lawfulness, fairness and transparency.
2. Purpose limitation.
3. Data minimisation.
4. Accuracy.
5. Storage limitation.
6. Integrity and confidentiality.

Although these principles are the direct successors of those outlined in the DPD, the Regulation notes that "the objectives and principles of [the DPD] remain sound, but it has not prevented fragmentation in the implementation of data protection across the Union, legal uncertainty or a widespread public perception that there are significant risks to the protection of natural persons, in particular with regard to online activity".[28] Because of this, organisations should have two primary concerns when ensuring they comply with the principles:

1. Understanding the full scope of the principles under the GDPR.
2. Ensuring that any distinctions between the previous principles and the new ones are identified and understood.

Although the GDPR has been in effect for more than a year, it is not uncommon for organisations to assume that one principle is much the same as its predecessor. Others might think that the fact they haven't been investigated by the supervisory authority is proof that they are getting things right. Regardless of how certain you might be that you are acting in accordance with the principles, it is absolutely essential that you confirm this before a data breach reveals that you are, in fact, not in compliance.

In the first instance, organisations need to appreciate that the scope of the GDPR is not the scope of the DPD. The Regulation applies more broadly and has a different scope from the laws that were developed in response to the DPD. (See chapter 4 for a discussion of the GDPR's scope and how it relates to the privacy compliance framework.)

In the second instance, organisations need to take care that their compliance programmes are sufficiently updated. Too

---

[28] GDPR, Recital 9.

often, updating compliance programmes results in little change; people are set in their habits, they assume the current practices are still 'good enough', and the people interpreting the Regulation may suffer from 'fatigue of repetition' and miss salient points.

Principle 1: Lawfulness, fairness and transparency

The three components of this principle are clearly linked: the data subject must be told what processing will occur (transparent), the processing must match this description (fair), and the processing must be for one of the purposes specified in the Regulation (lawful). The data subject should also be "informed of the existence of the processing operation".[29]

Fairness

Drawing on existing practice, "Fairness" requires that the controller:

- Is open and honest about its identity;
- Obtains data from someone who is legally authorised/required to provide it;
- Only handles data in ways the data subject would reasonably expect;
- Does not use the data in ways that might unjustifiably have a negative effect on them.

---

[29] GDPR, Recital 60.

Transparency

"Transparency" requires the data controller to tell people clearly and openly how (unless it is obvious) they intend to use any personal data that has been collected. These two are regularly linked in the Regulation, most notably in the statement that "the principles of fair and transparent processing require that the data subject be informed of the existence of the processing operation and its purposes".[30] For instance, it is obvious when buying something online that your name and address will be used to fulfil the purchase. It is not, however, reasonable to pass that information to a sister company that offers related products or services without first informing the data subject.

Lawfulness

The final component of this first data protection principle, "lawfulness", describes processing that meets one of the tests set out in Article 6. This is a complex area, and most organisations are likely to need specific legal advice in respect to the lawful basis on which they are processing data. Remember that, if there is no lawful basis, then by definition the processing will be illegal.

> Processing shall be lawful only if and to the extent that at least one of the following applies:
>
> (a) The data subject has given consent to the processing of his or her personal data for one or more specific purposes;

---

[30] GDPR, Recital 60.

(b) Processing is necessary for the performance of a contract to which the data subject is party or in order to take steps at the request of the data subject before entering into a contract;

(c) Processing is necessary for compliance with a legal obligation to which the controller is subject;

(d) Processing is necessary in order to protect the vital interests of the data subject or of another natural person;

(e) Processing is necessary for the performance of a task carried out in the public interest or in the exercise of official authority vested in the controller; or

(f) Processing is necessary for the purposes of the legitimate interests pursued by the controller or by a third party, except where such interests are overridden by the interests or fundamental rights and freedoms of the data subject that require protection of personal data, in particular where the data subject is a child.

Point (f) of the first subparagraph shall not apply to processing carried out by public authorities in the performance of their tasks.

Note that this only requires *one* of the conditions to have been met for the processing to be lawful. The Regulation makes it clear that lawfulness "does not necessarily require a legislative act adopted by a parliament", but that "such a legal basis or legislative measure should be clear and precise and its application should be foreseeable to persons subject to it".[31] Organisations that process personal data in the public interest or as a public authority, must ensure that the processing has "a basis in Union or Member State law".[32]

Point (a) – that the data subject has given consent to the processing of his or her personal data for one or more specific purposes – means that the data subject cannot reasonably be expected to consent without being in possession of the facts, nor can those facts be implicit (such as in fulfilment of a contract or compliance with a law). This is consistent with the Regulation's statement in Recital 50 that:

> The processing of personal data for purposes other than those for which the personal data were originally collected should be allowed only where the processing is compatible with the purposes for which the personal data were originally collected. In such a case, no legal basis separate from that which allowed the collection of the personal data is required.

In chapter 6 we deal, at some length, with the practical issues around consent. In short, consent should not necessarily be the first option selected to be the basis of lawful processing. The test for consent is relatively high. Consent must be:

> freely given, specific, informed and unambiguous indication of the data subject's wishes in which he or she by a statement or by a clear affirmative action, signifies

---

[31] GDPR, Recital 41.

[32] GDPR, Recital 45.

agreement to the processing of personal data relating to him or her.[33]

Consent should not be regarded as freely given if the data subject has no genuine or free choice or is unable to refuse or withdraw consent without detriment.[34]

Consent is presumed not to be freely given if it does not allow separate consent to be given to different personal data processing operations.[35]

These tests mean that employers are unlikely to be able to rely on consent in relation to the processing of most personal data relating to their employees. Any such consent would be invalid and the processing would therefore be unlawful.

Consent is accompanied by the right to withdraw consent, and by the rights of rectification and data portability. There may be circumstances in which organisations therefore wish to identify alternative lawful bases for processing, and these come from the other options set out in Article 6.

Organisations should use privacy notices and terms and conditions to give relevant context and transparency, provided that these are clear and accessible. The Regulation explicitly states that "the principle of transparency requires that any information addressed to the public or to the data subject be concise, easily accessible and easy to understand,

---

[33] GDPR, Article 4(11).

[34] GDPR Recital 42.

[35] GDPR Recital 43.

and that clear and plain language and, additionally, where appropriate, visualisation be used".[36] Simply including a link to detailed terms and conditions may not be adequate.

Clause 4 of Article 6 applies additional requirements for determining whether personal data can be processed without the data subject's consent. This essentially balances transparency (the data subject's knowledge of the processing) with lawfulness (providing exemptions for valid purposes) by applying a doctrine of fairness.

Where consent has not been gained for the specific processing in question, the organisation must address additional conditions to determine the fairness and transparency of the processing. These conditions include, but are not limited to, the below[37]:

(a) any link between the purposes for which the personal data have been collected and the purposes of the intended further processing;

(b) the context in which the personal data have been collected, in particular regarding the relationship between data subjects and the controller;

(c) the nature of the personal data, in particular whether special categories of personal data are processed, pursuant to Article 9, or whether personal data related to criminal convictions and offences are processed, pursuant to Article 10;

---

[36] GDPR, Recital 58.

[37] GDPR, Article 6(4).

(d) the possible consequences of the intended further processing for data subjects;

(e) the existence of appropriate safeguards, which may include encryption or pseudonymisation.

Although such safeguards may make processing more onerous, expensive or difficult, you should always consider a minimum level of security for personal data. Decisions on this matter should result from risk assessments and DPIAs, which are discussed later in this manual.

When processing data without consent, the organisation should determine the fairness of the processing by taking other factors into consideration, including the types of personal data involved, the specific reasons that consent is not available, and so on. The UK's ICO provides the following example[38]:

> Where personal data is collected to assess tax liability or to impose a fine for breaking the speed limit, the information is being used in a way that may cause detriment to the individuals concerned, but the proper use of personal data for these purposes will not be unfair.

In this instance, the personal data has been acquired likely without consent and without the subject being aware. However, this is wholly fair and legal because it is entirely

---

[38] *ico.org.uk/for-organisations/guide-to-data-protection/guide-to-the-general-data-protection-regulation-gdpr/principles/lawfulness-fairness-and-transparency/*.

reasonable for the state to collect taxes and levy fines for speeding.

Processing personal data without consent is also allowable under specific or extraordinary conditions, such as when national security or the protection of other data subjects is relevant to the processing.[39]

Demonstrating that the processing of personal data is lawful, fair and transparent will not be simple for many organisations. Your first consideration, however, should be to clearly document how you describe your processing when the data subject offers consent. Assuming you then do exactly as you say – and can prove it – and you are not in contravention of any other requirements of the GDPR or other laws, you should be confident that your processing is lawful, fair and transparent.

The supervisory authority might offer relevant information about the sort of proof they require to demonstrate compliance,[40] but you shouldn't rely on this: you have an obligation to keep appropriate records and evidence.

---

[39] GDPR, Article 23(1).

[40] The UK's ICO, for instance, has a number of articles and tools for determining whether your organisation complies with the law, as well as guidance on the implementation of the law. Cf. *https://ico.org.uk/for-organisations/guide-to-data-protection/*.

Principle 2: Purpose limitation

The Regulation states that personal data can only be collected for "specified, explicit and legitimate purposes".[41] That is, to comply with the purpose limitation principle, you must define up front what the data will be used for and limit the processing to only what is necessary to meet that purpose.

Privacy notices, terms and conditions, and consent forms should provide the data subject with unambiguous information about the extent of processing involved. These public statements should be reflected in the actual processing and the documentation of that processing.

For instance, many supermarkets collect personal information so that they can provide customers with targeted offers that match up with their usual spending habits. It would be a breach of this principle for those supermarkets to then hand this data to a sister company that sells holidays, as this is beyond the scope of the purpose for which the data was collected.

The Regulation does permit some further processing "for archiving purposes in the public interest, scientific or historical research purposes or statistical purposes".[42] Safeguards for processing this sort of information are laid out in Article 89, and you will need to examine both technical and organisational options in order to comply with the Regulation. Pseudonymisation and encryption, for instance, would be valid measures, as would restricting access to such

---

[41] GDPR, Article 5(1)(b).

[42] GDPR, Article 5(1)(b).

information on the basis of role and the requirements of a given set of procedures.

Principle 3: Data minimisation

The Regulation states that personal data you collect and/or process should be "adequate, relevant and limited to what is necessary in relation to the purposes for which they are processed".[43] This means that you should hold no more data beyond what is strictly required. After all, it is difficult to lose information that you don't have.

Some organisations are more prone to carrying excess information than others, particularly those in the healthcare industry or the financial services sector. The UK's ICO offers this example[44]:

A recruitment agency places workers in a variety of jobs. It sends applicants a general questionnaire, which includes specific questions about health conditions that are only relevant to particular manual occupations. It would be irrelevant and excessive to obtain such information from an individual who was applying for an office job.

In this instance, the purpose for processing is to ensure that the applicant is placed into an appropriate role for which they are qualified. As the indicated medical conditions are not relevant to office jobs, there is no need to collect this

---

[43] GDPR, Article 5(1) (c).

[44] *ico.org.uk/for-organisations/guide-to-data-protection/guide-to-the-general-data-protection-regulation-gdpr/principles/data-minimisation/*.

information, and the principle of data minimisation says that it should not be collected or processed.

Complying with this data protection principle will be facilitated by data mapping, which is discussed in chapter 9 of this manual, and by reviewing your procedures. Ensuring you know how data is used is critical to minimising the data that you collect and process, and should be integrated into the way your organisation works as part of a privacy-by-design approach.[45]

Data minimisation should also be taken into account in agreements with suppliers and data processors. This may include stripping out certain data before passing information over for external processing, then reattaching the data when it returns from the processor. Ensuring that data minimisation is accounted for in supplier agreements and binding corporate rules should be included in procurement and supply procedures.

Principle 4: Accuracy

The Regulation requires personal data to be "accurate and, where necessary, kept up to date".[46] Besides being good practice for any business, this protects the data subject from a number of threats, such as identity theft. It also ensures that any automated profiling decisions made regarding the data subject use accurate data.

---

[45] GDPR, Article 25.

[46] GDPR, Article 5(1)(d).

The Regulation clearly aims to regulate when, how and under what conditions profiling can be conducted.[47] If your organisation indulges in profiling of any kind – and especially if there are material impacts for the data subject – you need to ensure that you have processes in place to keep all personal data accurate and up to date.

The corollary to this principle is the data subject's right to rectification. This grants the data subject the right to "rectification of inaccurate personal data" and "the right to have incomplete personal data completed".[48] You should ensure not only that personal data is accurate, but also that you have a process by which data subjects can request correction or completion of their personal data. This could be linked to whatever method you use to give data subjects access to their data (which will be covered more fully in chapter 7 of this manual).

Maintaining personal data to ensure accuracy should be built into your regular processes. For instance, in a monthly process to archive redundant data, you could include steps to identify out-of-date or incorrect data, which then automates sending the data subject a request to provide accurate information. Alternatively – and more simply, perhaps –

---

[47] Recital 71 of the Regulation makes this abundantly clear: "The data subject should have the right not to be subject to a decision, which may include a measure, evaluating personal aspects relating to him or her which is based solely on automated processing and which produces legal effects concerning him or her similarly significantly affects him or her, such as automatic refusal of an online credit application or e-recruiting practices without any human intervention."

[48] GDPR, Article 16.

regular emails to data subjects could include the request that they log in to check and update any information. Other types of information or organisations in different relationships with the data subjects may require different solutions with potentially greater complexity.

It is not necessary to correct some forms of inaccuracy. For instance, if a customer places an order with an organisation and that order is fulfilled, it is not necessary to maintain an accurate record of the customer's address unless the customer makes other orders, in which case the order process should ensure that the address is accurate.

Other forms of inaccuracy may be valuable to retain. The ICO's *Guide to Data Protection* provides this example[49]:

> A misdiagnosis of a medical condition continues to be held as part of a patient's medical records even after the diagnosis is corrected, because it is relevant for the purpose of explaining treatment given to the patient, or for other health problems.

In this case, the original error is corrected (replacing the misdiagnosis with the correct diagnosis), but the record of the misdiagnosis is retained because it is information for the data subject's benefit.

---

[49] *ico.org.uk/for-organisations/guide-to-data-protection/guide-to-the-general-data-protection-regulation-gdpr/principles/accuracy/*.

Principle 5: Storage limitation

The Regulation requires that personal data is "kept in a form which permits identification of data subjects for no longer than is necessary for the purposes for which the personal data are processed".[50] The phrase "kept in a form" refers not to the medium on which it is stored (although that may be a factor) but to the way it is stored – whether, for instance, it is encrypted or split into separate databases to prevent identification of the data subject.

In simpler terms: if you no longer need the data, get rid of it. As you should be defining a purpose for all data collection, it should be quite simple to determine when the data is no longer required. Some organisations, however, may need to retain personal data for long-term purposes with intermittent processing – in healthcare, for instance – and in such cases summarily deleting data may not be possible.

Pseudonymisation – splitting personal data into sets that do not individually permit identification of the data subject – is one solution to secure storage of personal data, but presents its own issues with regard to usability. If that personal data must be regularly processed, the time spent reversing the pseudonymisation may be onerous or represent a poor ROI.

Wherever possible, it will be preferable to simply delete or destroy all personal data immediately following processing, and this will save having to implement additional measures.

Your approach to storage limitation should be enshrined in a data retention policy and supporting procedures. This must

---

[50] GDPR, Article 5(1)(e).

take into account legal and contractual requirements for retention periods – both minimum and maximum – and then trigger a process by which data is either securely disposed of or secured at the end of this period.

Many organisations have substantial quantities of old personal records. Unless there is a lawful basis for continuing to process this data, organisations should make arrangements to delete them (and to do so securely) as soon as possible. Remember that storing and archiving of data falls within the definition of processing and, therefore, any data subject access request (DSAR) can legitimately require copies of stored, archived or backed-up data. Seek guidance from your supervisory authority as to available options for demonstrating that archived digital data is not actually still being processed.

Principle 6: Integrity and confidentiality

This principle is perhaps the most important from a financial perspective. Although breaches of the other data protection principles can be damaging to data subjects, the impact is usually limited. Breaches of this principle, however, tend to result in data breaches, which make it very easy for supervisory authorities to prove that data has not been held securely – the fact that a data breach has occurred is compelling evidence in itself.

This final principle requires organisations to process personal data "in a manner that ensures appropriate security of the personal data, including protection against unauthorised or unlawful processing and against accidental loss, destruction or damage".[51]

In the parlance of information security, confidentiality is the "property that information is not made available or disclosed to unauthorized individuals, entities, or processes".[52] This means that personal data must be classified as confidential even within the organisation, as it is extremely unlikely that every single person in the organisation needs to have access to personal data. In many cases, there may be no requirement for anyone to access personal data.

Integrity is the "property of accuracy and completeness".[53] This clearly links to the fourth principle (accuracy) and is necessary for the same reasons: the data subject should not be jeopardised by inaccurate information. This also includes ensuring that personal data is correctly linked – such as keeping the correct address associated with the data subject – and making sure that data is not corrupted over time or by poor storage practices.

Meeting requirements for integrity and confidentiality are, mercifully, quite straightforward. Assuming you follow the advice of this manual, you will implement an information security solution such as an ISO 27001 information security management system to protect the confidentiality, integrity and availability of your organisation's information assets.

---

[51] GDPR, Article 5(1)(f).

[52] ISO/IEC 27000:2018, Clause 3.10.

[53] ISO/IEC 27000:2018, Clause 3.36.

These processes and frameworks will naturally link up with any necessary DPIAs or risk assessment activity (see Part 2 of this manual) in order to identify the critical risks to personal data and other sensitive information.

Accountability and compliance

Clause 2 of Article 5 is brief but extremely important:

> The controller shall be responsible for, and be able to demonstrate compliance with, paragraph 1 ('accountability').

This is a seventh principle, which asserts that the data controller is responsible for ensuring compliance with the previous six data processing principles and for being able to demonstrate this compliance. As such, the data controller needs to ensure that the data processing principles are met wherever the personal data goes: external processors and internal organisations/divisions must be required by contract and binding corporate rules to adhere to the data processing principles. There should be additional processes built into service agreements to demonstrate that the personal data is processed in compliance with these principles at every stage.

Failure to ensure that your suppliers meet the requirements of the principles can have a considerable impact. Because the GDPR makes the controller accountable for meeting its requirements, they will certainly take the brunt of enforcement actions, fines and reputational damage.

Embedding accountability into your organisation if you are the data controller may be difficult: you are asking your employees to be accountable for the suppliers' actions. Building a corporate culture that believes in the virtue of data protection, and in which responsibility and accountability are corporate values, will often be the difference between success and failure. An employee who feels they have ownership of the corporate relationship with the processor, or a duty to protect the information in question, should be encouraged to feel it a matter of professional pride to ensure personal data is protected.

A culture of accountability must be fed from the top down. It is very simple for an employee to feel no sense of responsibility if senior managers and the compliance manager don't show the same level of dedication. Training and staff awareness programmes should ensure that all staff understand their various duties and responsibilities in relation to privacy and data protection.

The GDPR makes explicit provision for codes of conduct. The expectation is that, over the course of the next few years, trade associations and representative bodies will prepare codes of conduct that are then put forward for approval, registration and publication by a national supervisory authority, or, where processing activities take place across Member States, by the EDPB. It is possible that the European Commission may then declare one or more of the codes recommended by EDPB to have general validity within the EU. Codes may be approved in relation to a wide range of topics and adhering to codes will, like implementing and complying with national or international management system standards, help controllers and processors demonstrate compliance with their GDPR obligations. Compliance with such codes will, of course, be subject to monitoring, carried out by suitably qualified and accredited bodies. Controllers and processors that are found to have infringed a relevant code may be blocked from claiming compliance with the code and reported to the relevant supervisory authority.

The UK's ICO recommends that codes of conduct should cover[54]:

- Fair and transparent processing;
- Legitimate interests pursued by controllers in specific contexts;
- The collection of personal data;
- The pseudonymisation of personal data;
- The information provided to individuals and the exercise of individuals' rights;
- The information provided to and the protection of children (including mechanisms for obtaining parental consent);
- Technical and organisational measures, including data protection by design and by default, and security measures;
- Breach notification;
- Data transfers outside the EU; and/or
- Dispute resolution procedures.

There is nothing stopping an organisation adopting its own code of conduct immediately and then adapting and improving it once more formal codes appear in the marketplace. A code of conduct is a solid starting point to inculcate a culture of accountability. It depends on the exact

---

[54] *http://ico.org.uk/for-organisations/guide-to-data-protection/guide-to-the-general-data-protection-regulation-gdpr/accountability-and-governance/codes-of-conduct/*.

nature of your business, its third-party suppliers and the industry in which you work, but a holistic approach is necessary to ensure the six data processing principles of the GDPR are understood and implemented across the organisation.

Of course, a good starting point is simply that: a starting point. In practice, organisations should establish a full suite of policies and procedures to ensure and demonstrate compliance with the Regulation and other relevant laws. This might include documentation around governance, management structures, roles and responsibilities, risk management, training and awareness, records management, physical and logical safeguards, data sharing agreements, or compliance and assurance programmes. In other words, an organisation will need to demonstrate it has records to prove that it is doing what it says it is. These are necessary to show that the principles and associated behaviours are fully embedded in the business.

CHAPTER 3: DATA SUBJECTS' RIGHTS

The GDPR sets out the rights data subjects have in relation to their personal data, the proper exercise of which allows them to have a better understanding of, and more control over, their personal data. The GDPR obliges organisations to provide transparency on their data processing methods and restore individuals' sense of control over their personal data. It sets time limits for organisations to respond to subject access requests and introduces new rights, such as the right to data portability, that address some of the outstanding issues that have arisen since the development of the DPD.

From an organisational point of view, the key issue is to fully understand these new or extended rights, and to determine the systems and processes that will need to be introduced or altered in order to comply with the GDPR.

It is especially crucial to ensure that data subjects' rights are protected because data subjects are entitled to complain to supervisory authorities[55] and seek judicial remedies[56] against controllers and processors for damages (both material and non-material) arising from breaches of the GDPR. In other words, the controller is directly liable for the damage caused by processing that infringes the Regulation. The controller is responsible for ensuring the security of any personal data that

---

[55] GDPR, Article 77.

[56] GDPR, Article 79.

is passed to a processor, whether that processor is inside or outside the European Union.

Fair processing

Article 12 of the GDPR describes what controllers have to do in terms of providing data subjects with information about the processing that is to occur, and about making them aware of their rights.

The information about the processing of personal data and the rights of the data subjects (and how to exercise those rights) are typically contained in a document called a privacy notice.[57] Privacy notices must be provided to data subjects when the data is collected or, if it is not collected directly from the data subject, before first use of the data and typically within 30 days of collection.

Articles 13 and 14 of the GDPR set out the minimum requirements for the content of such privacy notices. An Article 13 notice deals with data collected directly from data subjects and Article 14 deals with personal data collected other than from the data subject directly. Issuing updated and GDPR-compliant privacy notices should be seen as one of the most basic GDPR compliance practices.

A data subject is entitled to know what personal data of theirs is being processed, the lawful basis of that processing, whether or not their personal data is being processed by the

---

[57] Although note that the GDPR does not require this information to be in a privacy notice. If you have some other method of giving data subjects the same information as and when it is required, and if this method meets all of the requirements in Articles 12–14, then this is perfectly acceptable.

controller or by a third-party processor, the purposes of processing their data, including how long it will be stored by the controller, and to be provided with supplemental information about the processing.

The GDPR states that this information must be presented to the data subject "in a concise, transparent, intelligible and easily accessible form, using clear and plain language, in particular for any information addressed specifically to a child".[58] This statement expands on the sentiment of the DPD, which merely required such information to be "in an intelligible form".[59] Organisations will need to confirm that their practices meet these requirements for transparency.

Data subjects should also be told of their right to lodge a complaint with a supervisory authority against the controller under Article 77 if they believe the processing of their personal information infringes the Regulation.

If personal data is transferred to a third country outside of the EU or to an "international organisation" (which is any organisation governed by public international law or based on an agreement between two or more countries[60]), the Regulation stipulates that the data subject has the right to be informed of the safeguards put in place relating to this transfer.

---

[58] GDPR, Article 12(1).

[59] DPD, Article 12(a).

[60] GDPR, Article 4(26).

Furthermore, the data subject should be told of their right to request their information is rectified, removed or that its processing is restricted by the controller.

The right to access

The Regulation stipulates that the controller must give data subjects access to the following information: a copy of their personal data, the purposes of processing their data, the categories of the data being processed and the third parties or categories of third parties that will receive their data.[61] This is called a DSAR, and organisations should have in place tried and tested processes for identifying such requests and responding to them. An inadequate response might, after all, trigger either a complaint to a supervisory authority or a court action, or both.

The GDPR requires data controllers to respond to a DSAR "without undue delay and in any event within one month of receipt of the request".[62] The explicit one-month deadline could be a little tight for some organisations, particularly if a large number of requests are filed at one time, or complicated post-processing of the information is required to make it intelligible and identify the data subject. The Regulation, therefore, allows the period to be extended by two further months where necessary, but the controller must inform the

---

[61] GDPR, Article 15(1).

[62] GDPR, Article 12(3).

data subject of any extension within the original one-month time limit and explain the reasons for the delay.

If the information is requested electronically, it must be provided electronically. The information may be supplied in a variety of other formats, but this should generally be agreed with the data subject, and the controller must first confirm the identity of the data subject making the request.[63] These requirements could impose costs on organisations that use special formats to store data, or that only hold paper records.

Personal data provided in response to a DSAR must be provided free of charge under the GDPR. This is a marked change from the DPD. In the UK, for example, Section 7 of the Data Protection Act (DPA) 1998 allowed data controllers to charge up to £10 per information request, or up to £50 for paper-based health and education records.

Not all personal data is covered under the Regulation, and if an individual makes "unfounded or excessive" requests, the controller has the right to refuse an information request or to charge a "reasonable fee" to cover the resulting administrative costs.[64] The data subject must also be informed within at least one month of receipt of the request with the reasons for not taking action.

However, as the Regulation does not clarify these terms, it is up to the organisation to prove both that the requests are "unfounded or excessive" and that the fees they wish to

---

[63] GDPR, Recital 59 and Article 12(1).

[64] GDPR, Article 12(5).

charge are "reasonable". Failure to do so could be interpreted as obstructing the data subject's rights and freedoms, which is subject to the highest level of administrative fine.[65] There is potential, therefore, for high volumes of frivolous information requests. Organisations will have to assess the risk of this happening and put in place appropriate safeguards to manage such occurrences.

The GDPR extends this right to give data subjects access to additional information, including the period of time for which the data will be stored and, if this is not possible, the criteria used to determine the retention period.

The right to rectification

The data subject has the right to rectify any inaccuracies in the personal data held about them. Article 16 of the GDPR states that "the data subject shall have the right to obtain from the controller without undue delay the rectification of inaccurate personal data concerning him or her".[66] Inaccurate data includes incomplete data, so data subjects can also request that the controller completes any partial data, which might be achieved by providing the controller with a supplementary statement.

As this right is closely linked to the right to access, it would be sensible to link the processes used to support these two rights. For instance, if your customers view their personal

---

[65] GDPR, Article 83(5).

[66] GDPR, Article 16.

data online, you might use the same web interface to allow them to edit their personal data.

The right to be forgotten

Under Article 17 of the GDPR, data subjects can request that information be erased if they withdraw consent or there is an issue with the underlying legality of the processing.

This could be especially problematic for data collected over an extended period of time or in a variety of formats. It is vital either to establish a process or to review your current processing activities to ensure all such data can be permanently deleted as and when it is necessary. Data mapping, as described in chapter 9 of this manual, will also be essential to ensuring that you can identify all locations from which data will need to be erased.

It is important to note that this is not an absolute right. The right to erasure can only be exercised under a number of specific circumstances[67]:

1. When the personal data are no longer necessary for the purpose for which they were collected or otherwise processed.

2. If the data subject withdraws consent to processing, assuming there is no other legal justification for processing.

3. If the data subject objects to processing based on legitimate interests and the controller cannot

---

[67] GDPR, Article 17, Clause 1.

demonstrate any overriding legitimate grounds for the processing.

4. If the data must be erased under a legal obligation in the European Union or Member State law that applies to the controller.

5. If the data was collected in relation to "information society services".[68]

6. If the data has been unlawfully processed, in breach of the Regulation.

Although the conditions for erasure may seem relatively straightforward, the complete removal of an individual's personal data is more complicated, particularly in the online world. If the controller has made personal data public or passed the data onto other processors, it must inform those processors of the erasure request. Anyone who understands the Internet will recognise that removing all references to a person from every web page, news article, search results page or database is likely an impossible task.

The complexity of handling erasure requests is reflected in Article 17 of the GDPR, which states that the controller is obliged to erase the personal data that has been made available to the public by "taking account of available

---

[68] An information society service is defined in the EU's Information Society Directive (Directive 2001/29/EC) as "any service normally provided for remuneration, at a distance, by electronic means and at the individual request of a recipient of services". In other words, most services provided over the Internet.

technology and the cost of implementation, [and taking] reasonable steps, including technical measures, to inform controllers which are processing the personal data that the data subject has requested the erasure by such controllers of any links to, or copy or replication of, those personal data".[69]

The obligation to take "reasonable steps" makes erasure requests a more achievable goal for most organisations and strengthens the data subject's rights in the digital landscape.

Furthermore, organisations are not automatically obliged to fulfil deletion requests under the GDPR if holding or processing the personal data is necessary:

1. To protect the right of freedom of expression and information;
2. To comply with a European Union or Member State legal obligation;
3. To perform a task in the wider public interest or exercise of official authority;
4. For public health reasons;
5. For archiving, scientific or historical research, or statistical purposes; or
6. For the establishment, exercise or defence of legal claims.[70]

It is possible, of course, that the supervisory authority will disagree that your particular basis for refusing to erase the

---

[69] GDPR, Article 17(2).

[70] GDPR, Article 17(3).

data meets these criteria, so it may be necessary to liaise with it on the finer points of the exemptions.

The right to restriction of processing

Under certain circumstances, data subjects have the right to prevent controllers from conducting specific processing of their data. This right means that, although an organisation can store the personal data, it cannot process the data further unless the individual gives their consent to lift the restriction or the processing is necessary for the establishment of legal claims, to protect the right of another person or in the interests of the wider public.

An individual has the right to restrict the processing of their data if:

1. They contest the accuracy of the personal data, thereby restricting processing for long enough to allow the controller to verify its accuracy;
2. The processing of the data is unlawful, but the data subject does not want their data to be erased and instead requests the restriction of their use;
3. The controller no longer needs the personal data for the purposes of processing, but the data subject requires that data to establish, exercise or defend legal claims (this condition could require controllers working in certain sectors to retain records of former customers); or
4. They object to the processing of their data in accordance with the right to object, and restriction is used while the

controller seeks to verify the legitimate grounds for continuing processing.[71]

Your internal process for responding to restriction requests therefore needs to include a step where the grounds for the request are compared against criteria for restricting, and a formal sign-off process to ensure that appropriate decisions are taken and implemented.

Organisations may need to consider what changes are required to address the logistical issues presented by this right. For example, an organisation may have to segregate the affected data from standard data processing systems, which may require additional functionality and storage resources.

If the data has been disclosed to any third parties, these third-party recipients must be notified of the restriction to further processing as far as is reasonably possible.

Restrictions are not explicitly required to be permanent, so you should ensure that whatever mechanism you use to suspend processing of personal data can be reversed.

The right to data portability

Under the right to data portability, data subjects can request copies of their personal data in a useful electronic format. This right aims to improve the accessibility of information, and is stated in the GDPR as below:

---

[71] GDPR, Article 18, Clause 1.

The data subject shall have the right to receive the personal data concerning him or her, which he or she has provided to a controller, in a structured, commonly used and machine-readable format and have the right to transmit those data to another controller without hindrance from the controller to which the personal data have been provided.[72]

The right to data portability ensures that the data subject can see the specific data that the controller holds, as well as being able to transfer that data to another controller. For instance, if the data subject is trying to change banks, they will be able to readily obtain all of the pertinent information that their new bank needs.

This right only applies where the original processing is based on the data subject's consent or fulfilment of a contract they are party to, and if the processing is automated. It also only applies to data that the data subject has provided to the data controller themselves.[73] This is a reasonably narrow specification, so organisations shouldn't need to suddenly start digging out data that hasn't been processed using an automated system.

---

[72] GDPR, Article 20(1).

[73] The Article 29 Working Party has provided guidance in this area stating that it applies to information the data subject has knowingly and actively provided to the controller, as well as data that may be generated from the data subject's activity (*https://ec.europa.eu/newsroom/article29/item-detail.cfm?item_id=611233*).

Requests to transfer data between controllers are common practice throughout many parts of Europe, and are now required of many more organisations. Although it might not be particularly relevant to some businesses, it could be burdensome for others. Of course, this right also presents an opportunity to attract customers from competitors by, for example, removing the existing difficulties of setting up a new account.

The GDPR does not give specific guidance as to data transfer formats, but it is likely that common, readily accessible formats such as CSV will be acceptable to both the data subject and the supervisory authority.

If the data being transferred relates to more than one individual, the transfer must not "adversely affect the rights and freedoms of others".[74] Resolving this may require you to re-evaluate how data is stored so that individual data subjects can be segregated, it may involve applying some sort of anonymisation or, in some cases, determining whether it is even possible to provide this data without harming other data subjects' rights and freedoms.

The right to object

Under the GDPR, a data subject can object to having their personal data processed. When this occurs, that processing activity must be suspended and the onus is on the controller to demonstrate "legitimate grounds for the processing which override the interests, rights and freedoms of the data subject

---

[74] GDPR, Article 20(4).

or for the establishment, exercise or defence of legal claims".[75]

Individuals can object to specific types of data processing, including direct marketing, processing based on legitimate interests or in the wider public interest, and processing for research or statistical purposes. Only the right to object to direct marketing is absolute, so organisations that process data for the purposes of direct marketing should develop a simple method of removing an individual's personal data from the set of data being processed.[76]

Organisations are also obliged to inform data subjects of their right to object. This notification must "be presented clearly and separately from any other information"[77] when the controller first communicates with the data subject. For online services, there must be an automated way for individuals to exercise their right to object.

The Regulation obliges controllers to prove the need for data processing; to ensure clear and separate communication at the first point of contact; and to provide an automated method to object to processing as part of online services. You should address this obligation by conducting audits of your data protection notices and policies to ensure individuals are told about their right to object, and you should also put in place processes to enable you to respond to data subjects' requests. It will be difficult to comply with the law if you

---

[75] GDPR, Article 21(1).

[76] GDPR, Article 21(2)–(3).

[77] GDPR, Article 21(4).

cannot find ways to quickly and effectively suspend processing of an individual's personal data.

Rights in relation to automated decision-making

Data subjects have the right "not to be subject to a decision based solely on automated processing, including profiling, which produces legal effects concerning [them] or similarly significantly affects [them]".[78]

Under the Regulation, individuals must be able to trigger human intervention, express their point of view and obtain an explanation for a decision, and have the right to contest the resulting decision.

However, automated processing can take place if authorised by a European Union or Member State law.[79] The law itself must contain suitable measures to safeguard the individual's rights and freedoms, and ensure their legitimate interests are in place.

Further grounds on which automated processing can take place revolve around the fulfilment of a contract between the data subject and the controller, or if that individual has given explicit consent. To gain explicit consent, you'll need to ensure that it is very clear to the data subject what they are agreeing to: simply adding a reference to profiling into a consent form, for instance, isn't likely to pass any sort of legal test. In the UK, the ICO also recommends that this

---

[78] GDPR, Article 22(1).

[79] GDPR, Article 22(2)(b).

processing "be the least privacy intrusive way to reasonably achieve your objective".[80]

Where you are exempt from this right by contract or by consent, you'll need to ensure that you implement "suitable measures to safeguard the data subject's rights and freedoms and legitimate interests".[81] These should be assessed during any relevant DPIA and included as critical parts of your privacy compliance framework. Once again, remember that the data subjects' rights have primacy over almost all other concerns, and breaches of those rights can result in the largest administrative fines.

---

[80] *https://ico.org.uk/for-organisations/guide-to-data-protection/guide-to-the-general-data-protection-regulation-gdpr/automated-decision-making-and-profiling/when-can-we-carry-out-this-type-of-processing.*

[81] GDPR, Article 22(3).

Part 2: Building compliance

CHAPTER 4: PRIVACY COMPLIANCE FRAMEWORKS

Although understanding the fundaments of the GDPR is an excellent start, the first few steps of your compliance project can still be the most confusing. Where do you start? Who needs to be involved? How do you go about identifying and meeting all of your obligations? How will you prove that you're meeting all of the Regulation's requirements?

Such questions can distract you from the project's core requirements and make the entire process seem incredibly daunting.

For most organisations, a simple approach may be to ignore the specific, detailed requirements of the GDPR for now, and start instead by building a framework to ensure compliance both now and in the years ahead. The GDPR specifically requires that controllers should, "taking into account the nature, scope, context and purposes of processing as well as the risks of varying likelihood and severity for the rights and freedoms of natural persons, […] implement appropriate technical and organisational measures to ensure and to be able to demonstrate that processing is performed in accordance with this Regulation. Those measures shall be reviewed and updated where necessary".[82]

This clause is, in effect, saying that organisations should put in place a compliance framework that ensures they are

---

[82] GDPR Article 24(1).

implementing appropriate technical and organisational measures to ensure that data processing is performed in compliance with the GDPR.

The GDPR also explicitly requires organisations to demonstrate that they have embedded the principle of 'data protection by design and by default' into their organisational culture. Although there are a number of specific steps necessary to embed data protection by design, the starting point is undoubtedly to create an appropriate compliance framework that makes sure that data protection is at the core of the organisation's behaviour.

A 'compliance framework' is a structured set of guidelines and practices that bring together the regulatory compliance requirements that apply to an organisation, and the business processes, policies and controls necessary to meet these requirements. Technical measures include specific procedures, as well as staff training, audits and all the relevant technical and physical security controls that form part of an effective information security management system. These processes, policies and controls will generally outline how the organisation manages communication, risk and governance relevant to the compliance requirements. Because there will often be some overlap between different compliance requirements, the framework should identify this in order to eliminate redundancies and uncertainties.

All compliance frameworks have to include three categories of activity as illustrated in Figure 1: people, process and technology.

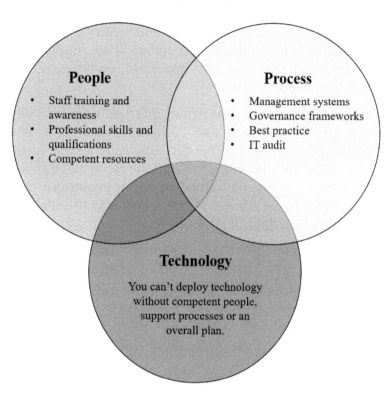

Figure 1: Three categories of activity: people, process and technology

A compliance framework could be developed for any set of legislative, regulatory or contractual requirements. For the GDPR, of course, it will be a privacy compliance framework.

The development of a privacy compliance framework is comparable to any other ongoing business project; you want to establish a set of practices and policies that make sure certain processes are always followed. Assuming those processes are aligned with the legal requirements, the framework should ensure that the organisation remains on the right side of the law. Importantly, all the necessary processes don't need to be defined from the start: they can be built into the framework at appropriate stages in order to achieve compliance. The most important step is getting the initial framework in place.

There are two ways of approaching this task: work it all out for yourself, or deploy and adapt a publicly available compliance framework. The first option relies on some combination of trial and error and (probably expensive) consultancy support; the second draws on established best practice and can be a faster and more cost-effective route to compliance than doing it all yourself.

There are several compliance frameworks and standards to choose from. The GDPR explicitly identifies the use of international standards and privacy marks as effective tools for demonstrating compliance with requirements, and it makes practical and commercial sense for a privacy compliance project to start off by drawing on such established best practice.

A privacy compliance framework is useful primarily because it provides a structured way of managing confidential data in such a way that the organisation is able to comply with often complex laws and, perhaps, on a multi-jurisdictional basis. Organisations that do not already have a privacy compliance framework can use a standardised framework to make the leap from exposure to compliance; organisations that do already have a privacy compliance framework can use national and international standards to obtain certifications that will enhance credibility with customers and stakeholders while also demonstrating to regulators and, perhaps, the courts that due diligence and compliance efforts have been made. There are currently two recognised standards or frameworks that could be used: ISO/IEC 27001:2013 and BS

10012:2017. There is an internationally recognised, accredited certification programme for ISO 27001. BS 10012 certification is relatively new and primarily available in the UK. ISO 27701 is also new and extends ISO 27001 to cover data protection more widely. Other standards and trust marks are also expected to emerge.

The three key areas of a privacy compliance framework are:

1. Governance, risk management and compliance objectives;
2. The data processing principles; and
3. Policies, procedures, controls and records.

In most management systems and frameworks, there is a sense that the various processes are related, and that they feed into and are informed by a common set of controlling processes. That is, like most business processes, these functions will have defined inputs and outputs, and the privacy-specific inputs will eventually result in privacy-specific outputs.

Material scope

Any framework applies to a specific scope, which is the area of the organisation and its operations that fall within it. For the purposes of compliance, the scope of the framework must be directly informed by the requirements of the Regulation, which is described in Article 2 as previously discussed.

This Regulation applies to the processing of personal data wholly or partly by automated means and to the processing other than by automated means of personal data which form part of a filing system or are intended to form part of a filing system.[83]

That is, your framework must cover all activities that involve the collection, use or other processing (such as deletion or modification) of personal data. For many organisations, this will cover almost all of their activities. Remember that this does not specify that the personal data is that of customers: you must also include personal data of your employees, contractors, etc.

There are some exemptions, but these typically relate to either high-level EU activities (such as Member States operating in the interests of national or Union security), in the pursuit of criminal justice by competent authorities or to very low-level activities (such as handling personal data as a natural person exercising activities that are exclusively personal or domestic, rather than as an organisation processing in pursuit of business objectives).

Territorial scope

As explained earlier, the GDPR is explicit[84] in saying that it:

> applies to the processing of personal data of data subjects who are in the Union by a controller or processor not established in the Union, where the processing activities are related to:

---

[83] GDPR, Article 2(1).

[84] GDPR, Article 3.

  (a) the offering of goods or services, irrespective of
      whether a payment of the data subject is required, to
      such data subjects in the Union; or
  (b) the monitoring of their behaviour as far as their
      behaviour takes place within the Union.

In other words, any organisation in the world may be subject
to the GDPR if it provides services to data subjects that are
within the EU. Please consider Recital 14: "the protection
afforded by this Regulation should apply to natural persons,
whatever their nationality or place of residence, in relation to
the processing of their personal data". GDPR confers the same
rights on all data subjects, wherever in the world they may live,
if that data is processed by a controller or processor within the
EU or by one that is providing services into the EU. This may
have significant implications for the scope of the privacy
compliance framework.

Furthermore, the GDPR requires organisations that are based
outside the EU to nominate in writing a representative
organisation within the EU.[85] This representative must be
located in one of the Member States where the target data
subjects are based and must be mandated by the data
controller or data processor to be addressed by the
supervisory authority or data subjects on all issues relating to
the processing of personal data. The appointment of such a
representative will not, however, enable the controller or
processor to avoid legal action for breaches of the GDPR.

---

[85] GDPR, Article 27.

In terms of the compliance framework, there may be other considerations, such as local or sector-specific laws and regulations, that may also have to be taken into account.

Governance

All organisations have an obligation to comply with the law. One of the fiduciary duties of directors is to ensure that their organisation has taken appropriate steps to comply with all relevant laws. Directors also have a fiduciary – and in many cases also a legal and contractual duty – to ensure that risks to the organisation are appropriately managed. Cyber risk is an example of the type of risk of which directors have to be aware. Cyber attack exposes organisations to significant reputational and operational damage, as well as the possibility of legal action by those whose personal data has been compromised. The GDPR gives any data subject the right to pursue judicial remedies for both material and non-material harm arising from the processing of their data. This, combined with the specific GDPR requirements around data breach reporting and the significant administrative penalties for compliance breaches (up to 4% of global turnover or €20 million, whichever is greater), should be on the radar of all directors and on the agendas of all board meetings. Boards should ensure that the privacy compliance frameworks that are put in place are capable of ensuring GDPR compliance and that they contain mechanisms for providing regular reports and assurance to the board on the state of compliance across the organisation.

One way that boards can approach their governance responsibility in respect of information and privacy risk is by appointing a board-level senior information risk owner (SIRO). The UK government originated the idea of this role as part of its extended strategy to tackle information risk across the public sector and described the role of SIRO to be managing information risk from a business not a technical perspective, focusing on the strategic information risks related to the delivery of corporate objectives. This means taking a holistic approach to information risk across the supply chain and managing it in line with the organisation's risk appetite. This is a useful role for a board to put in place. This role is expected to work with board colleagues to:

- Establish an information risk strategy that allows assets to be exploited and risks to be managed effectively;
- Identify business-critical information assets and set objectives, priorities and plans to maximise the use of information as a business asset; and
- Establish and maintain an appropriate risk appetite with proportionate risk boundaries and tolerances.

Clearly, this role has a broader responsibility than simply managing privacy risk. The reality, however, is that any framework you build to manage privacy risk must, perforce, be part of your wider framework for managing information risk. It therefore makes sense to tackle GDPR compliance as part of your wider strategy for managing information risk.

This governance element should manifest itself in appropriate resource commitment – in terms of personnel, financing and systems – to the GDPR compliance project, in demonstrable top management leadership and commitment, and in the corporate privacy policy and throughout internal communications.

All international management system standards published after 2013 contain, in Clause 5 and its sub-clauses, a number of specific requirements covering top management commitment; these provide a good starting point for any organisation in determining the leadership of a corporate governance framework. The Clause 5 requirements are detailed below.

Top management demonstrates leadership and commitment to the management system by:

a. Ensuring policies and objectives are established and are compatible with strategic direction;

b. Ensuring integration of the management system into the organisation's processes;

c. Ensuring resources needed for the management system are available;

d. Communicating the importance of effective management and of conforming to the management system requirements;

e. Ensuring the management system achieves its intended outcome(s);

f. Directing and supporting persons to contribute to the effectiveness of the management system;

g. Promoting continual improvement, and;

h. Supporting other relevant management roles to demonstrate their leadership as it applies to their areas of responsibility.

ISO/IEC 38500:2015 is a standard that deals specifically with the corporate governance of information and communications technologies. It, too, offers useful guidance for creating an effective technology governance framework.

Objectives

Your privacy framework will have a number of objectives. Obviously, the overall objective should be to comply with the Regulation and to avoid the 'dissuasive' fines and other punitive measures. Your framework should also identify specific subsidiary objectives relating to the rights of data subjects and the protection of personal data.

Objectives should be determined in a way that enables performance against them to be tracked and measured. An objective is only useful, after all, if you can determine how you stack up against it. The normal acronym used in relation to objectives is that they should be SMART:

- Specific
- Measurable
- Actionable (or achievable)
- Realistic
- Time-bound

The performance of information security controls should be capable of measurement and improvement, and ISO/IEC 27004:2016 provides specific guidance on control measurement. Although this standard is a useful starting point for tackling control performance, it does not contain specific guidance on measuring performance against specific data privacy objectives.

Key objectives could include:

- The ability to respond to subject access requests within the new prescribed timeframe (one month[86]);
- The ability to identify and report data breaches to supervisory authorities within 72 hours;
- Retention periods of personal data; and
- Staff awareness training.

Key processes

A privacy framework should have a number of key processes, some of which your organisation may already have, and others that may be new. These could include processes for incident management, change management, corrective action, risk management and continual improvement.

Incident management processes – which will be discussed in chapter 14 of this manual – are all about what you do when there is a data breach or some other information security incident.

Fundamentally, the incident management process will comprise several stages:

1. Realising that something has happened and reporting it.
2. Understanding what has happened.
3. Containing the event to minimise damage.
4. Repairing the damage.

---

[86] GDPR, Article 12.

5. Making sure that the event cannot recur.
6. Reviewing the organisation's response.

The outputs of the incident management process will inform how the organisation's framework evolves to meet its current and future challenges.

The organisation will also need **change management** processes. All organisations have to change and adapt to risks and events, and to changes in customer and market requirements. When changes are rolled out in an unstructured manner, new and unforeseen risks can be introduced. This is particularly true of ICT-related processes. Inadequate management of changes to business processes (or to departments or reporting structures) can create risks to personal information and possible breaches in existing privacy protection mechanisms. A change management process is an essential step in ensuring that rolling out a change is completely thought through, that possible deviations, problems and consequences have been identified and mitigated, and that roll-back options are in place.

A **corrective action** process is also necessary so that an organisation can make amends when something doesn't work as intended. This might be as obvious as a control being inadequate and failing to suitably protect an asset, or it might be a larger, systemic fault that prevents a whole process from functioning. In either case, the organisation will need a systematic method of identifying and remediating the fault.

You can see the obvious connection here with the incident management and change management processes. Once an incident has been dealt with, there should be an analysis of the cause of the incident, which should lead to the identification of amendments to or changes in existing controls or processes. These changes should be dealt with through the corrective action process, ensuring that corrections are reviewed and approved, that they're correctly implemented and that they're reviewed for effectiveness. This last point is worthy of note: a corrective action needs to correct the problem, so your process will need to include a review stage. This review might be a one-off confirmation or it might require ongoing attention – that's something the process will need to identify.

One of the more critical processes is **risk management**, which is dealt with in much greater depth in chapter 11 of this manual. All organisations face risks and, in the case of GDPR compliance, the focus will be on risks to personal data and to the systems and processes that interact with that data.

Risk management is very much at the core of any privacy compliance framework because the organisation needs to understand exactly what risks it needs to protect itself from. Just as a person might put on a suit of armour to save themselves from injury, that suit will be completely useless against poisonous gas, or might only have limited effectiveness against a bear. The organisation should ensure it invests its money and resources in the right areas, so having an effective risk management regime in place is a good way of ensuring that the return on investment is worthwhile.

Where privacy risk is concerned, though, the risk management programme must also look closely at risks to the 'rights and freedoms of natural persons' that might arise from the processing of their data. In a sense, the GDPR says to organisations that there is the risk of substantial administrative fines, as well as legal action from data subjects, if they fail to adequately manage risks to those data subjects. This tells the organisation that its risk management activities must account for both the risks to personal data should it be compromised and the risk to the organisation itself if it does not comply.

A framework or management system should also have an underlying continual improvement process. A continual improvement process assesses existing processes and their outputs for conformity with laws, regulations or other requirements, determines any necessary adjustments, and then feeds these into the originating processes that determine the framework or management system's inputs. In simpler terms, you might like to refer to the Plan-Do-Check-Act cycle (PDCA, also called the Deming Cycle), which is a popular process model for ensuring ongoing improvement.

Other continual improvement cycles, such as the COBIT® (Control Objectives for Information and Related Technologies) Continual Improvement Life Cycle or the ITIL®\ Continual Service Improvement process, could be applied instead of the PDCA cycle.

The PDCA cycle divides the standard processes and practices for a management system or development process into four distinct stages: planning, doing, checking and acting. As a cyclical process, each stage feeds into the one that follows and enables continual improvement.

In brief, the organisation:

- Plans what it is going to do;
- Does what it has planned to do;
- Checks whether what it has done has achieved what it planned; and
- Acts on those findings to improve how it achieves its objectives.

The PDCA cycle is illustrated in Figure 2, below.

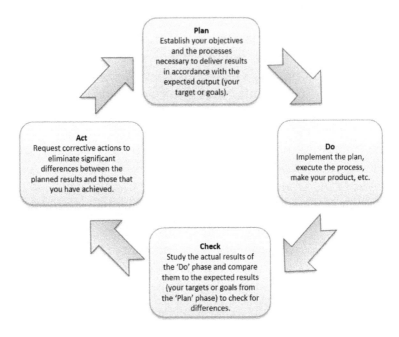

Figure 2: The PDCA cycle

Understanding how the processes and continual improvement of those processes all fit together is a critical feature of any effective compliance framework. Under the assumption that all of your processes are adequate and that they are being followed, such a framework provides assurance that you are continuing to adapt and improve your processes so as to continue meeting your compliance requirements.

Personal information management systems

Personal information management systems (PIMS) are a form of management system dedicated to the management of personal information. As such, they can form a good basis for a compliance framework.

It is important to note that, although a PIMS and a compliance framework are broadly similar, there are distinctions. For instance, a compliance framework is not necessarily a 'single object' but may be comprised of two or more management systems working in concert (a PIMS and an information security management system, or information security management system (ISMS), for example). A PIMS may also be focused on simply managing personal information rather than necessarily protecting it in line with legal or regulatory requirements. In this sense, the PIMS may only provide some of the processes necessary to ensure overall compliance.

Although a PIMS is not necessarily designed to ensure compliance with the GDPR specifically – or even with more specific laws such as the UK's DPA or Germany's Federal Data Protection Act (Bundesdatenschutzgesetz, BDSG) – standardised models will usually include a requirement to identify legislative, regulatory and contractual requirements relating to personal information, and to include those requirements in the PIMS.

There are several possible ways to achieve this and BS 10012:2017 – *Data protection – Specification for a personal information management system* – provides one such framework for doing so. It provides a well-defined, well-understood structure for managing data protection, and it is designed to follow the PDCA cycle to ensure continual improvement. Although the earlier version of the standard was specific to the UK's DPA, it has been redrafted and updated to reflect the requirements of the GDPR and, as such, BS 10012:2017 should be generally suitable as the core of a privacy compliance framework.

BS 10012 includes a requirement to "define the scope of the PIMS and set personal information management objectives, with due regard to the [...] applicable statutory, regulatory, contractual and/or professional duties".[87] Properly applied, this means that the processes described in BS 10012 should take the appropriate legal requirements into account.

However, BS 10012 may not on its own be an adequate framework, depending on how your organisation collects, stores and uses personal data. BS 10012 is narrowly focused on privacy protection, and if personal data is more widely used across your business processes, then a more comprehensive security framework would be appropriate. In this circumstance, you may need to define additional processes in order to comply with the Regulation. This is where an additional management system may be useful, such as ISO 27001, which is the international standard that describes best-practice requirements for an ISMS.

Regardless of the standard or business process model employed, a PIMS is likely to be a useful core for your privacy compliance framework. Figure 3 provides an overview of the typical components of a PIMS.

---

[87] BS 10012:2017, Clause 4.3.

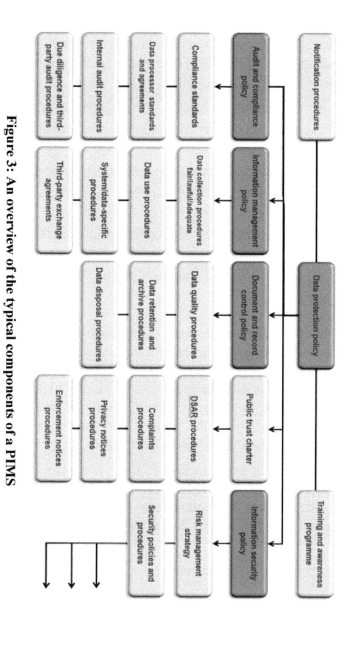

Figure 3: An overview of the typical components of a PIMS

ISO/IEC 27001:2013

The GDPR requires organisations to go further than simply putting in place a PIMS. There is an explicit requirement for organisations to have in place:

> (b) the ability to ensure the ongoing confidentiality, integrity, availability and resilience of processing systems and services;
>
> (c) the ability to restore the availability of and access to personal data in a timely manner in the event of a physical or technical incident;
>
> (d) a process for regularly testing, assessing and evaluating the effectiveness of technical and organisational measures for ensuring the security of the processing.[88]

This really does mean that organisations have to integrate data and privacy protection into 'business as usual' and that a more comprehensive approach to information security – one that deals with the processing systems and services, as well as with security, continuity and continual security testing (primarily in the form of penetration testing) – is essential. This is where ISO 27001 comes in.

ISO 27001 is sector-agnostic, does not favour any one technology or solution and can be used by organisations of any size. It sets out requirements for what must be done to secure information, but leaves room for organisations to

---

[88] GDPR, Article 32(1).

determine how they implement the requirements to meet their objectives and risk appetite.

This framework for information security can also be validated by accredited external certification. The assurance provided by such certification is widely recognised as proof that the organisation protects information assets, and it is a requirement in a growing number of contracts that involve valuable information.

Structurally, it is not too different from BS 10012: both are driven from the top of the organisation, describe processes that are critical to the protection of personal data and recognise that a number of processes are necessary to manage these processes as part of a wider structure. The distinction is that BS 10012 is specifically focused on personal information, while ISO 27001 is interested in information more generally. As such, an ISO 27001 ISMS could be used as a larger framework within which BS 10012 can sit. ISO 27001 encourages the organisation to seek out additional sources of best practice, and BS 10012 is certainly that.

Figure 4 shows the structure of an ISO 27001 ISMS.

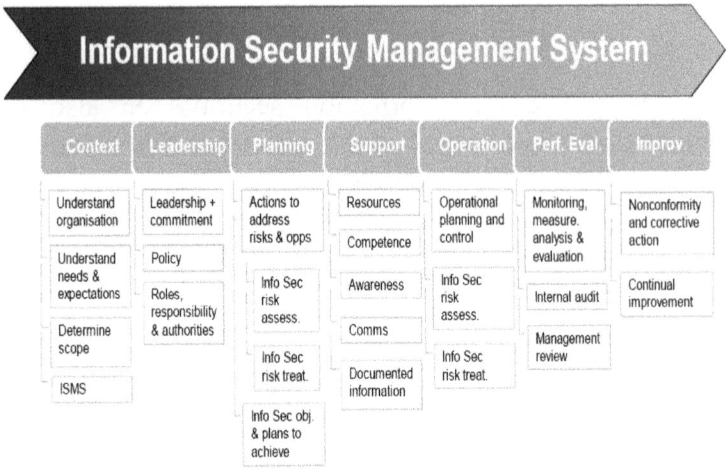

Figure 4: Structure of an ISO 27001 ISMS

ISO 27001 aims to safeguard the "confidentiality, integrity and availability of information by applying a risk management process and gives confidence to interested parties that risks are adequately managed".[89] In fact, information security is defined as the "preservation of the confidentiality, integrity and availability of information". In information security:

- Confidentiality is the "property that information is not made available or disclosed to unauthorized individuals, entities, or processes"[90];

---

[89] ISO/IEC 27001:2013, Clause 0.1.

[90] ISO/IEC 27000:2016, Clause 2.12.

- Integrity is the "property of accuracy and completeness"[91];
- Availability is the "property of being accessible and usable upon demand by an authorized entity"[92]; and
- Risk is the "effect of uncertainty on objectives".[93]

Confidentiality, integrity and availability are often called the CIA of information security because they are the key attributes of secure information. The GDPR itself mentions them explicitly on a number of occasions. Similarly, ISO 27001's approach to risk is in alignment with the Regulation's requirements for impact assessments, as you will see later in this manual.

ISO 27001 takes the approach that information security must be driven from the top down. As such, it contains the requirement that an information security policy, signed off by top management, is enacted through critical processes such as risk management, monitoring and review, corrective actions, and so on.

ISO 27001 Annex A lists 114 controls, in 14 categories, which can be used to identify what may be appropriate controls to help manage the security of personal information. Figure 5 shows the 14 control categories.

---

[91] ISO/IEC 27000:2016, Clause 2.40.

[92] ISO/IEC 27000:2016, Clause 2.9.

[93] ISO/IEC 27000:2016, Clause 2.68.

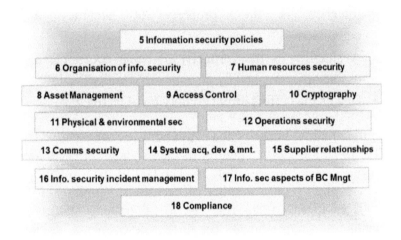

Figure 5: The 14 control categories of Annex A

The best book for detailed, practical guidance on implementing these controls is Alan Calder and Steve Watkins's *IT Governance: An International Guide to Data Security and ISO27001/ISO27002*,[94] now in its seventh edition. For a straightforward description of how to design and implement an information security management system that meets the requirements of ISO/IEC 27001:2013, turn to Alan Calder's *Nine Steps to Success: an ISO27001*

---

[94]*www.itgovernance.co.uk/shop/product/it-governance-an-international-guide-to-data-security-and-iso27001iso27002-7th-edition.*

Implementation Overview,[95] or Bridget Kenyon's *ISO 27001 Controls – A guide to implementing and auditing.*[96] IBITGQ also has relevant ISO 27001 implementation and audit qualifications available.

Organisations that implement ISO 27001 will naturally find themselves accruing evidence of their compliance with the Standard, especially if they have gone to the trouble of seeking external certification for their ISMS. This evidence is useful beyond simply getting certification or showing clients that your processes are secure. In the event that an organisation is subject to an investigation or audit, it will be able to draw upon this evidence to show that it has been following best practice, that it has taken appropriate steps to prevent incidents, that it recognises the risks it faces and that people at all levels throughout the organisation are appropriately trained, competent and responsible.

Other standards

Although ISO 27001 and BS 10012 are the most likely candidate standards to use as the basis of a privacy compliance framework, there are other standards and business process models that could also be used. Whichever you choose – and whether you decide to choose one of the standards or business processes mentioned here – will depend on your organisation and its specific processes, resources and requirements.

---

[95] *www.itgovernancepublishing.co.uk/product/nine-steps-to-success.*

[96] *www.itgovernancepublishing.co.uk/product/iso-27001-controls-a-guide-to-implementing-and-auditing.*

ISO 27701 has been developed as an extension of ISO 27001 to provide additional controls for data protection and to integrate data protection into information security processes. It is non-specific and relies heavily upon the organisation recognising its legal obligations, but it can be used to develop a framework capable of complying with any data protection regimes around the world.

COBIT is a control-based framework for the governance of IT and information. It may seem a slightly abstract approach to GDPR compliance, but establishing governance and oversight will be an important part of ensuring the security and privacy of personal data, as will asserting accountability and responsibility for maintaining this. COBIT is a widely used framework in some countries – particularly at the enterprise level – and so there are publications and experts available to provide advice and guidance, if necessary.

Other frameworks have been developed by government agencies to simplify the compliance process when working with complex sets of legislation. Although these may not be immediately relevant to GDPR compliance, they often contain an effective structure and processes that can be applied to meet European compliance requirements. The Privacy Management Framework[97] developed by the Office of the Australian Information Commissioner (OAIC), for instance, is a simple four-stage process that matches the PDCA cycle, and provides guidance at each stage to ensure compliance with the range of Australian law and other

---

[97] *www.oaic.gov.au/agencies-and-organisations/guides/privacy-management-framework.*

relevant requirements imposed by other nations that Australia regularly trades with.

The US National Institute of Standards and Technology (NIST) has also built an extensive collection of information security standards, known as the NIST Special Publication 800 series. Although it is not specifically an information security management framework, the NIST SP 800-53 model is used by US government agencies that need to comply with the requirements of Federal Information Processing Standard (FIPS) 200. Although NIST SP 800-53 may be intended for government agencies, the framework can certainly be applied to other industries.

Selecting and implementing a compliance framework

The decision to select, design or compile a particular framework to ensure compliance will be based on a number of critical considerations.

To begin, the scope of the compliance project will inform the level of detail and the breadth of the organisation that the framework will need to include. You will need to consider a variety of factors in this regard, including whether your organisation is a data controller or a data processor, the type and volume of personal data that your organisation collects and/or processes, the end-to-end processes within which personal data is processed, the different ways in which data is collected and processed and so on. Analysing this information in order to clearly define the scope of the project is an essential step, especially if you elect to use one or more management system standards (such as a PIMS) to develop your compliance framework.

As well as informing the scope, the personal data that your organisation collects, stores or processes will also influence your choice of compliance framework. If you work with special categories of personal information, such as health information, or process especially large quantities of data, the GDPR requires additional measures to ensure the data is secure. As such, your compliance framework may need additional processes to ensure that you meet these requirements and that you have sufficient evidence of compliance.

The complexity of your organisation will also influence your choice of compliance framework and its scope. A large organisation with a broad portfolio of processes will not necessarily want a framework that interferes with processes outside the data protection scope, for instance. In contrast, an organisation that makes extensive use of personal data for differing purposes across a range of functions will need a framework that accounts for data processing in relation to each of the various business objectives. The methods for protecting information in one process may be wholly incompatible with the methods for protecting it in another.

In addition to ensuring the framework is suitable to your organisation's specific needs, you should also consider the frameworks used by others in your industry or sector. This will help you to think about the sector-specific needs that other organisations have identified, as well as allowing you to leverage any existing experience or knowledge.

As previously noted, many organisations will be subject to a number of additional legal or regulatory requirements, as well as differing jurisdictional requirements in different parts of the world, in relation to personal data or information, ranging from freedom of information legislation to HIPAA data portability requirements. These should also be taken into account in your choice of compliance framework. Some laws and regulations will require specific evidence in order to demonstrate compliance, and this may overlap considerably with the requirements of the GDPR.

Your organisation's experience with management systems and frameworks will also influence your decision. For organisations with little such experience, we would generally recommend starting with established standards such as BS 10012 and ISO 27001, not least because of the wealth of standard-specific resources available to support your project. For organisations with more experience, the choice may be influenced by a desire to extend an existing management system to include personal information management. In this case, you will need to ensure that the organisation's internal pressures and documented processes do not interfere with the project's primary goal: having appropriate and proportionate controls in place to protect personal data and demonstrate compliance with the GDPR.

Finally, the availability of resources, support and guidance are important factors. Once again, organisations with less experience in either compliance or data protection will need to ensure there are appropriate resources available, both internally and externally, to ensure that the project will be viable.

Implementing the framework

Once you've decided on the starting point for your privacy compliance framework, you will need to establish how it integrates with your organisation. Who is responsible and accountable for each process? Who needs oversight? What sort of training is necessary? These sorts of questions, in conjunction with the requirements of the GDPR, will inform how you build out the framework from the core requirements.

Beginning from first principles, the framework should be driven by a formal organisational privacy and data protection policy, which should be published and made available to appropriate interested parties, including employees. The policy needs to specify the organisation's position on data privacy and protection, assert that it aims to comply with the GDPR and other relevant data protection laws and regulations, and be signed off by an appropriate top management authority, such as the board or CEO.

Beneath the data protection policy, you'll need to define and document the essential data protection processes that convert the policy into practice. You could do this with a set of process maps. Each specific process should be sufficiently documented so that anyone who has identified responsibilities within the process is clear about what has to be done, by whom, and by when, in a way that will deliver consistent outcomes. Typically, this is done by means of a RACI chart. A RACI chart defines, for each process (or step in a process), who is:

- Responsible
- Accountable
- Consulted
- Informed

The purpose of a RACI chart is to ensure that the process is designed and operates in line with business requirements, is consistently and reliably performed and is aligned with formal requirements, such that management can depend on it to deliver required results. Figure 6 shows what a simple RACI chart might look like.

Process	CEO	H of HR	H of IT	H of Fin	Legal	Users
A	R+A	C	I		C	I
B		C	R+A	I	C	
C		C	R+A		C	I (+ cleaners)
D		I		A	R (+reg)	I
E	C	I		I	R+A	I

Figure 6: A simple RACI chart

You will want the process outputs and activity records to confirm, first, that you are complying with the law and, second, that your framework is working in line with the organisation's requirements. So, you'll need to think about the metrics that will provide this information and how you can gather them. Some may be as simple as keeping a record of the number of times a certain process is performed, others might be based on staff surveys.

Developing a compliance monitoring programme is a logical extension of this approach, and would involve implementing a compliance testing process to monitor your system or framework. There are many ways of measuring the effectiveness of any management system or framework, and at least as many books on the topic. This evaluation process will feed your continual improvement process. This involves recognising when your organisation has failed to comply and working to amend that, or seeing that a process isn't working as well as it could and improving it.

Corrective action and continual improvement processes were discussed earlier. Such continual improvements are imperative to futureproof your compliance to the GDPR. As the business processes, policies and controls evolve, so must your framework.

CHAPTER 5: INFORMATION SECURITY AS PART OF DATA PROTECTION

An important component of data protection is also a wider concern for all organisations: information security. Not all data is personal data, but almost all data has value that the organisation has a vested interest in protecting. Although the GDPR and other data protection law focuses on protecting data subjects and preserving their rights, part of this necessarily includes information security, which has a much wider potential application.

Data security failures and cyber breaches can be catastrophic events for any organisation. Small organisations may well be wiped out simply by the nature of the breach or the immediate costs of dealing with it, and large corporations can be hit by enormous fines and class-action lawsuits, all of which can have significant repercussions and inflict significant damage on both the organisation's reputation and its bottom line.

Although the Regulation does not explicitly prohibit data breaches – that would be impossible to enforce – it does assert that organisations should seek ways to secure all personal data against loss and damage.

As the overwhelming majority of data security failures result from a common set of vulnerabilities, organisations should be aware of these vulnerabilities and act to eliminate them. There is no shortage of information on the topic, and the information security industry exists to support this approach. Despite these resources, the same set of vulnerabilities persists and organisations continue to suffer.

One of the more notable breaches in recent years was that of Target in the US. In late 2013, criminals gained access to around 70 million customers' personal information, and data on 40 million credit cards and payment cards. These details were stolen from Target's point-of-sale (POS) systems via malware. The attackers were able to gain access to Target's systems because of a number of flaws:

1. The attackers infiltrated the computer systems of Target's HVAC supplier; Target had not established an effective supplier security vetting process and this supplier's security processes were inadequate.

2. The interface between the building management system in one of Target's outlets and its customer payment systems was inadequately secured, and the attackers were able to move into those payment systems and then take advantage of inadequate control over access rights and privileges to escalate their access rights to get into what should have been an isolated and secure network.

3. Target ignored a number of automated warnings from its intrusion detection software (IDS).

As a result of the breach, Target was subjected to substantial fines and lawsuits, and both the CIO and CEO were forced to resign. The overall cost to Target was estimated to be in the hundreds of millions of dollars, not including the impact on revenues and profits that resulted from the loss in customer confidence.

Between July and September of 2018, there were 4,056 data security incidents reported to the Information Commissioner in the UK.[98] This is a significant increase over previous years,[99] which is likely to be partially due to the rise of the GDPR and mandatory reporting of data breaches. Although this number may still appear small in relation to the size of the British economy, it should be remembered that these are only the data breaches that were both identified and reported to the ICO. It is reasonable to assume that the true number is considerably larger.

The prevalence of cyber attacks is almost certainly down to organisations failing to address common security vulnerabilities.

According to the UK government's Cyber Security Breaches Survey 2018, barely half of all respondents had implemented the basic security controls recommended in the Cyber Essentials scheme.[100] These controls are intended to prevent around 80% of all Internet-based threats and, as such, should be considered a core component of data protection.

Personal data breaches

In the GDPR, a personal data breach "means a breach of security leading to the accidental or unlawful destruction,

---

[98] *https://ico.org.uk/action-weve-taken/data-security-incident-trends/*.

[99] By way of comparison, there were 697 such cases in the same quarter in 2017.

[100] *www.gov.uk/government/statistics/cyber-security-breaches-survey-2018*.

loss, alteration, unauthorised disclosure of, or access to, personal data transmitted, stored or otherwise processed".[101]

This is a key focus of the Regulation; it is less concerned with other forms of data breach except where they could impact the security of personal data. Note that breaches are not necessarily malicious, may not affect a significant number of people and may be caused by simple acts like losing a laptop.

Data breaches are unpleasant and undesirable, and all steps the organisation can take to secure its information will also shore up the security of the personal data of those inside and outside the boundaries of the organisation.

Anatomy of a data breach

Information can be compromised in a number of ways: it can be distributed outside the organisation (e.g. by theft and resale on the dark web), damaged or made inaccurate (e.g. by vandalism) or it can be rendered inaccessible (e.g. by ransomware). These are violations of the information's confidentiality, integrity or availability, also called the 'CIA' of information security.

Data compromises do not usually occur spontaneously. There will always be some action or inaction that undermines the security of the data and enables it to be breached.

---

[101] GDPR, Article 4(12).

The key components of a data breach are a threat and a vulnerability.

A threat is a "potential cause of an unwanted incident, which may result in harm to a system or organization".[102] In other words, a threat is anything that could cause something unwanted to occur. A threat could be as simple as a disgruntled ex-member of staff or a piece of malware.

Many threats are associated with threat actors – the entity that enacts the threat – such as a cyber criminal, a malicious insider, an oblivious member of staff, and so on, but there are other threats, such as natural disasters or environmental hazards, which are not associated with a threat actor.

A vulnerability is a "weakness of an asset or control that can be exploited by one or more threats".[103] Not all threats have a vulnerability to exploit, and both are necessary for there to be a breach. A threat without a vulnerability to exploit is no risk, and a vulnerability with no threat to exploit it is also not a risk. A data breach occurs when a threat successfully exploits a vulnerability and harms the organisation's information.

Sites of attack

All vulnerabilities have a location, although this should not be thought of in a purely physical sense. A web application, for instance, may have an SQL injection vulnerability

---

[102] ISO/IEC 27000:2018, Clause 3.74.

[103] ISO/IEC 27000:2018, Clause 3.77.

located in a virtual environment. That said, it is important not to forget the presence of physical vulnerabilities.

Beyond simply classifying each vulnerability as either physical or logical, organisations should ensure they know more specifically where the vulnerability is located. For instance, if you identify a vulnerability to heavy rain that only affects some rooms, then you need to know where those rooms are. Vulnerabilities that can be exploited by several threats may have multiple locations.

Your organisation has a number of perimeters, which are defined by the points at which your organisation meets the outside world. In physical terms, this is likely to be the walls of the building or offices; in logical or electronic terms, this will be your network perimeter and your endpoint devices, such as laptops and mobile phones. Each perimeter will have points of ingress and egress – doors, Internet connections, and so on– that make the perimeter porous and increase the potential harm. For example, an organisation's web application is linked to a database populated with sensitive information. A user interacts with this web application to manipulate a specific set of this information, such as their own address or contact details. If the user can modify their own details, a vulnerability in the web application might allow them to modify other users' details as well.

Securing your information

Vulnerabilities and threats are typically managed with controls. A control is a process or tool that mitigates the risk of the threat exploiting the vulnerability by reducing either the likelihood of the risk occurring or the impact if it does happen.

Securing your information is not something that can be achieved with technology alone. In simple terms, organisational operations depend on the effective interaction of people, processes and technology. Significant vulnerabilities can often be identified in each of those three areas, and trained personnel working to effective procedures are usually essential for the correct and secure configuration of software.

Security software, such as anti-malware software, must be correctly configured and deployed on the network as well as on endpoint devices if malware intrusions are to be contained. Correct configuration depends on clarity about the network design, where the interfaces are between the secure network and the outside world, as well as a trained and competent system administrator working to a clearly defined configuration standard.

This obviously requires an integrated and systematic approach, much like the compliance frameworks described in the previous chapter. It is generally considered good practice to implement an ISMS in order to manage risks to an organisation's information assets, and this approach is supported by the GDPR as asserted in Chapter IV, Section 5 ("Codes of conduct and certification").

ISO 27001

ISO 27001, which was described earlier, is the international standard for information security management systems. Organisations around the world have successfully used it to improve their information security posture, avoid data breaches, reduce insurance premiums, and so on.

It takes the form of a set of requirements against which an ISMS can be independently audited and certified.

Independent, accredited certification provides assurance – to the management and staff of the organisation as well as to its customers, suppliers and stakeholders – that the organisation protects its information assets using best-practice information security measures.

An ISO 27001-compliant ISMS has at its core a risk assessment, which ensures that the organisation takes a risk-based approach to securing its information. During the risk assessment process, the organisation identifies the threats and vulnerabilities that form a risk, determines the likelihood and impact of the risk materialising and applies controls to mitigate these risks.

Annex A of ISO 27001 lists a reference control set, comprising 114 controls that are expanded on in ISO 27002. Unlike ISO 27001, ISO 27002 is simply guidance: it provides advice and additional information about the controls without asserting any actual requirements.

Although other standards for information security exist, many are specific to certain industries, only offer a single set of controls or are less systematic. However, when implemented in conjunction with ISO 27001, these standards may provide additional security, further controls or access to specific markets or industries.

Ten Steps to Cyber Security

The UK's Department for Business Innovation and Skills (BIS) published its Ten Steps to Cyber Security[104] in 2012 as

---

[104] *www.ncsc.gov.uk/guidance/10-steps-cyber-security*.

an overview of cyber security for executives, and this is now maintained by the National Cyber Security Centre (NCSC). This guidance recognises that information is at the centre of business today, and that cyberspace provides the whole digital architecture of society. Cyberspace comprises both the Internet and the information systems that support and maintain infrastructure, business and services.

As a framework, the Ten Steps to Cyber Security focuses on a top-level understanding of cyber security. It relies on broad descriptions to explain the risks and provides defences and solutions that can be applied across the whole organisation, rather than providing a more specific set of controls that would require specialised skills or experience to implement. The Ten Steps can be achieved by applying other standards, and the organisation that can tick off all of the points raised in the Ten Steps can be reasonably confident in its ability to repel attacks.

It is not possible to be wholly immune to cyber attacks, of course, and the Ten Steps does not offer a certification or auditing scheme to confirm compliance. However, the framework gives a view of cyber security that senior management can readily communicate to the organisation. It does not rely on specific technical comprehension, it presents logically consistent goals, and it clearly explains the landscape in which cyber security operates. Given the preponderance of highly technical manuals on the topic, this is a useful framework.

Cyber Essentials

The Cyber Essentials scheme is functionally a control framework established by the UK government as a 'lighter' version of the Ten Steps. The Cyber Essentials framework asserts that "Around 80% of cyber attacks could be prevented if businesses put simple security controls in place",[105] and provides five controls to achieve this. It is supported by a certification scheme that provides organisations with a relatively easy way to give some form of cyber security assurance. Certification to Cyber Essentials is a requirement for UK government contracts that involve sensitive or personal information.

Adhering to the scheme provides an entry level for cyber security assurance. Organisations should, as a matter of common sense, implement the five Cyber Essentials controls and then move on to implement ISO 27001 or a similarly rigorous information security framework. Cyber Essentials certification should be an inexpensive option.

Cyber Essentials certification through a CREST-accredited certification body involves an external security scan of the in-scope externally-facing connections, which provides additional assurance that the organisation is secure. A more involved level of certification, Cyber Essentials Plus, requires additional internal testing, which provides assurance that individual device builds are secure and this is a significant enhancement in security.

Although Cyber Essentials certifications are technically only valid on the day of certification, in practice the assurance needs only to be renewed on an annual basis.

_____

[105] *www.gov.uk/government/news/cyber-security-boost-for-uk-firms*.

NIST standards

As mentioned previously, the NIST SP 800 series (and the forthcoming NIST SP 1800 series[106]) publications cover a great deal of ground in the field of information security. For US organisations, or those outside the US that do a lot of business with the US, using NIST frameworks and controls may make a great deal of business sense.

The NIST documents are available free of charge from the NIST Computer Security Resource Centre (*www.nist.gov*) and provide guidance for organisations seeking to comply with the US federal government's requirements in relation to the Federal Information Security Management Act (FISMA). They cover all of the procedures and criteria recommended by NIST for assessing and documenting threats and vulnerabilities, and the security measures deemed necessary to reduce the risk of data breaches.

The information security policy

At the core of any effort to secure the organisation's information assets should be a top-level declaration of the organisation's intent to implement an information security framework and its objectives in doing so. This declaration is the information security policy, which will drive all of your organisation's efforts to protect its information, including the personal data with which the GDPR is primarily concerned. It is worth noting that, although closely related, this is a

---

[106] *https://csrc.nist.gov/publications/sp1800*.

different document from the data protection policy described previously.

Getting the information security policy right is critical because it will form the basis of your organisation's whole approach to information security.

1. It should be signed off by the highest level of management, such as the CEO or the board.
2. It should assert the organisation's intentions for information security.
3. It should describe the information security objectives and how these align with the organisation's broader business objectives.
4. It should describe the scope of the policy. It could be that the policy only applies to one of the organisation's sites or only to certain types of information.
5. It should assert responsibility and accountability.
6. It should be communicated to everyone who needs to know about information security. This is likely to be the whole staff, contractors and, potentially, customers and other stakeholders.
7. It should be subject to a review, approval and reissue process to ensure that it remains accurate and relevant to the organisation.

Additional guidance on information security policies is contained in ISO/IEC 27002,[107] including a list of more

---

[107] ISO/IEC 27002:2013, Clause 5.1.1.

specific policies that could be established to support a primary information security policy.

Assuring information security

Part of establishing effective information security in order to comply with the GDPR will involve developing the evidence that you have done so. This serves two purposes: first, it allows the organisation to identify and react to any weaknesses or failings; second, it provides an auditable record of compliance.

As described in the previous chapter, the privacy compliance framework should operate in such a way to generate outputs that prove the processes are being followed. This is part of the 'people, processes and technology' mentioned earlier: well-documented processes carried out by trained staff using appropriate technology.

The outputs you generate should not expose the information you are seeking to protect. The output might be as simple as:

- A schedule for the process, indicating when it should be done and by whom, when it was done and who confirmed that it was done in accordance with the defined process.
- A collection of sign-off forms confirming that appropriate technology has been purchased and configured according to the organisation's standards.
- A log of access to confidential data, with automated checking to ensure that only authorised personnel have done so and only from authorised workstations.

The data collected only needs to be detailed enough to show that your processes and controls are functioning correctly. Any deviation from expected results can then be fed into your incident management and/or continual improvement processes.

Governance of information security

We have already identified the role of governance in a compliance framework. There should be top-level oversight of your cyber security and privacy protection programme (and, of course, your compliance programme). Senior managers and the board do not need to be involved at anything like the level of detail that most employees will be. The board doesn't need to see all of the logs or records; the board needs to see an analytical distillation of those logs and records at regular intervals so that it can evaluate them and provide direction. This is often described in shorthand as 'evaluate, direct and monitor', and is well-described in a number of frameworks.

The aim is to ensure that there is full support for the information security programme throughout all levels of the organisation. If the board regularly engages with it, the board can align its various goals and the information security programme gains importance in the eyes of the ordinary employee. In an ideal business, all functions should contribute positively to the organisation's goals and generate business enablers to improve the organisation's competitiveness.

As mentioned, there are a number of frameworks that give excellent coverage of governance as well as associated guidance. ISO/IEC 38500 and COBIT 2019 are notable examples, and further guidance can be taken from the King

Report on Corporate Governance, a South African standard that has influenced other governance codes internationally. The King Report is now in its third edition – King III – and King IV is soon to be approved and launched.

An effective governance regime is essential for effective information security and privacy and is therefore likely to be looked on favourably by regulators such as the GDPR's supervisory authorities.

Information security beyond the organisation's borders

As seen in the Target data breach, many organisations with otherwise impeccable information security measures still fall victim to data breaches. It is easy to forget that the organisation's perimeter is formed not just where it encounters the 'public' (such as through the Internet or the front door), but also where it deals with suppliers.

When establishing your relationships with other organisations, it is important to understand how the relationship could itself be a vulnerability and how that could be exploited by a threat. This is common business practice, of course, and agreements of various types usually provide a contractual assurance that each organisation's data is safe in the other's hands.

The primary problem with relying on such contracts is that they give no real assurance that your suppliers are following best practice or approved processes. You can confirm this through audit, but auditing is time-consuming and often expensive. Furthermore, you will need to do it for all of your suppliers. It is better by far to rely on standardised external certification audits for a management system such as ISO 27001.

If you make ISO 27001 certification a condition of the supply agreement, your suppliers will have to meet the same standards that apply to your own ISMS. The costs of audit will be borne solely by the supplier and a copy of the certificate more than adequately demonstrates that the supplier's ISMS meets the requirements of the Standard and assures your ability to preserve information security.

CHAPTER 6: LAWFULNESS AND CONSENT

Returning to the preservation of the data subject's rights and freedoms, it is critical to ensure, before almost anything else, that your processing activities are 'lawful'. There has been a lot of discussion around this, and in particular in relation to consent.

Consent is a key area in achieving GDPR compliance. Although consent is the simplest lawful basis available for processing personal data, it is also the easiest for data subjects to remove and the one most likely to generate legal difficulties for data controllers. The GDPR outlines the criteria for consent as the following:

> 'consent' of the data subject means any freely given, specific, informed and unambiguous indication of the data subject's wishes by which he or she, by a statement or by a clear affirmative action, signifies agreement to the processing of personal data relating to him or her.[108]

Like other elements involved in preserving data subjects' rights, the data controller is responsible for abiding by these criteria. Ensuring that data subjects consent to having their personal data processed (where this is possible) is a critical component to preserving their rights and freedoms, and adhering to the data protection principles.

However, consent is not the only available lawful basis for processing, so it is important to understand your duties in

---

[108] GDPR, Article 4(11).

relation to consent, the data subject's rights in relation to it and the processes by which both parties are satisfied.

Consent in a nutshell

Gaining consent is a simple way of ensuring that your processing is lawful (in accordance with the first privacy principle), so the Regulation has strict conditions to make sure that consent is fairly gained and not abused.

Consent must be freely given, as made clear by the Regulation, which states that "consent should not provide a valid legal ground for the processing of personal data in a specific case where there is a clear imbalance between the data subject and controller, in particular where the controller is a public authority and it is therefore unlikely that consent was freely given in all the circumstances of that specific situation".[109] Similarly, an employer/employee relationship would also be an imbalanced relationship, potentially rendering any consent given by the employee invalid.

When you request a data subject's consent, you therefore need to ensure that the data subject has the genuine option of refusal, and that there will be no repercussions for refusing to consent. Organisations – and particularly public authorities – that cannot meet this requirement will need to ensure that they have a valid legal basis for the processing under local or Union law.

---

[109] GDPR, Recital 43.

Consent must also be "specific", which means the consent must specify the exact purpose of the processing. An example of specific consent might be an insurance company requesting personal data to determine levels of risk.[110] In this instance, the insurance company would need to inform the data subject that all of the information supplied may be used to calculate premiums and offer targeted services.

However, specific consent need not be requested in all situations. For example, an online retailer that requests a customer for their address should not need to state that the address will be used for the purpose of delivering the customer's goods. This would fall under the general allowance for processing data in order to fulfil a contract. In this example, you would need to secure consent for the customer to set up their account – informing them that you will use the data to fulfil their orders, for instance – and anything that logically follows from that consent would be acceptable.

Ensuring that consent is "informed" is closely linked to it being "specific". A data subject cannot consent to something if they have not been adequately informed. It is your duty as a data controller to ensure that this information is clear, especially if you are using the personal data for commercial gain. Equally, the data subject must be "informed of the existence of the processing operation and its purposes",[111] which links to the principles of fair and transparent

---

[110] This would also likely constitute profiling, so there may be additional concerns beyond that of consent.

[111] GDPR, Recital 60.

processing. This means that you cannot hide another processing function behind one that you've obtained consent for.

Consent must be "unambiguous". In most instances, you will be providing the data subject with a written form of the consent itself, and all they need to do is to confirm that they understand and approve. This means that the consent as it is written must not be misleading, and that it must clearly indicate that the data subject is actually giving consent for the processing.

Consent must be granted in "a statement or a clear affirmative action". Although a statement should be obvious enough – whether written or spoken by the data subject or by the controller with clear agreement from the data subject – an "affirmative action" should perhaps be clarified. An affirmative action in this context is something that the data subject does, rather than something that they achieve through *inaction*.

For example, offering the data subject a statement of consent in a pop-up window with a check box to indicate their consent would require an affirmative action – the data subject performs an action to indicate their consent.[112] The same pop-up box with a statement that will *assume* consent

---

[112] In fact, the Regulation actually specifies this as an acceptable method of getting consent in Recital 32: "[Consent] could include ticking a box when visiting an internet website, choosing technical settings for information society services or another statement or conduct which clearly indicates in this context the data subject's acceptance of the proposed processing of his or her personal data".

if the data subject does nothing or has the box pre-checked would not constitute an affirmative action. Using confusing phrasing (e.g. "Please uncheck the box if you do not wish to have your personal data not processed") is likely to fall foul of the Regulation on a number of points.

Withdrawing consent

Data subjects have the right to withdraw any consent they have given, at which point the data controller must either stop processing the personal data or determine whether there are other grounds on which processing can be based.

Article 7 of the Regulation states:

> The data subject shall have the right to withdraw his or her consent at any time. The withdrawal of consent shall not affect the lawfulness of processing based on consent before its withdrawal. Prior to giving consent, the data subject shall be informed whereof. It shall be as easy to withdraw consent as to give it.[113]

What this boils down to is that the data subject's ability to withdraw consent is just as important as getting their consent in the first place, and should be capable of being done just as easily.

Handling withdrawal of consent is a new requirement and one that will force you to consider new methods for managing personal data. It is also important to remember that you will need to account for data subjects who have consented to a variety of processes simultaneously. For

---

[113] GDPR, Article 7(3).

instance, if a data subject consents to a number of different processing actions by means of a set of check boxes, they should be able to withdraw consent in a similarly simple manner. The implications of this for website and system design are significant.

Alternatives to consent

Article 6 sets out all the available lawful bases for processing personal data, the first of which is consent. The others are:

1. If the processing is necessary to fulfil a contract that the data subject is party to, or to take steps at the data subject's request prior to entering a contract. This would include gathering basic data about the data subject before the contract is established, or processing the personal data in order to meet the requirements of the contract. It does not extend to processing that does not fulfil the purposes of the contract. Most of the processing carried out within an employer-employee relationship is likely to be lawful on this basis.

2. If the processing is necessary in order for the controller to comply with a legal obligation. This may relate to banks processing information about their customers in order to provide relevant reports to tax authorities or public bodies providing annual reports, and so on. In all such cases, refer to the specific law that outlines the information required. An employer's processing of tax information in relation to its employees is likely to be lawful on this basis.

3. If the processing is necessary to protect someone's vital interests. This may be for security reasons or protection

of economic interests. For instance, processing personal data on everyone within a specific area to establish appropriate measures to prevent crime. Processing information about an employee's next of kin may be lawful on this basis.

4. If the processing is necessary for a task carried out in the public interest or in the exercise of official authority vested in the controller. This condition primarily relates to public authorities such as the police, border authorities, tax bodies and their agents. In these instances, the authorities are permitted to process personal data for the purposes of protecting public interests.

5. If the processing is necessary for the purposes of the legitimate interests of the controller or a third party, except where those interests are overridden by the interests, rights or freedoms of the data subject, especially if the subject is a child.[114] These legitimate interests include scientific or historical research purposes. In these cases, the Regulation recognises that it is extremely difficult to secure consent for such purposes and that such processing is generally a net benefit to society. Should the research prove detrimental to an identifiable data subject or class of subjects, however, this lawful basis will not apply.

---

[114] GDPR, Article 6(1).

Legitimate interests can also exist where there is a "relevant and appropriate" relationship between the data subject and the controller in situations such as where the data subject is a client or in the service of the controller.[115] At any rate, the existence of a legitimate interest would need careful assessment, including whether a data subject can reasonably expect that processing to take place at the time and in the context of the collection of the personal data. Recital 47 also allows that the processing of personal data strictly necessary for the purposes of preventing fraud also constitutes a legitimate interest of the data controller concerned. The processing of personal data for direct marketing purposes may be regarded as carried out for a legitimate interest.

Recital 48 allows that controllers that are part of a group of undertakings or institutions affiliated to a central body may have a legitimate interest in transmitting personal data within the group of undertakings for internal administrative purposes, including the processing of clients' or employees' personal data.

Recital 49 recognises that data controllers also have a legitimate interest in processing personal data "to the extent strictly necessary and proportionate for the purposes of ensuring network and information security".

---

[115] GDPR, Recital 47.

Practicalities of consent

Managing consent entails a number of practical considerations, including methods of collecting consent, processes for handling review and withdrawal of consent and means of demonstrating compliance.

The burden of proving consent is firmly on the data controller. As the Regulation says, "where processing is based on the data subject's consent, the controller should be able to demonstrate that the data subject has given consent to the processing operation".[116]

With that in mind, you will need to determine how to obtain proof. The obvious solution is to keep a record of all consent for each data subject. For data stored in a database, this should be relatively straightforward – you could even record when consent was given so that it can be reconciled against the data collected and the individual processes.

The actual manner of collecting consent also needs to be considered. Many organisations already have methods in place, but the increased scope for which consent applies, as well as the more stringent requirements, mean that this should be re-examined, even if only to confirm that it still complies.

Generally speaking, there are three ways in which consent can be gained: online using a form, on physical paper, or orally via a telephone or equivalent. In the first instance, the data subject will be presented with a statement explaining what data will be collected and what it will be used for, with

---

[116] GDPR, Recital 42.

some method of approving the consent. On physical paper, the method might be the same – a prepared statement that the data subject signs off and hands over to the data controller. The final option is slightly different; consent could be given in a literal recording, but this may be cumbersome (because file sizes or recording media are too large), or the data subject could express their consent orally, which is then marked into a physical or digital form on the subject's behalf by the other person on the call.

Regardless of the method you use to collect consent, you should ensure that it is readily accessible and readily editable to account for data subjects withdrawing their consent.

You should ensure that you also have processes for handling withdrawal of consent. Data subjects must be able to withdraw consent as easily as they provide it. In fact, because withdrawal of consent is so closely entwined with the data subject's rights, in some cases withdrawing consent may actually need to be *easier* than giving consent if your existing method is quite difficult. It may be that your primary business doesn't involve data processing, so you have never made much of an effort to make it streamlined and easy to obtain, and now you will need to manage consent to ensure that data subjects can exercise their rights.

For organisations with a more 'ordinary' business model, there should be simple ways of allowing data subjects to review and withdraw their consent. Using a set of online tools or a 'dashboard' that allows the data subjects to see an overview of all relevant processing, change their consent on the fly, and even update or correct their personal data, would solve a great number of issues under the GDPR.

Furthermore, an integrated solution like this will highlight to your data subjects how their personal data relates to the processing and provide them with control over how their personal data is used, thereby improving your approach to transparency and, in turn, your reputation.

You will need to ensure that whatever process or policy you choose in relation to withdrawal of consent is documented, and that you can measure how well this is being implemented.

Children

Children – anyone under 16 years of age[117] – are unable to consent to the processing of personal data for information society services, and so consent must be sought from the person who holds parental responsibility over the child. The Regulation explains that this is because "children merit specific protection with regard to their personal data, as they may be less aware of the risks, consequences and safeguards concerned and their rights in relation to the processing of personal data".[118]

This applies only to information society services, and only where consent is ordinarily necessary. If your processing is

---

[117] Note that the GDPR allows Member States to individually determine the age of consent, and that it could vary between 13 and 16 – the UK, for instance, has opted to set the age of consent for personal data processing at 13. Organisations operating across Member State borders will have to be aware of this and specifically deal with possible differences in the formal age of consent, and the evidence of compliance they need to obtain.

[118] GDPR, Recital 38.

lawful under other grounds, then you do not need to secure consent from the child. Of course, "information society services" are "any service normally provided for remuneration, at a distance, by electronic means and at the individual request of a recipient of services",[119] which is to say that children cannot consent to commercial contracts over the Internet.

Although this may provide quite a lot of wiggle room for organisations, such as those that provide services in person, it does mean that many businesses will need to ensure they have processes in place to confirm the age of the customer when collecting data online. The process you use to ensure that all consent is valid will need to take the age of the data subject into account, especially if you provide services that are likely to be of interest to children. This provision can be very difficult to implement effectively.

The simplest solution is to not collect any personal data, but this is unlikely to be a useful option for many organisations. Large, public organisations have in the past developed guidelines for securing parental consent, including the BBC in the UK, which provided examples of how the level of consent necessary was identified and the methods used to secure it.[120]

You should consult the supervisory authority if you have any concerns about how to secure parental consent. The BBC's example methods range from informal for data processing

---

[119] Directive 2015/1535/EU, Article 1(1)(b).

[120] *www.bbc.com/editorialguidelines/guidelines/children-young-people*.

that is likely to be appropriate for children of all ages and pose negligible risks to the child's rights and freedoms, through to more thorough vetting methods when the processing involves more data or greater risk, and include:

- Using simple wording asking a child to ask their parent for consent;
- Requiring the use of a clickable box to confirm that consent has been obtained before the child can proceed;
- Requiring parental consent via email (e.g. a parent confirms in an email with an address different from their child that they are happy for their child to upload a picture of themselves to the BBC site); and
- Requiring verifiable parental consent, e.g. a signed letter or logged personal telephone call from a parent or guardian.[121]

When explaining the nature of the processing to a child, even though consent will formally be given by an adult, you must use simpler, clearer language. The Regulation states: "any information and communication, where processing is addressed to a child, should be in such a clear and plain language that the child can easily understand".[122]

---

[121] *www.bbc.com/editorialguidelines/guidelines/children-young-people/guidelines#9.3.*

[122] GDPR, Recital 58.

You will also need to ensure that a process for withdrawal of consent is in place and that it is as simple to withdraw consent as it is to give consent. There are no special requirements relating to the withdrawal of parental consent beyond those of withdrawing ordinary consent.

Special categories of personal data

Processing special categories of personal data[123] is prohibited under the GDPR except under specific conditions. These require that there is a lawful basis for processing the personal information and that one of the specific Article 9 conditions must also be met. The first of these is the explicit consent of the data subject to the specific processing. As such, you will need to ensure that consent for any processing of special categories of personal data is very clearly documented. You should also ensure that your description of the processing itself is, if anything, even clearer than for other processing activities, as misuse of these categories of personal data can be extraordinarily damaging to the data subject.

Other conditions that allow the processing of special categories of personal data are generally based on the protection of the public good, or on the protection of the data

---

[123] GDPR, Article 9(1) defines this as "personal data revealing racial or ethnic origin, political opinions, religious or philosophical beliefs, or trade-union membership, [and] genetic data, biometric data [...] data concerning health or data concerning a natural person's sex life or sexual orientation".

subject and other natural persons. These exemptions will ordinarily be used by public authorities and their agents.

Data relating to criminal convictions and offences

The final category of personal data is data that relates to criminal convictions and offences, and there are no rules in place for consenting to processing of this type of data. There is, however, the requirement that such processing "shall be carried out only under the control of official authority or when the processing is authorised by Union or Member State law providing for appropriate safeguards for the rights and freedoms of data subjects".[124]

If any of your existing processing activities rely on this type of data, you will need to ensure that you are operating under an official capacity. There is no room in the Regulation for private or commercial processing of this data.

---

[124] GDPR, Article 10.

CHAPTER 7: SUBJECT ACCESS REQUESTS

As we have already seen, a data subject has the right to request the personal information held about them by a data controller. These requests are known as DSARs, and the GDPR states that they enable the data subject "to be aware of, and verify, the lawfulness of the processing".[125]

In making a DSAR, an individual is exercising their right to obtain confirmation that their data is being processed by the data controller, and to have access to that personal data and any other supplementary information to help explain the data revealed to that individual.

The right to access personal information allows data subjects access to additional information, within a timeframe of just one month, and includes specific information on, for example, providing online services for subject access requests.[126]

The Regulation also highlights the importance of a data subject's access to information concerning their health. This includes any data in their medical records such as diagnoses, examination results, medical assessments and any treatments or interventions that have been provided.[127]

---

[125] GDPR, Recital 63.

[126] GDPR, Article 12(3).

[127] GDPR, Recital 63.

Receiving a request

Any organisation that holds personal information could receive a subject access request.

It is important to note that, although you might provide a method for data subjects to make access requests, they are not required to use that. A request could come in any format (it does not have to be in writing), be part of a high-volume bulk request or require the information to be returned in a format that is not used by the organisation.

DSARs under the GDPR can place an administrative burden on organisations. They need to identify, respond and have suitable systems in place to answer all DSARs within just one month.

The controller must also give individuals the opportunity to make a DSAR and "to exercise that right easily and at reasonable intervals".[128] This could necessitate a review of customer-facing processes, procedures and additional staff training to ensure they can meet the Regulation's data access and portability rules.

The information to provide

The data controller must provide the data subject with "a copy of the personal data undergoing processing".[129] This simple statement has many implications for the data

---

[128] GDPR, Recital 63.

[129] GDPR, Article 15(3).

controller in terms of the range of information they must provide when responding to a subject access request.

More specifically, the data subject has the right to access the following information in addition to the relevant personal data:

- The purposes of the data processing;
- The categories of personal data;
- To whom the data has been or will be disclosed, particularly recipients in third countries or international organisations;
- How long the personal data will be stored or, if an estimate is not possible, the criteria used to determine that period of time;
- The data subject's rights in relation to the data, including the right to lodge a complaint with the supervisory authority;
- Any available information on the source of the data, if the personal data was not collected directly from the data subject; and
- Whether any automated decision-making processes, such as data profiling, have been applied to the individual's personal data. If they have, the controller must provide "meaningful information about the logic involved, as well as the significance and the envisaged

consequences of such processing for the data subject"[130].

This list is quite extensive compared to requirements under previous laws.

Data portability

Under the GDPR, data subjects have the right to data portability. This is a new requirement that was not covered under the DPD, but it is an important premise of the GDPR, which states that:

> data controllers are encouraged to develop interoperable formats that enable data portability. That right should apply where the data subject provided the personal data on the basis of his or her consent or the processing is necessary for the performance of a contract. It should not apply where processing is based on a legal ground other than consent or contract.[131]

This right is fundamentally about allowing data subjects to change providers freely, but it complements the right of access, and a data subject can request that their data is provided in a "structured, commonly used and machine-readable format".[132]

---

[130] GDPR, Article 15(1).

[131] GDPR, Recital 68.

[132] GDPR, Article 20(1).

If the subject access request is made in electronic form, then the information should also be provided in a commonly used electronic form, unless the data subject specifically and reasonably requests an alternative format.[133] The format the information is presented in could have a significant financial impact on controllers that use special formats or only hold paper records. It may, therefore, be necessary for data controllers to develop formatting capabilities to comply with the GDPR.

It is important to remember that this applies to all information requested from the data controller in exercising a data subject's rights. You must endeavour to provide the information in a common format, and you must offer to reply electronically if you allow data subjects to make requests electronically. For many organisations, this won't be a problem: the data is packaged in a machine-readable database format, and you can provide it via a user account web application or similar. For organisations that handle data in other ways, it would be sensible to invest in tools to convert data into a useable format, and to consider offering a web application or similar solution. Note, however, that you only have to offer the information electronically *if* you allow the data subject to make the request electronically.

Responsibilities of the data controller

Responsibility for complying with a subject access request lies with the data controller. Data controllers need to ensure that data processors are able to provide all relevant

---

[133] GDPR, Article 12(3).

information within the one month allotted by the Regulation. It would make sense to design, document and deploy a subject access request process that complies with the specific GDPR requirements, and to train relevant staff in its use, in advance of receiving any such requests.

Building guarantees of responsiveness into service level agreements (SLAs) is one method of getting processors to help you meet the requirements of the Regulation. You might also be able to arrange direct access to the data as it is held by the processor, or to establish a system whereby you can request relevant data to be fulfilled automatically or with a minimum of human interaction.

The data controller must also provide the data subject with explanations of their rights to rectification or erasure of their personal information, or to object to processing activities, as well as their right to lodge a complaint with the relevant supervisory authority. These are all possible results of providing data subjects with their personal data and relevant related information.

The controller must identify where they have collected a requester's personal data from, if it has not been sourced directly from the individual. The requester also has the right to obtain details of the safeguards applied where their information is transferred outside of the EU and international organisations.

Transparency is a core component of the GDPR. Data controllers have a responsibility to facilitate this transparency at every stage of a subject access request.

Processes and procedures

The GDPR places pressure on data controllers to provide more information in response to subject access requests in a shorter timeframe than allotted under previous directives such as the DPD. Controllers should outline a specific process for handling subject access requests as soon as is possible, and review the current processes, procedures and tools available to customer-facing teams to ensure they are sufficient to deal with the GDPR's data access rules.

The controller must ensure staff are sufficiently trained to identify that a request from an individual constitutes a subject access request, which could be made in any format and not just through the channels provided by the data controller. The controller should also ensure that staff are prepared to handle potentially high volumes of requests, given that data subjects cannot generally be charged for an initial subject access request under the GDPR.[134]

If the subject access request is valid, the data must be exported in a structured and machine-readable format. Depending on the nature of the request, the data may need to be delivered in additional formats. The data controller should take reasonable steps to develop new systems, improve existing architecture or establish a process for converting data to common formats in order to assure data portability.

For many organisations, the simplest solution will be to expand an existing data access portal to allow the data subject to directly exercise their access rights. This has the

---

[134] GDPR, Article 12(5).

advantage that the organisation can contextualise the personal data and would also meet the intent of Recital 63, which states that "where possible, the controller should be able to provide remote access to a secure system which would provide the data subject with direct access to his or her personal data".

The Regulation also states that the right to access personal data or obtain a copy of information through a remotely accessed secure system should also not adversely affect the freedoms and rights of others. To ensure that this is the case, the controller should review the nature of remote access provided and the data that is held there. The controller will need to address, among other considerations, how the system proves the user's identity, the sensitivity of the data available and whether there are any additional privacy concerns or legal restrictions to making the personal data accessible over the Internet.

Options for confirming the requester's identity

Confirming the requester's identity is critical to complying with the Regulation, and the Regulation explicitly enables controllers to require proof of identity from the data subject before they release personal information. It also helps to reduce the risk of unscrupulous third parties gaining access to personal data unlawfully.

The data controller must ask for sufficient information to judge whether the person making the request is the individual to whom the personal data relates to (or a person authorised to make a subject access request on their behalf). The controller cannot ask for excessive amounts of information if the identity of the individual is obvious. This point is particularly applicable if the data controller has an ongoing relationship with the data subject.

For example, if an organisation receives a written subject access request from a current employee, it would seem excessive to go through the usual channels to verify their identity by asking for a copy of their passport or utility bill. Because the organisation knows the person making the request, it is reasonable to grant this request automatically and deliver the information directly to the data subject.

If, on the other hand, an organisation receives a written subject access request from a customer where there is no longstanding relationship, it would be reasonable to verify that individual's identity by asking them to submit specific documentation and information such as date of birth, address, photographic identification, utility bills, and so on.

However, although the data controller must use reasonable means to verify that the individual making the subject access request is the data subject, they must not retain information specifically to meet such data requests, as stated in Recital 64: "The controller should use all reasonable measures to verify the identity of a data subject who requests access, in particular in the context of online services and online identifiers. A controller should not retain personal data for the sole purpose of being able to react to potential requests."

Historically, supplemental information might have been the data subject's mother's maiden name, the school they attended or some other piece of personal information that was otherwise unrelated to the data subject's business with the organisation.

Where the controller has reasonable doubts as to the identity of the data subject, they are permitted to request additional information. The controller should also not refuse to take additional information from the data subject if it is provided "in order to support the exercise of his or her rights".[135]

Balancing the need to authenticate data subjects against the demand not to hold supplementary information can be difficult for data controllers, and online services that have no physical contact with the data subject may struggle with such verification processes. The Regulation provides some direction on online authentication in Recital 57, which states that:

> identification should include the digital identification of a data subject, for example through authentication mechanism such as the same credentials, used by the data subject to log-in to the on-line service offered by the data controller.

Multi-factor authentication is one option for verifying a data subject's identity online, whereby the individual must present several separate pieces of evidence to the system. This evidence usually constitutes at least two pieces of information from the following categories: knowledge (something the subject knows, such as a PIN or password), possession (something the subject has, such as a credit card or physical token) and inherence (something the subject is, which includes biometric data such as fingerprints or vocal patterns).

An individual can also make a subject access request through a third party, which includes (and is often) a solicitor acting

---

[135] GDPR, Recital 57.

on behalf of a client. This adds another layer of complexity to the authentication process, as the data controller must be satisfied that the third party making the request is entitled to act on behalf of the data subject. In this case, it is the third party's responsibility to provide this evidence in the form of, for example, a power of attorney or other written form of authority.

Records to examine

A key consideration is the records that must be examined to comply with a subject access request. This depends on the nature of the request and of the data controller, but the following records may need to be examined:

- Any information held, or which will be held, on an electronic database or repository;
- Records of correspondence, whether in the form of physical letters, emails, text messages or other formats;
- Records held in a manual filing system, which is highly structured so that information can be easily retrieved;
- Health, education, social service or housing records;
- Any other information held by a public authority;
- Video footage and audio recordings; and
- Records of processing activities carried out on the individual's personal information.

The data controller does not need to provide information where the "subject proves to be impossible or would involve a disproportionate effort".[136] For example, information held in a sprawling archive with a large number of data subjects where a high level of processing has been carried out to anonymise those subjects, could prove too costly or time-consuming, or could impinge on the rights of the other data subjects whose information is held in that repository.

Time and money

The data controller must comply with a subject access request "without delay and at the latest within one month of receipt of the request",[137] although it is possible to extend this period under certain circumstances, as stated in the Regulation:

> That period may be extended by two further months where necessary, taking into account the complexity and number of the requests. The controller shall inform the data subject of any such extension within one month of receipt of the request, together with the reasons for the delay.[138]

The controller cannot ask for payment to fulfil the subject access request, which was previously permitted under the DPD. Under the Regulation, the first copy must be provided to the data subject free of charge, which is a change for UK-based controllers that could previously charge up to £10 for

---

[136] GDPR, Recital 62.

[137] GDPR, Article 12(4).

[138] GDPR, Article 12(3).

every copy. The controller can then charge "a reasonable fee based on administrative costs" for any additional copies.[139]

Dealing with bulk subject access requests

An organisation may receive multiple subject access requests within a short timeframe or even multiple requests from one source if a management company is acting on behalf of multiple data subjects.

If a bulk request is received, then each subject access request must be considered individually and responded to appropriately. There are many potential resource implications here, so it is vital that the data controller can assess whether all, or any, of the requests are valid. A data controller can also extend the one-month timeframe to respond by a further two months if it receives an excessive number of requests. Whatever the case, the data controller must be prepared to respond to peaks in the volume of subject access requests.

Bulk subject access requests were highlighted in the Information Commissioner's Annual Report and Financial Statements 2015/16[140] for requests relating to compensation claims for health conditions. The ICO "advised Her Majesty's Revenue and Customs and the Ministry of Defence about the importance of upholding information rights when dealing with high volumes of subject access

---

[139] GDPR, Article 15(3).

[140] Information Commissioner's Annual Report and Financial Statements 2015/16, *https://ico.org.uk/media/1624517/annual-report-2015-16.pdf*.

requests". A lack of resources is not a valid excuse for not complying with the GDPR.

Right to refusal

If the data controller does not intend to comply with a subject access request, they must provide reasons for this refusal within one month of receiving the request. Grounds for refusal include if the information required for the subject access request may "adversely affect the rights and freedoms of others".[141] In other words, the protection of trade secrets or intellectual properties could be a valid reason to refuse to disclose information under the GDPR.

If a data controller decides to refuse a request, it needs to have policies and procedures in place to demonstrate why the request meets the criteria for exemption.

The process flow

The following is a simple high-level diagram setting out the key stages for receiving and responding to a subject access request. Note that many requests will require more or less care, and varying needs for tracking or recording the process.

---

[141] GDPR, Article 15(4).

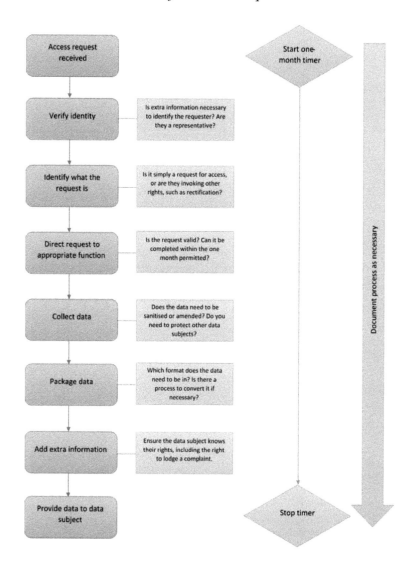

Figure 7: A subject access request process

CHAPTER 8: ROLE OF THE DATA PROTECTION OFFICER

The GDPR takes a role that already exists in some organisations, that of the DPO, and gives it statutory importance.

Articles 37–39 of the GDPR lay out the requirements for appointing a DPO, as well as their specification, role, duties and relationships with other entities (such as data subjects, controllers and processors, etc.).

Whether or not your organisation needs to appoint a DPO comes down to three basic conditions, according to the Regulation:

The controller and the processor shall designate a data protection officer in any case where:

(a) the processing is carried out by a public authority or body, except for courts acting in their judicial capacity;

(b) the core activities of the controller or the processor consist of processing operations which, by virtue of their nature, their scope and/or their purposes, require regular and systematic monitoring of data subjects on a large scale; or

(c) the core activities of the controller or the processor consist of processing on a large scale of special categories of data pursuant to Article 9 and personal data relating to criminal convictions and offences referred to in Article 10.[142]

The EU's Working Party 29 (WP29, now replaced by the EDPB has provided guidance on key definitions within these requirements, which we summarise,[143] although it is worth noting that the definitions as implemented may vary between Member States.

The Regulation also allows individual Member States to pass additional laws regarding DPOs.[144] For example, an individual Member State may make DPOs a requirement for a larger range of organisations under its jurisdiction and, as such, it is possible that many more organisations may have to appoint DPOs in the future.[145]

Although you are not required to appoint a DPO if you don't meet these conditions, there may be good business reasons for doing so: perhaps to streamline the compliance project, to be on hand to provide expert advice or guidance or to be at the ready in case conditions change and you are required to have one. In the same way that organisations of all sizes

---

[142] GDPR, Article 37(1).

[143] WP29, "Guidelines on Data Protection Officers ('DPOs')", April 2017, *https://ec.europa.eu/newsroom/article29/item-detail.cfm?item_id=612048*.

[144] GDPR, Article 37(4).

[145] Germany, for instance, requires organisations to appoint a DPO on the basis of the number of people involved in non-automated processing.

now usually give one or more individuals specific responsibilities around HR and health and safety, so it is likely that data protection responsibilities will become a basic operational competence required in all cases.

Core activities

The GDPR makes several references to the "core activities of the controller or the processor".[146] WP29 defined core activities as "the key operations necessary to achieve the controller's or processor's goals". However, core activities also include processing that is an inextricable part of the controller's or processor's activity. For example, the core activity of a hospital is to provide healthcare; it could not do this without processing health data, such as patient health records. Processing this type of data is therefore a core activity and a DPO must be appointed.

Activities that can be regarded as support functions to these core activities, such as payroll or IT support, although necessary and/or essential, are considered ancillary functions rather than core activities.

Large scale

The GDPR requires that a DPO be appointed when processing of personal data is carried out on a large scale,[147] but does not define what constitutes large-scale data processing. The guidance from Recital 91 is that "large-scale

---

[146] Article 37(1) (b) and (c), and Recital 97.

[147] Article 37(1) (b) and (c).

processing operations which aim to process a considerable amount of personal data at regional, national or supranational level and which could affect a large number of data subjects and which are likely to result in a high risk" would be included. On the other hand, the recital also specifically provides that "the processing of personal data should not be considered to be on a large scale if the processing concerns personal data from patients or clients by an individual physician, other health care professional or lawyer".

The EDPB is yet to provide more precise guidance for 'large scale', either with regard to the amount of data processed or the number of individuals concerned. The WP29 did, however, recommend that the following factors should be considered when determining whether the processing is carried out on a large scale:

- The number of data subjects concerned – either as a specific number or as a proportion of the relevant population.
- The volume of data and/or the range of different data items being processed.
- The duration, or permanence, of the data processing activity.
- The geographical extent of the processing activity.

WP29 also stated that large-scale data processing would include:

- Processing of patient data in the regular course of business by a hospital;
- Processing of travel data of individuals using a city's public transport system (e.g. tracking via travel cards);

- Processing of real-time geo-location data of customers of an international fast food chain for statistical purposes by a processor specialised in providing these services;
- Processing of customer data in the regular course of business by an insurance company or a bank;
- Processing of personal data for behavioural advertising by a search engine; and
- Processing of data (content, traffic, location) by telephone or Internet service providers.

Examples that do not constitute large-scale processing include:

- Processing of patient data by an individual physician; and
- Processing of personal data relating to criminal convictions and offences by an individual lawyer.

Regular and systematic monitoring

Regular and systematic monitoring is also not defined in the GDPR. The concept of "monitoring of the behaviour of data subjects" is discussed, however, and includes all forms of tracking and profiling on the Internet, including for the purposes of behavioural advertising.[148]

---

[148] Recital 24.

WP29 is clear that monitoring is not restricted to the online environment and online tracking is only an example of monitoring the behaviours of data subjects.[149]

WP29's guidance provided its interpretation of the elements. 'Regular' should be taken as meaning one or more of the following:

- Ongoing or occurring at particular intervals for a particular period.
- Recurring or repeated at fixed times.
- Constantly or periodically taking place.

'Systematic' means one or more of the following:
- Occurring according to a system.
- Prearranged, organised or methodical.
- Taking place as part of a general plan for data collection.
- Carried out as part of a strategy.

Examples of regular and systematic monitoring:

- Operating a telecommunications network.
- Providing telecommunications services.
- Email retargeting.
- Profiling and scoring for purposes of risk assessment (e.g. for purposes of credit scoring, establishment of

---

[149] Recital 24; there is also a difference between the wording "*monitoring their behaviour*" (Article 3(2)(b)) and "*regular and systematic monitoring of data subjects*" (Article 37(1)(b)), which could be seen as constituting a different notion.

insurance premiums, fraud prevention, detection of money-laundering).

- Location tracking, such as by mobile apps.
- Loyalty programmes.
- Behavioural advertising.
- Monitoring of wellness, fitness and health data via wearable devices.
- Closed circuit television.
- Connected devices, e.g. smart meters, smart cars, home automation, etc.

Voluntary designation of a data protection officer

Every organisation has to make a rational assessment, taking into consideration such factors as the size, complexity and diversity of its business operations, in conjunction with the acceptable level of risk to their business and risks to the rights and freedoms of data subjects, whether to appoint a DPO. In most cases, most organisations would be well-advised to make such an appointment: the risks are significant and the compliance complexities are not insubstantial.

When an organisation designates a DPO on a voluntary basis, the same requirements under the GDPR apply to his or her designation, position and tasks as if the designation had been mandatory.

Unless it is obvious that an organisation is not required to designate a DPO, WP29 recommends that controllers and processors document the internal analysis carried out to determine whether or not a DPO is to be appointed, in order to be able to demonstrate that the relevant factors were all properly taken into account.

It should be noted that you do not need a dedicated DPO in-house. It is entirely reasonable to share a DPO with other organisations, perhaps through a third-party service provider such as a specialist consulting or legal firm.

Undertakings that share a DPO

The GDPR allows a group of undertakings to designate a single, shared DPO, provided that the DPO is "easily accessible from each establishment".[150]

The notion of accessibility refers to the DPO's role as a contact point with respect to data subjects and supervisory authorities, but also internally within the organisation, considering that one of the tasks of the DPO is "to inform and advise the controller and the processor and the employees who carry out processing of their obligations pursuant to this Regulation".[151]

In order to make sure that the DPO (whether internal or external) is accessible, it is important to make sure that their contact details are available in accordance with the requirements of the GDPR.[152]

The DPO must be in a position to efficiently communicate with data subjects and cooperate with the supervisory authorities concerned. This also means that this

---

[150] Article 37(2).

[151] Article 39(1)(a).

[152] Article 37(7).

communication must take place in the language or languages used by the supervisory authorities and the data subjects concerned.

A single DPO may be designated for several public authorities or bodies, taking account of their organisational structure and size.[153] The same considerations with regard to resources and communication apply.

Given that the DPO is responsible for a variety of tasks, the controller must make sure that a single DPO can perform these efficiently despite being responsible for several public authorities and/or bodies.

The personal availability of a DPO (whether physically on the same premises as employees, via a hotline or other secure means of communication) is essential to making sure that data subjects are able to contact the DPO.

The DPO is bound by secrecy or confidentiality concerning the performance of their tasks, in accordance with Union or Member State law. However, the obligation of secrecy/confidentiality does not prohibit the DPO from contacting and seeking advice from the supervisory authority.[154]

DPO on a service contract

The function of the DPO can also be exercised on the basis of a service contract with a third-party individual or

---

[153] Article 37(3).

[154] Article 38(5).

organisation. In this latter case, it is essential that each member of the organisation exercising the functions of a DPO (e.g. a DPO-as-a-Service offering) fulfils all relevant requirements of the GDPR (e.g. it is essential that no one has a conflict of interests).[155]

It is equally important that each such staff member be protected by the provisions of the GDPR (e.g. no unfair termination of the service contract for activities as DPO, but also no unfair dismissal of any individual member of the organisation carrying out the DPO tasks). At the same time, individual skills and strengths can be combined so that several individuals working in a team may more efficiently serve their clients.

For the sake of legal clarity and good organisation, there should be a clear allocation of tasks within the DPO team, with a single individual assigned as a lead contact and person 'in charge' for each client. Organisations contracting such services should ensure that these arrangements are specified in the service contract.

Publication of DPO contact details

The GDPR requires the controller or the processor:

- To publish the contact details of the DPO; and
- To communicate the contact details to the relevant supervisory authorities.[156]

---

[155] Section 4 – Data protection officer.

[156] Article 37(7).

These requirements make sure that data subjects (both inside and outside of the organisation) and the supervisory authorities can directly and confidentially contact the DPO without having to contact another part of the organisation.

The contact details of the DPO should include information allowing data subjects and the supervisory authorities to reach the DPO in an easy way (a postal address, a dedicated telephone number and a dedicated email address). When appropriate, for purposes of communications with the public, other means of communications could also be provided – for example, a dedicated hotline, or a dedicated contact form addressed to the DPO on the organisation's website.

The GDPR does not require the published contact details to include the name of the DPO. Although it may be good practice to do this, it is for the controller and the DPO to decide whether this is necessary or helpful in the particular circumstances.

As a matter of good practice, an organisation should inform the supervisory authority and employees of the name and contact details of the DPO. For example, the name and contact details of the DPO could be published internally on the organisation's intranet, internal telephone directory and on organisational charts.

Position of the DPO

The GDPR says that the controller and the processor must make sure that the DPO is "involved, properly and in a timely manner, in all issues which relate to the protection of personal data".[157]

It is therefore crucial that the DPO is involved from the earliest stage possible in the development of the privacy compliance framework and in all issues relating to data protection. In relation to DPIAs, the GDPR explicitly provides for the early involvement of the DPO and says that the controller must seek the advice of the DPO when carrying out such impact assessments.[158] Making sure that the DPO is informed and consulted at the outset will facilitate compliance with the GDPR and ensure a data protection by design approach, and should, therefore, be standard procedure within the organisation's governance. It is also important that the DPO is seen as someone within the organisation with critical input on all data processing activities, so they should, therefore, be part of any of the organisation's working groups that deal with data processing activities.

The organisation should make sure, for example, that:

• The DPO is invited to participate regularly in meetings of senior and middle management;

• They are present where decisions with data protection implications are taken;

---

[157] Article 38(1).

[158] Article 35(2).

- All relevant information is passed to the DPO in a timely manner in order to allow him or her to provide adequate advice;

- The opinion of the DPO is always given due consideration and, where conflict and disagreement arise, that the parties document the reasons for not following the DPO's advice; and

- The DPO is promptly consulted when a data breach occurs.

Where appropriate, the controller or processor should develop formal guidelines that describe clearly when the DPO must be consulted.

Necessary resources

The GDPR places a legal obligation on organisations to support the DPO by "providing resources necessary to carry out [their] tasks and access to personal data and processing operations, and to maintain his or her expert knowledge".[159]

The following would be key to meeting this obligation:

- Active support of the DPO's function from the board of directors.

- Sufficient time for DPOs to fulfil their duties. This is particularly important where the DPO is appointed on a part-time basis or where the employee carries out data protection in addition to other duties. Otherwise,

---

[159] Article 38(2).

conflicting priorities could result in the DPO's duties being neglected. Having sufficient time to devote to DPO tasks is paramount. It is good practice to establish a percentage of time for the DPO function if it is not a full-time role. It is also good practice to determine the time needed to carry out the function, the appropriate level of priority for DPO duties and for the DPO (or the organisation) to draw up and follow a formal work plan.

- Adequate support in terms of financial resources, infrastructure (premises, facilities, equipment) and staff, where appropriate.

- Officially communicating the designation of the DPO to all staff to make sure that their existence and function are known within the organisation.

- Access to other services where necessary, such as human resources, legal, IT, security, etc., so that DPOs can receive essential support, input and information from those other services.

- Ongoing training. DPOs should have the opportunity to stay up to date regarding developments in data protection. The organisation should aim to constantly increase the DPO's level of expertise, and they should be encouraged to participate in training courses on data protection and other forms of professional development, such as participation in privacy fora, workshops, etc.

- Given the size and structure of the organisation, it may be necessary to set up a DPO team (a DPO and his/her staff). In such cases, the internal structure of the team and the tasks and responsibilities of each of its members should be clearly documented.

In general, the more complex and/or sensitive the processing operations, the more resources must be given to the DPO. The data protection function must be effective and sufficiently resourced in relation to the data processing being carried out.

Acting in an independent manner

The GDPR sets out clear protective guarantees to help make sure that DPOs are able to perform their tasks with a sufficient degree of autonomy. In particular, controllers/processors are required to make sure that the DPO "does not receive any instructions regarding the exercise of [his or her] tasks".[160] Furthermore, it says that DPOs, "whether or not they are an employee of the controller, should be in a position to perform their duties and tasks in an independent manner".[161]

This means that, in fulfilling their tasks under the GDPR, DPOs must not be instructed how to deal with a matter. For example, they must not be told what result should be achieved, how to investigate a complaint or whether to consult the supervisory authority. Furthermore, they must not be instructed to take a certain view of an issue related to data protection law, such as a particular interpretation of the law. The autonomy of DPOs does not, however, mean that

---

[160] Article 38(3).

[161] Recital 97.

they have decision-making powers extending beyond their tasks pursuant to the GDPR.[162]

The controller or processor remains responsible for compliance with data protection law and must be able to demonstrate compliance with the principle of accountability. If the controller or processor makes decisions that are incompatible with the GDPR and the DPO's advice, the DPO should be given the opportunity to make his or her dissenting opinion clear to those making the decisions.

Protected role of the DPO

The GDPR protects the role of the DPO; it requires that DPOs should "not be dismissed or penalised by the controller or the processor for performing [their] tasks".[163]
This requirement also strengthens the autonomy of DPOs and helps make sure that they act independently and enjoy sufficient protection in performing their data protection tasks.

For example, a DPO may consider that a particular processing presents a high risk to the rights and freedoms of data subjects and advise the controller or the processor to carry out a DPIA but the controller or the processor may not agree with the DPO's assessment. In such a situation, the DPO cannot be dismissed or otherwise penalised for providing this advice.

---

[162] Article 39.

[163] Article 38(3).

All of the ways that organisations might attempt to penalise an individual whose advice they dislike would be illegal. These illegal penalties can take a variety of forms and may be direct or indirect. They could consist, for example, of absence or delay of promotion, prevention from career advancement or denial of benefits that other employees receive. It is not necessary that these penalties actually be carried out: a mere threat is sufficient if they are used to penalise the DPO on grounds related to his/her DPO activities.

As a normal management rule – and as would be the case for any other employee or contractor – a DPO could still be dismissed legitimately for reasons other than for performing his or her tasks as a DPO (for instance, in case of theft, physical, psychological or sexual harassment or similar gross misconduct).

In this context, it should be noted that the GDPR does not specify how and when a DPO can be dismissed or replaced by another person. However, the more stable a DPO's contract is, and the more guarantees exist against unfair dismissal, the more likely they will be able to act in an independent manner.

Conflicts of interest

The GDPR has a provision that allows DPOs to "fulfil other tasks and duties". It requires, however, that the organisation makes sure that "any such tasks and duties do not result in a conflict of interests".[164]

The absence of conflicts of interest is closely linked to the requirement to act in an independent manner. Although DPOs are allowed to have other functions, they can only be entrusted with other tasks and duties provided that these do not give rise to conflicts of interest. In particular, this means that the DPO cannot hold a position within the organisation that leads him or her to determine the purposes and the means of the processing of personal data, or be responsible for service delivery. Because of the specific structure in each organisation, this has to be considered on a case-by-case basis. In broad terms, however, this will tend to mean that it is not possible for an IT manager, CIO or CISO to also be the DPO.

Depending on the activities, size and structure of the organisation, it can be good practice for controllers or processors to:

- Identify the positions that would be incompatible with the function of the DPO;
- Draw up internal rules to this effect in order to avoid conflicts of interest;
- Include a more general explanation about conflicts of interest;

---

[164] Article 38(6).

- Declare that the DPO has no conflicts of interest with regard to its function as a DPO as a way of raising awareness of this requirement; and

- Include safeguards in the organisation's rules, and make sure that the vacancy notice for the position of DPO or the service contract is sufficiently precise and detailed in order to avoid a conflict of interest. In this context, it should also be borne in mind that conflicts of interest may take various forms depending on whether the DPO is recruited internally or externally.

Specification of the DPO

The Regulation describes the DPO in Article 37, stating that "the data protection officer shall be designated on the basis of professional qualities and, in particular, expert knowledge of data protection law and practices and the ability to fulfil the tasks referred to in Article 39".[165] This description is quite broad and it is therefore open to organisations to determine how they specifically meet this requirement.

The 'ability to fulfil the tasks' is at least as important as is a knowledge of the law. After all, legal advice can always be obtained from professional advisers; the key requirement for DPOs is that they be able to fulfil a set of specific tasks, which requires a significant level of practical knowledge and experience about implementing and operating an effective privacy compliance framework. In terms of appropriate qualifications and experience, here is a brief (and non-exhaustive) list of some of the attributes and knowledge a

---

[165] GDPR, Article 37(5).

DPO may require, depending on the significance of the specific role:

- A law degree, ideally with specialisation in data privacy law, and specifically with the GDPR.
- Professional qualifications/certifications relating to data protection and/or information security, and specifically to the GDPR.
- Professional qualifications/certifications relevant to the industry or sector in which they are working.
- Experience implementing data protection measures and/or frameworks.
- Experience managing the key systems and processes involved in securing personal data.
- Experience with risk management standards and frameworks.
- Experience and knowledge of information security management and key cyber security assurance certifications.

Earlier in the Regulation is some additional information: "a person with expert knowledge of data protection laws and practices should assist the controller or processor to monitor internal compliance with this Regulation. […] The necessary level of expert knowledge should be determined in particular according to the data processing operations carried out and the protection required for the personal data processed by the controller or the processor".[166] Although it is clear that a legal qualification is not a requirement for the role of DPO, an understanding of data privacy law is essential. This understanding could be gained through experience. The DPO should ensure that they are *au fait* not just with the relevant laws (including the GDPR), but also with the nature of the processing itself and how it relates to the organisation's business operations.

Typical qualifications for DPOs include the ISO/IEC 17024-certificated EU GDPR Practitioner (C GDPR P) and Certified Data Protection Officer (C-DPO) qualifications from IBITGQ (*www.ibitgq.org*), the International Board for IT Governance Qualifications. For more information, see *www.ibitgq.org/candidates/certificates.aspx*.

Duties of the DPO

The DPO is a protected and independent role, as the Regulation itself states:

> The controller and processor shall ensure that the data protection officer does not receive any instructions regarding the exercise of those tasks. He or she shall not be dismissed or penalised by the controller or the processor for performing his tasks. The data protection officer shall directly report to the highest management level of the controller or the processor.[167]

---

[166] GDPR, Recital 97.

[167] GDPR, Article 38(3).

It is clear that the DPO is to be permitted a high degree of autonomy to pursue their duties, with the full support of the controller and/or processor, and with recourse to the highest level of management.

The DPO's primary tasks are outlined in Article 39.[168] The first is to:

> inform and advise the controller or the processor and the employees who carry out processing of their obligations pursuant to this Regulation and to other Union or Member State data protection provisions.

That is, the DPO is responsible for ensuring that the controller, processor and employees who process personal data understand their obligations, and for providing advice on meeting those obligations. Although this obligation explicitly applies to the GDPR and other requirements under Member State and EU law, it would make sense that the DPO should also be responsible for providing advice for any other data protection laws that might apply. The DPO should advise controllers and processors to implement staff awareness and training programmes to help meet this requirement.

Some of the more important information that the DPO should be able to advise upon relates to Articles 12, 13 and 14, which cover the controller's/processor's duties regarding transparency and how personal data is collected from data subjects. These can be especially complex, and may require

---

[168] GDPR, Article 39(1).

the organisation to think carefully about how those processes should be managed to minimise the impact on other business processes.

Furthermore, the organisation will need to be aware of any additional legislation that may apply in the relevant Member State or the Union. The Regulation states elsewhere that "Member States should be able to lay down the rules on criminal penalties for infringements of this Regulation, including for infringements of national rules adopted pursuant to and within the limits of this Regulation".[169] This is reiterated when the Regulation encourages Member States to establish further "effective, proportionate and dissuasive penalties"[170] where necessary. It will often fall to the DPO to ensure that controllers and processors are made aware of such additional laws and their penalties and, in many cases, this will also need to be communicated clearly to staff.

The DPO's second task is to:

> monitor compliance with this Regulation, with other Union or Member State data protection provisions and with the policies of the controller or processor in relation to the protection of personal data, including the assignment of responsibilities, awareness-raising and training of staff involved in processing operations, and the related audits.

The DPO should have oversight of the privacy compliance framework described in the previous chapter. The

---

[169] GDPR, Recital 149.

[170] GDPR, Recital 152.

documentation produced by the framework should produce evidence that it is effective, including records, reports, schedules, and so on, which the DPO can use to monitor data protection activities. Assuming the compliance framework is thorough and effective, the DPO will also be able to confirm that the organisation's processes meet the requirements of the Regulation, from the policy down to the actual day-to-day application of documented procedures.

This relates to Article 30 of the Regulation in particular (which requires the controller to maintain a record of processing activities), so it will be incumbent on both the controller/processor and the DPO to ensure that the compliance framework generates adequate, suitable and accurate records. Such records will be necessary for the DPO to confirm the efficacy of the organisation's compliance programme.

The DPO's third task is to:

> provide advice where requested as regards the data protection impact assessment and monitor its performance pursuant to Article 35.

Part 3 of this manual (Chapters 10–12) covers DPIAs in detail. The DPO has a significant role in DPIAs, so should pay close attention to this section of the manual. This is related to risk management, which the DPO should also be involved in (as noted in Clause 2 of this Article).

The DPO's fourth and fifth tasks are:

> to cooperate with the supervisory authority; and
> to act as the contact point for the supervisory authority on issues relating to processing, including the prior consultation referred to in Article 36, and to consult, where appropriate, with regard to any other matter.

The DPO is essentially the organisation's immediate liaison with the supervisory authority. Because organisations required to have a DPO are typically involved in processing large volumes of personal data or special categories of data, they are likely to be subjected to increased attention from the supervisory authority. The DPO, therefore, operates as a single point of contact between the organisation and the supervisory authority, minimising disruption for the organisation.

The DPO will need to pay due regard to high-risk processing, taking into account the nature, scope, context and purposes of any such processing. The appointment of a DPO is mandatory for organisations involved in high-volume data processing because the processing of large quantities of personal data comes with an inherent risk commensurate to the volume.

It is also worth understanding the relationship between the DPO and the data subject. Because organisations are required to publish the DPO's details, they will often be a point of contact for data subjects asserting their rights under the Regulation. The DPO should therefore ensure that they have appropriate (and documented) processes in place to respond to DSARs and complaints to the controller or processor, and to operate as a mediator in any resultant discussions or responses.

This will involve some overlap with the controller's/processor's duties to uphold data subjects' rights. Because of the potential complexity of the interaction between the Regulation and the organisation's business processes, especially where "modalities [are] provided for facilitating the exercise of the data subjects' rights under this

Regulation",[171] the DPO will be affected by the twin pressures of helping the organisation to comply with the Regulation, and supporting and assuring the data subjects' rights.

The DPO and the organisation

As noted previously, the DPO is a largely independent role, even if it stands in addition to an individual's other duties within the organisation. The role is about delivering compliance, and you can't have compliance under the direction of the delivery team because of the conflict of interest. The DPO should, therefore, have the primary objective of ensuring compliance with the law, while the delivery team's main objective will be to maximise productivity, which may sometimes be counter to the requirements of legal compliance.

To ensure autonomy and oversight, the DPO should sit within a risk management, compliance or governance function. Such roles are generally independent of other business functions and usually have direct access to senior levels of management and/or the board. Ensuring that the DPO has this access is crucial to ensuring that compliance with the Regulation is discussed and directed at that level.

On the other hand, the DPO must also be allowed to conduct their tasks with complete confidentiality and secrecy, when required, which brings a layer of separation between the DPO and the organisation to achieve compliance.

---

[171] GDPR, Recital 59.

An effective DPO will ensure that data protection, privacy and the organisation's legal obligations are on the board's agenda. Although boards have traditionally been disinterested in data protection and cyber security, the size of the potential fines and ramifications of data breaches now place a fiduciary duty on directors to ensure these risks are properly identified, assessed and managed.

As well as providing guidance on compliance with the Regulation, the DPO should also be capable of providing guidance on appropriate best-practice frameworks to assure compliance. This may be in addition to such guidance from the EDPB.[172]

The DPO and the supervisory authority

Just as the DPO has a specific relationship with the organisation, it also has a specific relationship with the supervisory authority.

The DPO operates as a kind of intermediary in many instances, providing a single point of contact, and ensuring that any communications between the supervisory authority and the controller/processor are clearly understood (because the DPO must be suitably qualified, as noted earlier).

The controller or processor must make the DPO's contact details available to both the supervisory authority and to the public. The DPO must also respond directly to requests from the supervisory authority addressed to them, and ensure that

---

[172] GDPR, Recital 77.

requests from the supervisory authority addressed to controllers are acknowledged.

The DPO must also cooperate fully with the supervisory authority if it asks the DPO to, for example:

- Supplement information that was provided in a notification for prior checking with respect to a complaint concerning the DPO's organisation;
- Monitor progress on the implementation of recommendations from the supervisory authority; or
- Gather information on behalf of the supervisory authority on an issue undergoing examination.

It is good practice to respond to the supervisory authority within one month, and the DPO should also address any requests to controllers within the same timeframe If this is not possible, the DPO must inform the supervisory authority when a reply will be sent.

Of particular importance will be the DPO's mediation between the supervisory authority and the controller/processor in the event of a data breach. By operating as a go-between, the requirements of Article 33 can be fulfilled while allowing the controller/processor to focus on responding to and recovering from the incident.

Data protection impact assessments and risk management

The DPIA is a key tool for the DPO.

DPIAs are a tool for risk management, but are only part of the whole process. The DPO should ensure they understand risk management as a process and how it fits into the compliance framework. This is especially important if the DPO is an external contractor, as they may not otherwise appreciate the organisation's risk management stance and processes, or how data protection fits into the wider whole.

The DPO should also ensure that they understand the organisation's risk appetite and how this intersects with the supervisory authority's expectations. An organisation may, for instance, be willing to accept certain risks that the supervisory authority would expect to be rejected. Should a data breach occur as a result of taking such a risk, the supervisory authority is unlikely to respond kindly.

Many of these issues should be resolved during the consultation phase that may follow a DPIA, as described in Article 36 of the Regulation. Because this procedure relates to potential breaches of the Regulation (and, possibly, other relevant Member State legislation), the DPO will need to be fully prepared to advise the controller or processor, and to respond to any queries or recommendations from the supervisory authority.

In-house or contract

Larger organisations are likely to employ one or more DPOs to create strength in the data protection team and to provide adequate resource to cover for holidays, illness and succession planning. For smaller organisations, the DPO may in reality not be a full-time activity. As we've seen, the organisation has two options for fulfilling the role in such cases:

1. Assign it to an existing member of staff.
2. Buy it in from a third party.

Assigning the role to a current member of staff has the advantage that the costs will almost certainly be lower than if a separate individual is employed, and the DPO will be more readily available because of being on-site. However, you must ensure that the projected privacy workload is appropriate to a part-time role and, even more importantly, that it does not occasion any conflicts of interest. It should also be noted that the requirements of the DPO role may in any case make it difficult to fill, and that writing the DPO's duties into another job description may make your DPO more difficult to replace.

Despite being the seemingly more expensive option, contracting the role out to a third party may prove to be the ideal solution. A contracted DPO (or a DPO-as-a-Service) has more incentive to remain up to date with current practices and technologies, and to maintain any relevant professional certifications. Furthermore, as a contracted DPO could fulfil the same role for a number of organisations within the same industry or sector, they will have greater insight into the specific data protection issues affecting that industry/sector. Contractors usually command daily rates of pay, which means they can be called upon as and when they are needed. If your compliance frameworks are properly implemented and followed, you may find you need your DPO's services less than you anticipated, making a contracted DPO a more cost-effective solution than it may at first appear.

CHAPTER 9: DATA MAPPING

In order to fully appreciate the scope of the GDPR and your duties in relation to it, it is essential to understand the personal data you are collecting and that you already hold. This is especially important for DPIAs, for the simple reason that a DPIA relies on having a comprehensive understanding of the data lifecycle.

There's no explicit requirement for data mapping in the Regulation, but it would be extraordinarily difficult to meet all of the GDPR's requirements without establishing the lifecycle of personal data in your organisation. In particular, Article 30's requirement for a record of processing activities could be nearly impossible to meet without some sort of data mapping process.

Data mapping is generally considered best practice for any data protection or privacy compliance programme, because you can't protect your information if you don't know:

a) That it exists;

b) Where it is; and

c) The conditions under which it is kept.

Though simply put, data mapping can prove challenging for organisations that haven't examined their processes before, work with a great deal of personal information or rely on data held in a variety of formats. Even well-organised businesses rarely keep a centralised map of all their data-collection and data-processing activities; it is generally left as disparate pieces of information held in process documentation and contracts.

Regular data mapping exercises are essential to protecting personal data in line with the GDPR. It gives the organisation a clear overview of its data processing activities, which can be leveraged for continual improvement across a number of the organisation's business interests.

Objectives and outcomes

As with any new process, you need to identify the objectives and desired outcomes of data mapping before you begin. The overall objective of data mapping as part of GDPR compliance is to identify and address potential privacy issues.

The process of data mapping is not always as simple as just figuring out where the data is and what it is used for; in many instances, the mapping process includes analysis on the go. For instance, if the data passes through a storage phase, you might identify that the server where it resides is not behind a locked door.

The output of the data mapping should record key aspects of a data workflow that will inform the measures that you take to comply with the GDPR.

You are also aiming to identify the specific risks to personal data, so your data mapping process should help you to identify unforeseen or unintended uses of the data. Because you generally need to inform data subjects about what you are doing with their data, any additional uses are likely to be in breach of the Regulation.

It is quite possible that the data mapping process can be rewarding for the organisation. In addition to identifying where efficiency can be improved, it can also draw your attention to potentially lucrative or useful processing opportunities.

Finally, and quite significantly, the data mapping process should help you to recognise who is involved at each stage in data processing activities and who *should* be involved. This will ensure that the people who will be using the information can be consulted on the practical implications of compliance with the Regulation (including the impact controls or other measures might have).

Four elements of data flow

There are four key elements in data mapping: data items, formats, transfer methods and locations. These elements are essentially all that you need to build your data map.

Data items are the information itself. An individual data item could be a single data point (e.g. a name) or a collection of related data (e.g. all of the information the organisation holds about a data subject). You will typically define the data items on the basis of the process itself. If the process only uses a person's address, for instance, then that would be the data item for that process.

Formats are the state in which the data items are stored. For an increasingly large proportion of organisations, this will be digital information stored in remote locations (e.g. in the Cloud), but you should aim to identify all of the formats that you actually use, including paper, photographs, backup tapes, USBs, etc.

Transfer methods are the explicit methods by which the data items move from one location to another, whether those locations and transport are physical or electronic. A process might include carrying physical files from a filing cabinet to a fax machine so that they can be faxed to another location. In this instance, both the act of carrying the files and faxing them are transfer methods, and a new data item (the printed fax at the other end) is created when the physical file is faxed.

Locations are the sites where data items are stored and where processing happens. Depending on the complexity of your processes, it may be useful to identify several locations at different levels of granularity for each step. For instance, you might specify that information is stored at the head office site, in the secure office and in the locked filing cabinet. This approach allows you to define varying levels of precision, which may be useful if some of your data items are spread across physical or digital locations.

Smaller organisations may prefer to simplify these elements as appropriate to their business. If you're a business based in one office and you do all processing on-site, for instance, you might declare that all locations are that office – there's no real need to be more specific because the data can be easily located when needed. Any transfers that aren't into or out of the organisation might also be ignored.

Data mapping, DPIAs and risk management

Data mapping is an important part of the risk management process. Your data map doesn't need to have incredible granularity or detail to be accurate; the level of detail that you go into should be *relevant*. By identifying all of your collection and processing activities, you will gain an overview of the risks to personal data and a relatively easy way of identifying activities worthy of closer inspection as part of a DPIA or risk management process.

It should be quite obvious when you're looking at a data map which areas could cause privacy issues. Examples might include when data is transferred to a third party, or when it interacts with several different individuals or entities, each of which could damage or inappropriately modify the data. These are risks, and should be processed and mitigated under your risk management methodology.

What you want to collect

You need a good understanding of your processing activities to develop a data map. In order to get to this state, there are a few questions you can ask about your process:

- How is the personal data collected? Personal data can be collected in a number of ways: paper forms, web applications, call centres, etc. Each of these methods also has a location – paper forms are often completed outside the business, for instance.

- Who is accountable for the personal data? Each processing activity should have an owner who is responsible for the data being processed. It is possible you will also assign other people to be responsible for various elements of the processing, and they may have varying levels of responsibility for the data at different points.

- Where is the personal data stored? As described earlier, personal data can be stored in both digital and analogue forms, and in several locations simultaneously, so it is important to track all sites that store it.

- Who has access to the personal data? This may include employees who do not need access, which should therefore be reviewed. It may also include the data subject themselves, or their friends and family.

- Is the personal data disclosed or shared with anyone? This includes other parties such as suppliers and data processors.
- Does the system share data with other systems? Sharing data between systems can lead to unintended or excessive processing, but can also offer significant business benefits.

Methods of data mapping

One of your first considerations in approaching data mapping will be creating a schedule of data mapping exercises. Initially, you should run a data mapping exercise covering all of your processing activities to ensure that you are complying with the Regulation. Following on from this, later data mapping exercises should coincide with your regular risk assessments. Beyond this, as with any other risk management process, you should map information flows when there is a significant change or a new processing activity has been designed.

You also need to identify the scope of the mapping. Like risk assessments, the first time you conduct a mapping exercise, you should be looking to map the lifecycle of all of the personal data your organisation holds. Depending on the size and complexity of this data, it may be valuable to break this down into phases, perhaps splitting the process up according to division or prioritising it based on the value and significance of each process.

With the context of the mapping pinned down, you can start the data mapping exercise. The method you use for tracking information flows will depend on the complexity of the organisation's processes and preferences.

It is simplest to begin with creating a visual representation of the information flow. You can use almost anything that lets you draw or arrange information, such as a whiteboard, Post-it notes, software or other mind-mapping tools.

There are several ways to map information flows. You might prefer to focus on how data moves between specific sites. A very simple example is shown in Figure 8.

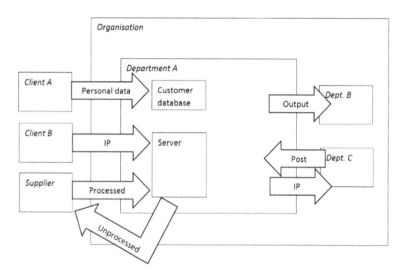

Figure 8: A simple way to map information flows

This method shows how Department A uses data, including its relationships with internal and external bodies, indications of data that have been processed, where data is stored within the department, and so on. For many organisations, this mapping method may be entirely adequate, or could form a high-level view of the range of processes within the organisation or department.

A process map, on the other hand, focuses on how data is used in the process itself. An example can be seen in Figure 9.

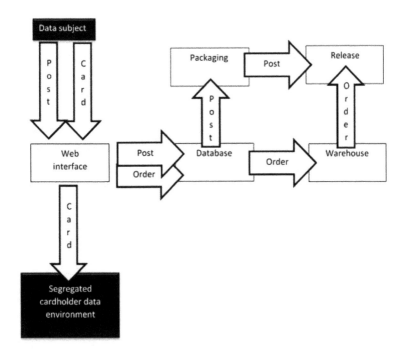

Figure 9: An example information process map of an online retailer

This is a simple example of what an online retailer might be doing with personal data, including payment card data. The retailer takes in the customer's name, postal address and credit card details. The credit card details go to the segregated cardholder data environment (CDE), which is subject to a different process and specific, contractual, regulatory and legal requirements. Meanwhile, the customer's order is separated from the postal address and both are sent to the fulfilment database. The database processes this information and sends the order to the warehouse, while the postal information is sent to be attached to the packaging. Customer address and order details are then reunited for release.

A more complex version of this diagram might show that the order and customer data are also sent to a separate process that tracks the customer's purchasing habits, it might include more specific details about the personal data collected (street address, postcode, etc.), or you might get around this by referring to a spreadsheet that tracks the specific data and use the map as a quick reference or overview.

Whichever method you choose, you will need to be able to transfer the information in your data map over to your risk management process. In many cases, this means your data map needs to be converted to something tabular such as an Excel spreadsheet.

If you are looking for further guidance on the data mapping process, the UK's NHS has published a particularly useful and practical guide to information mapping,[173] which was written to support a focused information mapping tool. This document was developed to help healthcare organisations comply with a number of legal and ethical obligations relating to the handling of personal and sensitive

---

[173] Look for "Information Mapping Guidance" on *www.igt.hscic.gov.uk/datamappingguidance.aspx*.

information. Although it is quite likely that your organisation isn't subject to the same obligations, the process and fundamental concerns that the tool presents are fairly universal.

Other sectors and jurisdictions are likely to have their own versions of this tool or something comparable, so do keep them in mind when developing your organisation's data mapping process.

Vigilant Software, the IT Governance software development subsidiary, has a data flow mapping tool that allows this exercise to be simplified and supported over time. More information can be obtained from: *www.vigilantsoftware.co.uk*.

Part 3: Data protection impact assessments and risk management

CHAPTER 10: REQUIREMENTS FOR DATA PROTECTION IMPACT ASSESSMENTS

The DPIA is one of the specific processes mandated by the GDPR. Many organisations will be required to conduct DPIAs and, in many instances, an organisation may find it a valuable process even when a DPIA is not required by the Regulation.

DPIAs are used to identify specific risks to personal data as a result of processing activities and the significance of their role in a PIMS could be compared to that of the information security risk assessments required by ISO/IEC 27001 and described in ISO/IEC 27005 (see chapter 11). DPIAs naturally have a greater focus on data protection and privacy, of course, so a more focused model is valuable. The Regulation describes the purpose of DPIAs:

> In order to maintain security and to prevent processing in infringement of this Regulation, the controller or processor should evaluate the risks inherent in the processing and implement measures to mitigate those risks, such as encryption. […] In assessing data security risk, consideration should be given to the risks that are presented by personal data processing, such as accidental or unlawful destruction, loss, alteration, unauthorised disclosure of, or access to, personal data transmitted,

stored or otherwise processed which may in particular lead to physical, material or non-material damage.[174]

The GDPR also sets out what must, as a minimum, be contained in a DPIA[175]:

- A description of the processing and purposes;
- Legitimate interests pursued by the controller;
- An assessment of the necessity and proportionality of the processing;
- An assessment of the risks to the rights and freedoms of data subjects;
- The measures envisaged to address the risks;
- All safeguards and security measures to demonstrate compliance;
- An indication of timeframes if processing relates to erasure;
- An indication of any data protection by design and default measures;
- A list of recipients of personal data;
- Confirmation of compliance with approved codes of conduct; and
- Details of whether data subjects have been consulted.

Before the GDPR, privacy impact assessments (PIAs) were widely considered best practice by regulators, including the

---

[174] GDPR, Recital 83.

[175] GDPR, Article 35(7).

UK's ICO. Given the wide acceptance of PIAs and the availability of resources supporting them, the PIA model can be taken as a good foundation for GDPR-compliant DPIAs. For any practical purpose, PIAs and DPIAs are the same thing.

DPIAs

A DPIA is a process that helps organisations identify and minimise privacy risks, and is usually conducted ahead of implementing new processes, projects or policies. DPIAs aim to seek out potential problems so that they can be mitigated ahead of time, thereby reducing the likelihood of occurrence and the associated costs. Furthermore, DPIAs should directly benefit the organisation by improving policies, processes and systems, and securing relationships with customers and stakeholders.

The UK's ICO produced a comprehensive code of practice for DPIAs,[176] and several other European agencies have also produced documents relating to DPIAs.[177] Approaches are generally identical, with some varying commentary based on local laws and historic data protection practices. It is important to remember that DPIAs currently do not have a

---

[176] *ico.org.uk/for-organisations/guide-to-data-protection/guide-to-the-general-data-protection-regulation-gdpr/data-protection-impact-assessments-dpias/*.

[177] France's CNIL, for instance, maintains regularly updated guidance: *www.cnil.fr/sites/default/files/atoms/files/cnil-pia-1-en-methodology.pdf*.

specification: there is no central source to explain, in detail, how they must be done.[178]

For ease of reference – and to avoid issues with translation – we will refer to the ICO's DPIA guidance. If you are implementing GDPR compliance elsewhere in Europe, you should consult your local supervisory authority in case there is alternative regionally appropriate guidance.

The ICO recommends seeking advice on DPIAs from your DPO, but not all organisations have their own DPO, so it makes sense to ensure you have access to an independent adviser. . Because DPOs (where they exist) are also required to monitor DPIAs, they should not be directly involved in running the DPIA itself as that would constitute a conflict of interest.

The ICO's guidance defines a number of specific steps in the DPIA:

1. Identify the need for a PIA.
2. Describe the processing.
3. Consider consultation.
4. Assess necessity and proportionality.
5. Identify and assess risks.
6. Identify measures to mitigate the risks.
7. Sign off and record outcomes.

---

[178] Article 35 of the GDPR does describe what needs to be included in the DPIA, but not *how* the DPIA should be conducted. This is an important distinction.

These simple steps provide a good overview of the process and are relatively straightforward for anyone to follow. Given that the guidance is simply that – guidance, not a prescribed method – most organisations could reasonably put together their own DPIA methodology based on these steps. Some additional research may be necessary to understand the finer points of data protection and privacy, but it should be well within the means of most organisations to actually achieve this. We will now go through these phases briefly in order to introduce the various topics and considerations relevant to DPIAs.

1. Identify the need for a DPIA

Identifying the need for a DPIA is the critical first step, as the organisation will need to determine whether a) the law requires one, or b) the needs of the organisation demand one. In the first case, this will be determined by examining the relevant laws. For our purposes, this would be the GDPR, which states[179]:

> Where a type of processing in particular using new technologies, and taking into account the nature, scope, context and purposes of the processing, is likely to result in a high risk to the rights and freedoms of natural persons, the controller shall, prior to the processing, carry out an assessment of the impact of the envisaged processing operations on the protection of personal data.

---

[179] GDPR, Article 35(1).

This is the short version, of course, and there are several references throughout the Regulation that clarify when DPIAs should be conducted, notably in Recital 91. There are three primary conditions for conducting a DPIA[180]:

1. When the processing involves a systematic and extensive evaluation of personal aspects relating to natural persons based on automated processing, including profiling, and on which decisions are based that produce legal effects concerning a data subject or similarly significantly affect them.

2. When processing special categories of data on a large scale, or personal data relating to criminal convictions and offences.

3. When systematically monitoring a publicly accessible area on a large scale.

It should be noted that the Regulation states that these are required "in particular" – you should not assume that these are the only times that DPIAs are necessary. Recital 91 provides more detail on the context for the use of DPIAs:

1. When there is large-scale processing across a geographical area, e.g. an organisation wants to collect information on everyone in Scotland who falls within a specific demographic.

2. When new technologies are being used on a large scale, e.g. an organisation has developed a new algorithm for

---

[180] GDPR, Article 35(3).

sorting large quantities of personal data prior to the data being encrypted.

3. When there is a high level of risk to the data subjects' rights and freedoms, or to their ability to exercise their rights and freedoms, e.g. processing personal information that results in a list of people who could then be targeted by criminals.

4. When processing based on profiling is used to make decisions regarding specific natural persons, e.g. automated processing that collates information about someone's socio-economic status so that they can then be ordered into groups for future education opportunities.

5. When processing of special categories of personal data, biometric data or data on criminal convictions and offences is used to make decisions regarding specific natural persons, e.g. automated processing that collates information about someone's medical history so that their health insurance rates can be adjusted.

6. When monitoring publicly accessible areas on a large scale, especially when using optic-electronic devices (such as CCTV, infrared cameras, etc.) or the competent supervisory authority considers there to be a high risk to the rights and freedoms of data subjects, e.g. a fitness club wants to put a range of cameras around its car park, which also serves customers of a vegan food supply store and a community centre.

WP29 has expanded on this, publishing guidelines explaining the nine criteria that may act as indicators of high-risk processing[181]:

1. Evaluating or scoring data subjects, especially based on "aspects concerning the data subject's performance at work, economic situation, health, personal preferences or interests, reliability or behaviour, location or movements".[182]

2. Automated decision-making that produces "legal effects concerning the natural person" or "similarly significantly affects the natural person".[183]

3. Systematic monitoring – processing used to observe, monitor or control data subjects, including through data collected through networks or from "a systematic monitoring of a publicly accessible area".[184]

4. Processing sensitive data or data of a highly personal nature, including both special categories of personal data and data relating to criminal convictions or offences.

---

[181] WP29, "Guidelines on Data Protection Impact Assessment (DPIA)", October 2017, *ec.europa.eu/newsroom/article29/item-detail.cfm?item_id=611236*.

[182] GDPR, Recitals 71 and 91.

[183] GDPR, Article 35(3)(a).

[184] GDPR, Article 35(3)(c).

5. Large-scale data processing (see chapter 8 for a discussion of what constitutes 'large scale').
6. Matching or combining data sets, such as when combining data that has been processed for different purposes or by different controllers and could exceed the data subject's reasonable expectations.
7. Processing data concerning vulnerable data subjects, which may include processing where there is an imbalance in the relationship between the data subject and the controller.
8. When using innovative processing techniques or applying new technologies. DPIAs for this purpose should also seek to understand any unintended or novel results from processing.
9. When the processing in itself "prevents data subjects from exercising a right or using a service or contract".[185]

Under the GDPR, the primary concern of DPIAs is to reduce the risk of harm to the data subject.

The key terms throughout the recital are "large scale" and "high risk", the criteria for which could be difficult to determine. The simple option is to consult a DPO, who should have sufficient experience and expertise to determine such things. If you don't have access to a DPO, the alternative is to ask the supervisory authority.

---

[185] GDPR, Article 22, Recital 91.

The supervisory authority should generally be considered the primary source for clarification on questions like these, and supervisory authorities are required to produce "a list of the kind of processing operations which are subject to the requirement for a [DPIA]" and may also produce "a list of the kind of processing operations for which no [DPIA] is required".[186]

In addition to the listed requirements for DPIAs, Member States may require public authorities to conduct DPIAs covering specific processing operations, which are likely to relate to specifically regulated areas.[187]

A DPIA may also be necessary to meet the organisation's risk management requirements. It is quite likely that many companies will establish their own additional criteria to trigger a DPIA, perhaps where the processing in question is extremely expensive and any risk of a breach might make it a risky business decision, or if the organisation has a very low risk appetite or simply wants to ensure it stays on the right side of the law. Whatever your reasons, you should document your criteria or define a repeatable process for determining whether a DPIA is necessary.

You may also wish to consider voluntarily conducting one in a number of situations to support good practice in complying with the Regulation, especially with regard to data protection by design and by default. In some instances, you may be able

---

[186] GDPR, Article 35(4) and (5).

[187] GDPR, Recital 93.

to look into DPIAs on similar processing or technologies to discover whether there are any notable findings.

A more obvious condition for a voluntary DPIA would be in preparing for or validating compliance with the GDPR. Every organisation should examine their current and planned processing activities and technologies to determine whether any of them warrant examination via a DPIA. Identifying all of your current processes will come as part of your initial data mapping exercise, which will be discussed in chapter 7.

2. Describe the processing

The second step, describing the processing and information flows, relates to data mapping, which we looked at in much more detail in chapter 9.

It is also worth mentioning that a DPIA can examine a number of processes at once. This is obviously simpler when those processes are related or linked, but it is quite acceptable for a single assessment to determine the impact of a range of data processing operations/functions.

3. Consider consultation

This refers to consulting individuals who might be affected by the processing activity. The ICO recommends seeking out their views (or those of their representatives) unless there is a good reason not to. WP29 supports this position, and notes that the controller should record any justification for not consulting data subjects, as well as any decision that goes against the data subjects' views.

4. Assess necessity and proportionality

This stage determines whether the processing activity is necessary at all and whether there is a safer way of achieving the same results. The organisation might consider other processing activities that it already conducts safely, alternative methods of achieving the same results, how the processing can be explained to the data subject, and so on.

5. Identify and assess risks

This is a common component in all risk management strategies: know your threats and how they might exploit your vulnerabilities. In essence, you should be attempting to catalogue the range of threats, and their related vulnerabilities, to the rights and freedoms of the data subjects whose data you collect and/or process.

6. Identify measures to mitigate the risks

For each identified risk to the personal data, you should make what is called a 'risk decision': do we accept or reject the risk, or do we take steps to reduce the impact or likelihood of the threat successfully exploiting the vulnerability by selecting and implementing one or more controls? The value of ISO 27002, the standard that provides guidance on implementing the controls listed in Annex A of ISO 27001, is that its control set is comprehensive and covers all the most likely areas of required activity, from HR through to physical and logical security.

The decision to select and apply controls will depend on a number of factors: the likelihood of the risk and its potential impact, the cost of remediation, and so on. Some of these cannot be thoroughly examined without knowing also how to control the risk, so you may need to identify both the risk and the solution(s) before deciding whether it is appropriate to remediate the risk. Once a risk decision is made, you can create a RTP, which essentially outlines the operational steps to be taken – together with details of accountabilities, measures, etc. – to translate the risk decision into reality.

7. Sign off and record outcomes

The outcomes of the DPIA (steps 1–6) should be recorded and signed off by whoever is responsible for those decisions. This means that you should record the risk decision and the corresponding RTP alongside each risk. If you have a DPO, you should ensure they review this and confirm that the risks have been appropriately accounted for and that the processing is acceptable. Provide a copy of the consolidated RTP to top management for sign-off and resource commitment. Implement the RTP, report to top management on progress, maintain the RTP and ensure – through internal audit and, where relevant, testing – that the selected controls continue to meet the organisation's risk management objectives. This is, of course, related to the organisation's risk management approach, which is discussed later in this manual.

The importance of recording good information and producing a formal report cannot be understated. A formal report will outline the measures to address the data protection issues raised by the DPIA, and gives organisations accountability and transparency for such issues, allowing individuals to learn more about how the DPIA affects them and their work.

The report can also form the basis for further audits and post-implementation reviews, as well as a reference for future PIAs, so it is vital that all information and the subsequent outcomes of the PIA are recorded to a high standard.

After the DPIA

With the DPIA complete, recorded and approved by top management, your earlier decisions become defined actions. This may entail prioritising the decisions or reviewing the DPIA in more detail to correctly and effectively mitigate the identified risks.

This also feeds into the project plan for the processing function(s) that the DPIA examines. This means that the implementation plan will be modified and updated to include the results of the DPIA. Depending on the nature of the processing function(s), this may require more or less technical work (such as programming/coding work, etc.), and may require you to re-examine project deadlines and dependencies.

Furthermore, some measures that you implement may require maintenance or periodic observation, so these should be accounted for in the relevant operational procedures.

The ICO also states that it is good practice to publish your DPIAs in order to aid transparency and accountability. Obviously, there must be a sensible limit to the information revealed by publishing a DPIA – as the ICO recognises: "If you are concerned that publication may reveal commercially sensitive information, undermine security or cause other risks, you should consider whether you can redact (black out) or remove sensitive details, or publish a summary".[188]

---

[188] *ico.org.uk/for-organisations/guide-to-data-protection/guide-to-the-general-data-protection-regulation-gdpr/data-protection-impact-assessments-dpias/how-do-we-do-a-dpia/*.

Consulting with stakeholders

Regardless of your approach to the DPIA, you should always remember that you are attempting to minimise the impact of your processes on the rights and freedoms of data subjects, and stakeholders should be consulted appropriately throughout the process. The ICO's guidance also recommends seeking advice from other independent experts, such as lawyers, IT experts, sociologists or ethicists, which you might consider depending on the specific nature of the processing and the risk to data subjects.

You should also ensure that you have access to a resource that represents the data subjects themselves as stakeholders. Depending on the processing in question, this may be someone within the organisation who operates as a devil's advocate, an external consultant with expertise in data protection and privacy or a group of anonymous data subjects – anyone capable of appreciating the data subjects' concerns.

Who needs to be involved?

It is the responsibility of the data controller to ensure DPIAs are carried out where required by the GDPR, or by other Union or Member State law. It is the controller's responsibility because the controller determines the purpose of the processing.

The DPO is a central figure in DPIAs. The Regulation states that "the controller shall seek the advice of the data protection officer, where designated, when carrying out a data protection impact assessment".[189] What this should also say is that seeking out a DPO (or someone with comparable expertise) should be considered best practice for any DPIA. The Regulation specifies certain aspects of your DPIA, but it doesn't tell you how to actually do one, or provide the insight necessary to really get to grips with privacy and data protection.

Asset and process owners should certainly be involved. They will be responsible for the actual processing and/or the personal data being processed, so it is critical that they have a thorough understanding of all of the risks, including those that you might consider negligible and leave untreated.

A whole range of functions within the organisation might also be involved: risk management, service delivery, infrastructure, and so on. It will all depend on the organisation, the scale and nature of the processing, its criticality to the business, and, of course, the organisation's stance with regard to compliance.

It is also quite likely that you will want to involve a number of stakeholders. These don't need to be involved in any great depth at all stages of the DPIA, but they will need to be available at the key moments to provide feedback or input.

It is worth remembering that, like any other business process, having too many people directly involved can ruin the process; it gets bogged down in irrelevant details, decisions are made by committee instead of by authority, the objectives of the process are lost as internal politics derail the discussion

---

[189] GDPR, Article 35(2).

and decisions that should have taken days end up taking weeks. This sort of 'paralysis by analysis' will be familiar to most organisations.

The DPIA process should be proportional to the size of the organisation, its turnover and the scale of the processing. It is reasonable to assume that the CEO of a major international organisation will hurl bodies at the problem quite happily if it will save 4% of global turnover. As long as the DPIA process is well managed and led, this should not pose too great a problem.

Data protection by design and by default

The Regulation states that "the controller should adopt internal policies and implement measures which meet in particular the principles of data protection by design and data protection by default".[190]

DPIAs are an important part of data protection by design and by default, which is a process of ensuring that all personal data collection, processing, storage and destruction measures are designed to secure privacy. The UK's ICO describes data protection by design as "an approach that ensures you consider privacy and data protection issues at the design phase of any system, service, product or process and then throughout the lifecycle".[191] This is expanded in the GDPR to include "by default", which essentially insists that the

---

[190] GDPR, Recital 78.

[191] *ico.org.uk/for-organisations/guide-to-data-protection/guide-to-the-general-data-protection-regulation-gdpr/accountability-and-governance/data-protection-by-design-and-default/*.

organisation ensures that *all* such projects take data protection into account.

According to the Regulation, the controller should establish whatever measures are necessary to "implement data-protection principles [...] in an effective manner and to integrate the necessary safeguards into the processing in order to meet the requirements of this Regulation and protect the rights of data subjects".[192] This is expanded more clearly in the following clause to encompass each of the data protection principles:

> The controller shall implement appropriate technical and organisational measures for ensuring that, by default, only personal data which are necessary for each specific purpose of the processing are processed. That obligation applies to the amount of personal data collected, the extent of their processing the period of their storage and their accessibility. In particular, such measures shall ensure that by default personal data are not made accessible without the individual's intervention to an indefinite number of natural persons.[193]

The Regulation mandates putting measures in place to ensure that the data subjects' rights and freedoms are preserved simply because the processing has been designed that way. It is quite a logical step, and often applied to other design practices that, depending on the industry, are also seen as

---

[192] GDPR, Article 25(1).

[193] GDPR, Article 25(2).

essential, such as safety by design in an industrial setting, or hygiene by design in healthcare practices.

Conducting DPIAs is an important part of this. If you know what the risks are to the data subjects' rights, it is much simpler to establish measures that will protect them. As such, you should ensure that your DPIA methodology will provide outputs that can be turned into preventive measures and applied to the processing design from the very start.

In the 1990s, the Information and Privacy Commissioner (IPC) of Ontario, Canada, developed a comprehensive primer on privacy by design, which has been regularly updated and remains an authoritative source on ensuring privacy in business applications by default.[194] It establishes seven key principles around which data protection by design should be built:

1. Proactive not reactive; preventative not remedial.
2. Privacy as the default setting.
3. Privacy embedded into design.
4. Full functionality – positive-sum, not zero-sum.
5. End-to-end security – full lifecycle protection.
6. Visibility and transparency – keep it open.
7. Respect for user privacy – keep it user-centric.

The *Privacy by Design* document formed the foundation of many further publications and additional guidance focusing on the concept of promoting privacy and data protection

---

[194] Ann Cavoukian, *Privacy by Design,* January 2018, *www.ipc.on.ca/guidance-documents/.*

compliance from the start of a project and throughout its lifecycle. The document itself has also been translated into a range of languages to improve its worldwide reach.

With the prevalence of materials and support available to help you establish data protection by design and by default, your final concern will be generating evidence that this takes place and is appropriately applied. Much like anything else associated with your privacy compliance framework, some records should be generated to provide this evidence. The Regulation, however, provides a second option: certification schemes.

The Regulation states that "an approved certification mechanism […] may be used as an element to demonstrate compliance".[195] It is only "an element", but the Regulation actually allows quite a lot of compliance to be proven through certification schemes. If you would like to pursue this, you should contact your supervisory authority to find out if any certification schemes are available in your jurisdiction.

---

[195] GDPR, Article 25(3).

CHAPTER 11: RISK MANAGEMENT AND DPIAs

The Regulation notes that controllers and processors "should evaluate the risks inherent in the processing and implement measures to mitigate those risks".[196] This same consideration is mentioned several times throughout the Regulation, requiring the controller and the processor to take risks into account at many stages throughout the lifecycle of the personal data in question. Although it stops short of saying that the organisation should have an explicit risk management programme, it is clear that a systematic and comprehensive approach is the best way to ensure compliance.

Risk management is now a near-universal expectation of corporate management and, although smaller organisations might manage risk relatively informally, most organisations of any size will have a formal approach to the subject. This will include, for instance, a board risk register and regular board reviews of corporate risk. Risk management is not necessarily complicated, but there are a variety of ways you might approach it, along with associated standards, models, training opportunities, consultants, and so on.

Effective risk management is also an important tool for achieving GDPR compliance. The Regulation reinforces the risk management that organisations must execute in order to

---

[196] GDPR, Recital 83.

build the necessary preventive measures against data breaches and other forms of cyber attack.

DPIAs as part of risk management

DPIAs are essentially a form of risk management. You use them to identify risks to the data subject's privacy, the security of their personal data, and their rights and freedoms in relation to their data. Data protection risks (the risks to data subjects) should now be identified and managed alongside risks to the organisation as part of business as usual. A DPIA should therefore inform and be part of your larger corporate risk management activity. The DPIA identifies a set of risks specific to personal data or the data subject's rights. The risk management programme then categorises and analyses these risks, and finally determines an appropriate response. This is all part of the privacy compliance framework.

Risk management standards and methodologies

Risk management is a vast field. For decades, organisations around the world have been dealing with ideas about managing risks to almost every facet of business, so there are a variety of methodologies and standards that account for different industries and sectors, geographical or political regions, languages and corporate ideologies. You could likely find a new risk management model in every Member State of the EU.

Because of this variety, and because your organisation may already have a risk management model in place, we will focus here on the more common methodologies espoused by ISO standards – ISO 27001, ISO 27005 and ISO 31000 in particular. ISO standards are appropriate because they can be integrated with many management systems, they are based on decades of studying best practice and they are widely popular, which makes finding support or resources relatively simple.

ISO 31000

ISO 31000:2018, *Risk management – Guidelines*, is the central repository for risk management practices in the ISO standards. It is widely used across the world. Many disciplines that ISO has developed standards for will have their own variety of risk management, but ISO 31000 provides a framework into which these more specific risk management methodologies can fit, enabling the organisation to consolidate diverse risk management activities.

For an organisation that needs to comply with the GDPR, ISO 31000 can provide a model framework to integrate your various risk management processes. This may not be necessary at all for organisations that already manage a variety of types of risk, but for smaller organisations or those that haven't historically taken a systematic approach to risk, the framework could be a useful tool. At the very least, the Standard provides valuable guidance.

ISO 31000's definition of "risk" is the "effect of uncertainty on objectives".[197] ISO 31000 goes on to clarify that "an effect is a deviation from the expected. It can be positive, negative or both, and can address, create or result in opportunities and threats", which provides some additional

---

[197] ISO/IEC 31000:2018, Clause 3.1.

clarity. Essentially, a risk is something that can impact your ability to meet objectives. In the context of the GDPR, those objectives would be to protect personal data, and to comply with the Regulation and relevant local laws.

In accordance with this definition, the risk management framework that ISO 31000 espouses is focused on reducing the threats to your objectives. It quite clearly states this in its discussion of the principles of risk management: risk management "improves performance, encourages innovation and supports the achievement of objectives".[198]

ISO 31000 asserts a triple structure for risk management, with principles informing both the risk management framework and the risk management process. The framework and process then inform one another. This structure is illustrated, in a marginally simplified format, in Figure 10.

---

[198] ISO/IEC 31000:2009, Clause 4.

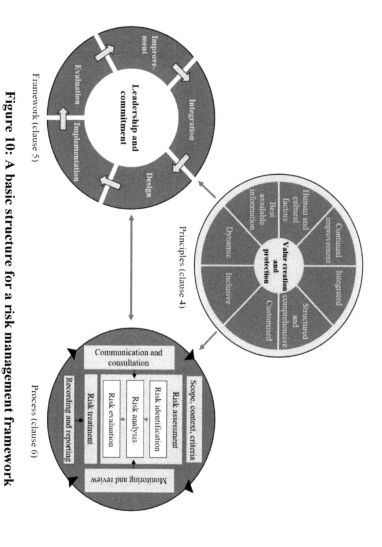

Figure 10: A basic structure for a risk management framework

The principles, framework and processes operate at different levels within the organisation. The principles, being constants, are simply objectives for risk management; the framework is operated from the governance level by senior management and/or the board; and the processes are managed at the procedural level by appropriately skilled and qualified staff.

You will also note that the framework very closely aligns with a PDCA cycle as described in chapter 4. It includes a single additional phase – 'integration' – which describes the process of integrating risk management across the organisation and could be read as part of the 'Act' phase in PDCA.

Critically, ISO 31000 provides a common approach in dealing with specific risks and sectors. That is, the framework and principles should be taken as universal – an overarching approach to risk management, if you will – while the processes will be informed by whatever processes are necessary for the types of risk under consideration. For GDPR compliance, these will be privacy and information security risks.

Even when it describes the "process" level, it does so by providing guidance on appreciating things such as the internal context, how to define risk criteria, evaluating risks, and so on. In short, it simply recognises that all risk management processes have a broadly similar set of inputs and outputs, and processes to derive those outputs from the inputs, and gives the reader some context. It is not a specification and it cannot be certified; ISO 31000 is simply guidance.

The process of risk management laid out in ISO 31000 is strikingly simple once you pare it down to the core:

1. Ensure that communication and consultation take place throughout the risk management process (Clause 6.2 of ISO 31000). People will be informed and asked for input, others may proffer information or experiences that had not been considered. You should ensure that those who are involved in risk assessment and treatment are open to such communication and that they understand the need for consultation.[199]

2. Establish the context of the risk assessment, both internally and externally (Clause 6.3). Who are the stakeholders? What is important? What is the legal, regulatory and contractual environment? What are the organisation's objectives? Understanding the context is an important feature of many management systems; it informs how you go about your risk assessment, how you determine risk criteria, what you deem to be a risk, the resources you have to mitigate risks, and so on.

3. Identify the risk (Clause 6.4.2). This can be approached in a number of ways. You could examine your information assets to identify the threats that are likely to impact them, or you could consider scenarios that could cause harm to an asset or assets. We will look more at asset- and scenario-based risk assessments a little later in this chapter. Regardless, you should be

---

[199] You may recall the RACI matrix described in chapter 4. Risks related to information assets or processes, for instance, should trigger some form of communication/consultation with the relevant asset or process owner.

aiming to identify all of the relevant risks within the context of the risk assessment. In the case of a GDPR risk assessment, it should be risks to personal data and the rights and freedoms of data subjects.

4. Analyse the risk (Clause 6.4.3) by identifying how likely it is and the potential impact on the organisation should the risk occur.
5. Evaluate the risk (Clause 6.4.4) against the risk criteria. ISO 31000 states that the risk criteria "should reflect the organization's values, objectives and resources".[200] This should include your organisation's attitudes to GDPR compliance. Risk criteria will be used to determine how important a given risk is, which will be based on your organisation's risk appetite. The criteria are the measure of the risk, and the results of how a risk is evaluated against the criteria will inform how you choose to respond to the risk.
6. Treat the risk (Clause 6.5). Your risk treatment will be based on the outputs of the risk evaluation, taking into account the severity of the risk, where it sits in relation to the risk criteria, the organisation's risk appetite and the availability of treatment options for the risk.
7. Develop a RTP (Clause 6.5.3) to formally document the identified risks, your chosen responses and how the responses are to be implemented. This should include

---

[200] ISO/IEC 31000:2009, Clause 5.3.5.

noting who is responsible for the treatment of each risk, when the treatment should be completed, and so on.

8. Subject the risk assessment to monitoring and review (Clause 6.6). You will need to determine how to measure the state of implementation as well as metrics to ensure that the treatment is in place and active. These measurements should be subject to formal review and any discrepancies with the planned results should then receive corrective action. Like almost everything else, the risk treatments should also be looked at as part of continual improvement.

9. Record the risk management process and its outcomes, and report those to top management (Clause 6.7).

ISO 27001 and ISO 27005

ISO 27001, which has been mentioned several times already in this manual, is the ISO standard for information security management. Part of the specification relates to information security risk assessment and treatment, which is clearly of interest in relation to the GDPR. It is broader than a privacy risk assessment, and it could easily be argued that such a risk assessment in conjunction with a DPIA should be adequate for compliance.

ISO 27001 leaves the detail of the risk assessment methodology up to the organisation, stating that "the organization shall define and apply an information security risk assessment process".[201] As you will see, this process isn't much different from that outlined in ISO 31000.

ISO 27001 requires you to establish a set of criteria for the risk assessment (Clause 6.1.2 a). These should include the organisation's risk acceptance criteria and the criteria under which the organisation will perform information security risk assessments. These are both derived from the organisation's risk appetite, which should reflect the organisation's attitude to the repercussions of a data breach.

The risk assessment methodology needs to produce "consistent, valid and comparable results" (Clause 6.1.2 b). This is necessary to ensure that the organisation can accurately apply appropriate treatments: if the same risk could be assessed multiple times and achieve different outcomes, there could be no confidence in the risk assessment and the resulting treatments.

ISO 27001 also requires that the risk assessment process identifies the risks to the confidentiality, integrity and availability of information assets (Clause 6.1.2 c). The focus on identifying risks to confidentiality, integrity and availability ensures that risks are not identified simply for the *perceived* risk of harm: the organisation must have a reasonable expectation that there is a risk to at least one of the three attributes of information security.

Each risk should be assigned a risk owner (Clause 6.1.2 c) whose job is to ensure that the selected risk response is properly implemented. In most cases, this involves

---

[201] ISO/IEC 27001:2013, Clause 6.1.2.

implementing the measures that were selected to mitigate the risk. It is worth noting that a single risk may impact a number of assets, so the risk owner should ensure that all of the relevant assets are protected from the risk.

As in ISO 31000, the process includes risk analysis (Clause 6.1.2 d). This analysis should focus on three factors: the consequences of the risk occurring; the "realistic likelihood" of the risk occurring; and, as a factor of impact and likelihood, the levels of risk. In most risk assessment programmes, this will be represented by a table mapping impact against likelihood, as shown in Figure 11.

Very high impact	Medium risk	Medium risk	High risk	High risk	Critical
High impact	Low risk	Medium risk	Medium risk	High risk	High risk
Medium impact	Low risk	Low risk	Medium risk	Medium risk	High risk
Low impact	Very low risk	Low risk	Low risk	Medium risk	Medium risk
Very low impact	Very low risk	Very low risk	Low risk	Low risk	Medium risk
	Very unlikely	Unlikely	Moderately likely	Likely	Very likely

Figure 11: Impact vs likelihood

In this method, mapping the risk's impact against its likelihood provides the level of risk.

Measures of impact and likelihood are typically qualitative but might be linked to a more concrete monetary value. For instance, you might decide that "very low impact" is annualised damages of less than £100, while very high impact is annualised damages of more than £50,000. Equally, "very unlikely" might be taken to mean "it will occur less than once per year" and "very likely" as "it will occur every day".

Once you have analysed the risks, evaluate them against the risk acceptance criteria (Clause 6.1.2 e). One approach might be to decide that risks categorised as "low" or "very low" fall within the organisation's appetite for risk, but that more severe risks will require an appropriate response. The actual response may even be related to this table, such as deciding to terminate all activities that face "critical" risks.

The next stage of the risk assessment, just as in ISO 31000, is to determine the responses to the risks and to document the RTP (Clause 6.1.3). This comprises two main stages: selecting an appropriate response for each risk, and determining the controls necessary to implement those responses. This RTP should be clearly documented. It should also be signed off by the risk owners.

ISO 27001 also mandates the creation of a Statement of Applicability, which is a record of all of the controls that the organisation has selected, whether they have been implemented and justifications for excluding any controls from Annex A of the Standard. This is an exercise in ensuring that the organisation has considered the full set of best-practice controls.

Controls are processes or practices that you put in place to reduce the impact or likelihood (or both) of a risk. They are often considered best practice, and there are a number of sources that provide more information.[202] Controls are often very broad, of course (such as a "secure perimeter"), so you will need to determine for yourself just how the control should be implemented in your organisation. The risk owner will also be responsible for making sure that controls are implemented effectively and that they are monitored to ensure they continue being effective.

ISO 27005 is a related standard that focuses explicitly on information security risk management. It provides additional context and guidance for organisations that want to establish a more complete risk management framework to support their information security efforts.

Risk responses

You will need to respond to each risk that exceeds your organisation's risk acceptance criteria. This is sometimes called risk treatment, and comprises four broad categories of response:

1. Treat (also called "control" or "risk modification").
2. Tolerate (also called "risk acceptance" or "risk retention").
3. Terminate (also called "risk avoidance").
4. Transfer (also called "risk sharing").

---

[202] Annex A of ISO 27001 is the obvious source; each of the controls listed there has extensive guidance available in ISO 27002, the companion code of practice. Other sources include COBIT, the Cloud Security Alliance's Cloud Controls Matrix, NIST's SP 800-53, and so on.

'Treat' involves applying controls to reduce the level of risk. A control might reduce the impact of the risk or its likelihood, or it might reduce both; it might even eliminate the risk entirely (although that's almost certainly impossible for most risks). The goal when applying controls is to reduce the risk until it falls within your risk acceptance criteria.

Very high impact	Medium risk	Medium risk	High risk	High risk	Critical
High impact	Low risk	Medium risk	Medium risk	High risk	High risk
Medium impact	Low risk	Low risk	Medium risk	Medium risk	High risk
Low impact	Very low risk	Low risk	Low risk	Medium risk	Medium risk
Very low impact	Very low risk	Very low risk	Low risk	Low risk	Medium risk
	Very unlikely	Unlikely	Moderately likely	Likely	Very likely

Figure 12: The organisation's risk acceptance criteria (line) vs the level of a given risk (circle)

In the example shown in Figure 12, the line represents the organisation's risk acceptance criteria, while the level of a given risk is circled at the top. To treat this risk, the organisation could take a couple of routes: they could apply controls to reduce both the impact and the likelihood, or apply enough controls to reduce the impact considerably. In either case, once the controls are applied, the risk should then fall within the risk acceptance criteria.

'Tolerate' is an informed decision to do nothing. This is generally the default response to risks that already fall within the risk acceptance criteria, but it may also be applied to risks where the cost of treatment outweighs the business benefits. A risk that could come to pass 50 times a day, for instance, may only have an annualised financial impact of £10. Alternatively, it could have a significant impact but be so vanishingly unlikely that you have to wonder why you even included it as a risk in the first place.

'Terminate' is the elimination of the risk in its entirety. This is normally done by simply removing the target of the risk, such as by terminating the process or getting rid of the asset in question. You might choose this response if the cost of treating the risk is excessive and the return on investment would not be worth the effort.

'Transfer' is the act of sharing the risk with other parties. There are several ways to do this, such as by outsourcing the process or asset to another company so that they have to face the risk themselves (but note that transferring a data protection risk in this way will not absolve a data controller of its accountability under the GDPR for protecting personal data), or by purchasing insurance to reduce the impact of the risk, and so on.[203] You might choose to transfer the risk if the cost of treating it is excessive but the process or asset is too valuable to terminate.

Risk relationships

When considering something abstract such as privacy risks, it is important to understand the full range of actual risks and

---

[203] For the purposes of GDPR compliance, transferring the risk by taking out insurance is unlikely to be considered an adequate way of dealing with the risk.

how seemingly disparate forms of risk can have significant impacts on privacy.

In particular, you should remember that physical risks can also be privacy risks. For instance, having information visible on a screen close to a window, unlocked doors and physical damage are all physical risks that could also be privacy risks.

Cyber risks, which are risks related to information and communication technologies, have a more obvious overlap with privacy risks. Given the modern reliance on and saturation of IT in processing information, any significant cyber risk is likely to also be a significant privacy risk, and the speed with which cyber risks can come to pass and the volumes involved can make them significantly more dangerous than other kinds of risks.

Continuity risks can prevent an organisation from operating, either permanently or temporarily. As the GDPR requires you to give data subjects access to their information, this can quickly become a privacy risk. If you suffer a continuity incident and cannot give data subjects that access for any extended period of time, you are not just suffering from your own loss of access, you are also incidentally inhibiting the data subject's ability to act on their rights.

A loss of continuity could raise other risks. If a continuity incident results in electronic doors failing to lock, they pose a physical risk to the premises that is, as we've seen, a potential privacy risk.

As your organisation gains experience in conducting risk assessments, you will find that the relationships between different types of risk become more apparent, and that a comprehensive risk management framework that can take these risks into account and deal with them appropriately is the best way to protect both the organisation and the personal data that it holds.

Risk management and personal data

The key additional step that an organisational risk management framework has to make to accommodate GDPR compliance is to recognise that the risks to the rights and freedoms of data subjects of any particular processing activity may have a different profile than it does in relation to the organisation. The corruption of the data of one data subject may have a minimal impact on an organisation processing thousands of data records but it may have a significant impact on that individual. The GDPR requires organisations to consider that impact on the individual and to determine appropriate controls that will reduce those individual impacts to levels that are likely to be acceptable both under the law and to the data subjects. This additional thought process is critical for the organisational risk manager and will have to be documented and appropriate evidence retained to demonstrate that the organisation has dealt with its obligation to identify and implement appropriate organisational and technical controls.

CHAPTER 12: CONDUCTING DPIAs

It is important to recognise the very real benefits of conducting a DPIA, and they are not just limited to complying with the law. A DPIA builds trust. You can publish the results of a DPIA in order to show both that your organisation is keeping personal data secure and that you have taken a rigorous approach to ensuring this. In doing so, you will also demonstrate your commitment to transparent processing.

Consistently using DPIAs raises awareness of your compliance with the Regulation. Internally, this translates to a greater awareness of the individual's duties; externally, it translates to an improved reputation and increased trust. Furthermore, taking advantage of this awareness can contribute to the effectiveness of your overall privacy compliance framework.

A DPIA also helps you to identify problems early on – often before you have spent a considerable amount of time and money implementing a project – and to find other efficiencies. This may extend to revising the actual data you collect in accordance with the principle of data minimisation.

The overall procedure for DPIAs can be long and complex, especially for large organisations or those that handle large volumes of complex data. The DPIA is an integral part of the organisation's risk management framework, so there are some core principles that can be applied to any such project.

Five key stages of the DPIA

The key stages of the DPIA are:

1. Identify the need for the DPIA.
2. Describe the information flow.
3. Identify privacy and related risks.
4. Identify and evaluate privacy solutions.
5. Sign-off and record the outcome.

Identify the need for the DPIA

First and foremost, you should conduct your DPIAs when it is still possible to have an impact on the project in question. If you conduct DPIAs at the start of your compliance project, of course, you could well be examining existing processes, but this is an instance of "better late than never", and stakeholders will be pleased to see that you are taking compliance seriously.

You can use a set of questions about your project to determine whether a DPIA may be necessary:

- Will the project involve the collection of new information about individuals?
- Will the project compel individuals to provide information about themselves?
- Will information about individuals be disclosed to organisations or people who have not previously had routing access to the information?
- Are you using information about individuals for a purpose it is not currently used for, or in a way it is not currently used?

- Does the project involve using new technology that might be perceived as privacy-intrusive?
- Will the project result in decisions being made or taking action against individuals in ways that could have a significant impact on them?
- Is the information about individuals of a kind likely to raise privacy concerns or expectations?
- Will the project require you to contact individuals in ways they may find intrusive?

Answering "yes" to any of these questions is a good indication that a DPIA may be a useful exercise, if only as part of due diligence. If you fail to perform a DPIA when one is required under the Regulation, there could be severe repercussions, so you should ensure that your processes require you to consider whether or not a DPIA might be necessary for any new or amended processing activities.

As established in chapter 10, there are a range of scenarios that require you to conduct a DPIA. The Regulation itself sets these out in Article 35 and in several of the recitals. The data maps you construct will highlight processing activities that require you to conduct a DPIA under the Regulation. The UK's ICO also offers guidance on when it may be advisable to conduct a DPIA.[204]

---

[204] *https://ico.org.uk/for-organisations/guide-to-data-protection/guide-to-the-general-data-protection-regulation-gdpr/accountability-and-governance/data-protection-impact-assessments*.

You will need to keep track of any additional conditions under which DPIAs are deemed necessary by the supervisory authority.

You may wish to conduct a DPIA for your organisation's benefit rather than out of necessity or an abundance of caution. As noted earlier in this chapter, there are distinct benefits to DPIAs that can be motivations in themselves.

Even if you elect not to perform a DPIA, you should retain any records you create indicating why you chose not to. This in itself demonstrates that you have performed due diligence, and may minimise the impact of any actions taken against you in the event of a personal data breach.

Objectives and outcomes

Like any other project, the DPIA should have a set of objectives and defined parameters for the outcomes. As described earlier, the Regulation specifies a minimum set of outcomes:

(a) a systematic description of the envisaged processing operations and the purposes of the processing, including, where applicable, the legitimate interest pursued by the controller;

(b) an assessment of the necessity and proportionality of the processing operations in relation to the purposes;

(c) an assessment of the risks to the rights and freedoms of data subjects [affected by the processing operation]; and

(d) the measures envisaged to address the risks, including safeguards, security measures and mechanisms to ensure the protection of personal data and to demonstrate compliance with this Regulation taking into account the rights and legitimate interests of data subjects and other persons concerned.[205]

In simpler terms, the desired outcomes of a DPIA can be reduced to:

- A description of the processing and its purposes;
- The legitimate interests you are pursuing with this processing;
- An assessment of the necessity and proportionality of the processing;
- An assessment of the risks to the rights and freedoms of data subjects;
- The measures envisaged to address the risks;
- All of the safeguards and security measures to demonstrate compliance with the Regulation;
- Indications of timeframes if the processing will include erasure of personal data;
- An indication of any data protection by design and by default measures;
- A list of the recipients of personal data;
- Compliance with approved codes of conduct; and
- Details of whether the data subjects have been consulted and have consented.

---

[205] GDPR, Article 35(7).

These should be established as the minimum outputs of any DPIA. In addition to this, there may be specific outcomes that you determine necessary on the basis of your organisation's needs or the nature of the processing itself.

For instance, you might require the DPIA to determine how little personal data is needed to achieve the intended outcome of the processing, thereby improving efficiency and (as noted earlier) living up to the principle of data minimisation. Alternatively, you might require a given DPIA to pay special attention to a specific element of the processing because the organisation has had an issue with it in the past.

As the DPIA is part of the larger risk management process, you should also seek to frame the "measures envisaged to address the risks" in terms consistent with your broader risk management framework. Because these measures are necessary in order to meet legal requirements, they become part of the baseline security criteria – the set of controls and business processes that the business puts in place as an ordinary part of doing business.

Consultation

Throughout the DPIA process, you will need to consult a number of people or entities. Some will provide input or insight, others will be experts in the processing or scope of the project, and others will have vested interests in the processing. Equally, you may need to consult both internally and externally.

Internal stakeholders are likely to be involved in the processing or the project in some way, and may be consulted in order to get a better idea of the risks involved, the impact of treating the risks or for their opinion on risk responses and treatment options. Such stakeholders might include the project management team, the DPO themselves, engineers, the IT team, procurement, customer support, legal counsel, and so on.

The Regulation stipulates that "where appropriate, [data controllers] shall seek the views of data subjects or their representatives on the intended processing".[206] The Regulation doesn't specify precisely what makes this "appropriate", but it is safe to assume that if you are seriously considering whether it is appropriate then it probably is. It is best to assume the supervisory authority will side with the data subjects in most instances.

Consulting external stakeholders such as the data subjects improves transparency by making people aware of how the information about them is being used. Of course, it is also very easy for external stakeholders to lose sight of the project: they are not invested in it, they may not have a complete understanding of it and they may not be interested at all. As such, it is important to frame this consultation to get results that you can use in the DPIA.

When consulting external stakeholders, you should follow a set of principles:

- **Make it timely.** Consult at the right stage and give stakeholders enough time to respond. If you are expecting answers from an online survey, you need to account for traffic and conversion rates to get enough responses.

---

[206] GDPR, Article 35(9).

- **Make it clear and proportionate.** Present the information necessary – no more and no less. Providing too much information or context will confuse people, and withholding information will only result in vague or useless responses.
- **Consult appropriate representatives.** You should ensure that those you approach fairly represent those who could be impacted, or those who should have input (such as local authorities or regulatory bodies).
- **Be objective and realistic.** Offer external stakeholders realistic options and present the information without bias. If you find you are having to dodge around the issues, it could be a sign of larger problems with the project.
- **Feedback goes both ways.** You are getting feedback, so ensure that you also offer feedback in turn. In many cases, the stakeholders will end up consulting on a number of projects for a variety of organisations and bodies, so feedback will prove valuable in the long term, especially if you need to consult them again.

The most important external stakeholder to consult will be the supervisory authority. Article 36 of the Regulation states that the controller must consult the supervisory authority if the DPIA "indicates that the processing would result in a high risk in the absence of measures taken by the controller to mitigate the risk".[207] This means that the supervisory authority would be permitted to extend or even suspend the length of its consultation following the DPIA, potentially holding up the organisation indefinitely.[208]

To avoid such a situation arising, the supervisory authority should be consulted when determining how to treat privacy risks during the DPIA. This may involve terminating whole parts of the process and redesigning them in order to avoid such significant risks.

Describe the information flow

Your data mapping exercise is crucial here. You need to be able to describe how personal data is collected, stored, used and deleted, and this should be available in an abstract form from your data mapping.

Although data mapping will provide you with a large-scale overview of all your processing activities, it could also produce more granular maps of individual processes. A thorough assessment of privacy risks is only possible if your organisation fully understands how information is actually being used.

For some DPIAs – notably when the processing is complex or multi-stage – you may need to go into greater detail than the mapping exercise. You may also need to translate it into another format, such as a spreadsheet or written report.

---

[207] GDPR, Article 36(1).

[208] GDPR, Article 36(2).

Identify privacy and related risks

Risk identification can be an art in itself, and there are a number of training opportunities that offer qualifications and certifications available to help you get a background in risk identification (and risk management more generally).

You should aim to identify risks to the rights and freedoms of the data subjects in accordance with the data protection principles. This means looking for sites where data could be:

- Inaccurate, insufficient or out of date;
- Excessive or irrelevant;
- Kept for too long;
- Disclosed to the wrong people or entities;
- Used in ways that are unacceptable or unexpected to the data subject; or
- Stored or transmitted insecurely.

These are broad categories, of course, and not particularly useful if you want to mitigate those threats. The actual risks to personal data might include:

- Hacking;
- Viruses and other malware;
- Intruders stealing or damaging data;
- Phishing scams;
- Inadequately trained staff;
- Unencrypted laptops outside the premises;
- Poor access control; or
- Weak passwords.

Some of these risks will continue to exist regardless of what you do (malware, hackers, natural disasters, etc.), while others can essentially be eliminated (weak passwords, unlocked doors, etc.). The former can be treated to reduce the likelihood or potential impact of the risk. Many of the latter, as noted, can be completely eliminated. For example, weak passwords may be eliminated by improving the password policy to force users to create strong passwords that are changed every three months.

When identifying a privacy risk, you need to assess the potential impact. In a DPIA, this impact is harm to the data subject rather than harm to the organisation, which would be covered in a broader information security risk assessment. It is also worth considering whether you want your DPIAs to reveal information about harm to the organisation if you intend to distribute the results outside of the organisation.

One of the first considerations for harm is whether the data involved can identify a data subject. This will depend on the data in question, and some sets of personal data cannot be used to identify a specific individual. For instance, data comprising dates of birth, postcodes or gender usually won't provide enough information for direct identification, but context and sample size could increase the possibility. Meanwhile, data comprising names, fingerprints or national identity numbers can identify individual data subjects.

A second consideration for harm is the quantity of data involved. If, for instance, the specific risk results in the loss of 25 records, there is limited harm to society (and to the organisation). In conjunction with the identifiability of the data, it may even be harmless. Hashed data, for instance, is usually quite secure, but if the hashing method is flawed, it may be possible to crack the hash with a large enough sample to identify patterns.

A third consideration for harm is the sensitivity and variety of the data. Some information is naturally sensitive, such as medical information and political allegiances. The "special categories of personal data"[209] that the Regulation refers to are always sensitive. Data regarding a data subject's criminal convictions and offences, as referred to in Article 10, should also be treated similarly here.[210] Less sensitive information could have secondary uses or be significantly more sensitive in context. For instance, possession of both the data subject's national identification number and their mother's maiden name could be used to gain access to more sensitive information and commit fraud or identity theft.

Harm is often tangible and quantifiable, and may be predictably obvious when you are conducting a DPIA. Harm may take the form of financial or job loss, or damage to personal relationships and social standing from disclosure of sensitive information. This information can be quite easily translated into harm to the data subject and to the organisation (in terms of compensation payments, etc.).

---

[209] GDPR, Article 9(1): "personal data revealing racial or ethnic origin, political opinions, religious or philosophical beliefs, or trade-union membership, and the processing of genetic data, biometric data for the purpose of uniquely identifying a natural person, data concerning health or data concerning a natural person's sex life or sexual orientation."

[210] GDPR, Article 35 (3)(b) states that a DPIA would be required for "processing on large scale of special categories of data [...] or of personal data relating to criminal convictions and offences".

Harm may not always be tangible and quantifiable, however. The fear of identity theft after personal data has been breached is harmful. This sort of harm can be more difficult to identify because it often does not derive directly from the actual data. Accounting for this, case law in many jurisdictions has developed to allow the courts to make awards for "distress".

It is also important to recognise that harm can be done by damage to or loss of data – it is not always about theft or what criminals might do. For instance, a healthcare organisation might mix up patient data, resulting in an incorrect diagnosis, a failure to treat a serious illness, accidental disclosure of sensitive information to the wrong patient, and so on.

Identify and evaluate privacy solutions

These are the measures you put in place to prevent the risks from doing harm. In chapter 11, we identified four possible responses to risk:

1. Treat.
2. Tolerate.
3. Terminate.
4. Transfer.

These apply equally here, and just as in 'ordinary' risk management, your decisions will be informed by a variety of considerations. The cost of treating a risk may exceed the cost of the risk coming to pass. Remember that the cost isn't simply the cash value of implementing the control, but also includes the impact on the project's outcomes. If the risk slows the process by 20%, or reduces the value of the output at the end, then this should be factored into your decision. In instances where the cost of treatment is excessive, other options, such as terminating the risk, may be preferable.

It is possible to apply multiple treatments or even mix responses. For example, consider a process that entails five risks, two of which are minor, and three more serious risks, the last of which relates to a critical part of the process. The risk assessor might decide to tolerate the two minor risks, terminate the two non-essential serious risks and apply a combination of treatments to reduce the impact and likelihood of the final, business-critical risk, potentially also transferring part of that risk via insurance.

It is not necessary to eliminate all privacy risks. The key is to reduce risk to an acceptable level (based on your risk acceptance criteria) while still allowing a useful project to go ahead. In a DPIA, remember that 'acceptable' risk should be assessed against what is acceptable to data subjects, not just what is acceptable to the organisation.

A variety of sources catalogue different risk responses, but the following are typical examples of actions an organisation might take to treat, transfer or terminate risks to personal data[211]:

- Reduce the amount of data collected.
- Develop a retention policy governing how long and in what format personal data is stored.

---

[211] Tolerating the risk would be done after treatments, transfers and terminations are applied – for instance if your various responses cannot reduce the risk enough but the process is essential.

- Securely destroy information when it is no longer needed.
- Access control policies and procedures to minimise access to personal data.
- Introduce a training and awareness programme to reduce accidental exposure of or damage to personal data.
- Anonymise the personal data.
- Draw up contracts or data sharing agreements.
- Develop a subject access request process to protect data subjects' rights.
- Demand that suppliers conduct risk assessments and supply you with the results.

The results of this process should be recorded in a data protection risk register. Like other risk registers, this should record not just the risk, but also explain what action has been taken or will be taken in response to the risk, and identify who is responsible for approving and implementing any solutions that have been chosen. This is comparable to a RTP, and might look something like the example in Figure 13.

Risk	Impact	Likelihood	Response	Action	Owner
Employee misuse of personal data	High	High	Treat	Develop privacy policy. Communicate and test via training and awareness programme.	Information Security Manager
Information is collected and stored indefinitely	Moderate	Low	Treat	Develop retention policy.	Operations Manager
Third-party data breach	High	Moderate	Tolerate	Appropriate clauses in existing contracts.	Relationship Manager and Legal
Accidental theft or loss of data	High	Moderate	Transfer	Insurance policy	CFO

Figure 13: A sample risk register

Your risk register should be tailored to your business needs. It might automatically calculate the risk score and colour-code risks that exceed the risk acceptance criteria for ease of reference, or it might feature additional columns to record other data relevant to your organisation, the processing or your responses to risks.

You should ensure that any risk that you choose to tolerate is explained. This applies not just to risks that you simply tolerate outright, but also to residual risks that remain after treatment.

Sign off and record the outcome

Many of the documents you produce as part of the DPIA will be of limited use to stakeholders outside the organisation, such as the supervisory authority, partners, clients or the wider public. These are precisely the entities you need to impress, however, so you need to ensure that you have a final DPIA report suitable for external distribution.

Whatever the nature of the project and the information you are providing, your DPIA report should include a project overview, which should indicate what personal data is involved, what you are doing with it and why, and how long the data will be held. This project might be a set of processing functions, a single process or a business project that will only run for a defined period.

The DPIA report should also provide information to demonstrate that you have adequately assessed the impact of the project on data protection, including a description of the data flows and identified privacy risks, and details of how the privacy risks will be handled. Your supervisory authority may apply further conditions to the DPIA report.

The report should be sanitised to protect the data subjects and the organisation itself, and to meet the requirements of its audience. If you are simply submitting the report to your organisation's board for its approval, you might exclude information that is excessively technical. The board relies on the expertise of the company's employees and only need a good, reliable overview in order to make strategic decisions.

Before being sent out, the report should be signed off by the appropriate authority. Internally, this should typically be the DPO. Other external approval could be supplied by the supervisory authority, and may in fact be required under law in some instances.

Once you have received external sign off, the report is ready to publish or be made available in summary form to stakeholders. If you wish to release the full details, a second round of sanitisation may be necessary. Publishing the DPIA report is what earns you real trust and builds a reputation for transparency. In the UK, the ICO encourages organisations to consider publishing material relating to DPIAs. It is good advice: the more organisations within an economy that publish such reports, the more transparent the economy becomes and the easier it is to secure international business and investment.

Integrating the DPIA into the project plan

The outcomes of the DPIA need to be integrated into the project plan. You will need to continually refer back to the DPIA to ensure that it is being followed and that its responses to the risks have been effectively implemented.

You should define metrics for effectiveness against which risk responses may be measured. In some cases, the metric will be as simple as "the information is still intact", while for others it might be more complex, perhaps "number of times the log has been accessed by non-admin staff".

In any case, you will need to ensure that your privacy compliance framework takes effectiveness into account. ISO 27001, for instance, applies a set of checks against the information security management system to ensure that all necessary processes are both functioning and effective. Even if you don't choose to implement ISO 27001, it would be valuable to look at clauses 9 and 10 of the Standard to see how they approach monitoring, measurement, analysis and evaluation of information security, as well as the review and response to the results of monitoring.

The DPIA is a written record of your determination to protect personal data throughout the project, and external stakeholders – including the supervisory authority – will hold you to this. Furthermore, if you have chosen to publish your DPIA reports, those same external stakeholders will be able to ask specific questions about the effectiveness of your security measures.

Part 4: International transfers and incident management

CHAPTER 13: MANAGING PERSONAL DATA INTERNATIONALLY

To enforce the Regulation outside the bounds of the EU, the GDPR has a number of elements designed to control how organisations within the EU are able to transfer personal data internationally.

The term "third countries" is not defined in the GDPR but comes from the EU's primary treaties in order to refer to countries that are not party to those treaties. It is a common term in EU law and is normally taken to refer to any country that is not part of an organisation that is to be held under that law – so, because the GDPR applies as law to the EU and EEA, "third countries" refers to those countries that are not Member States of the EU or EEA. It is not separately defined in the GDPR, but it is safe to assume that the same definition applies. Given that the Council of Europe includes 17 distinct groups such as the EU, EEA, Eurozone and the EFTA, with a complex set of overlaps, it is critical to understand who "in Europe" you are allowed to send information to, and what rules need to be in place to do so.

For ease of reference, the EU and EEA countries are shown in Table 2.

Table 2: EU and EEA Country List

Austria	Greece	Norway
Belgium	Hungary	Poland
Bulgaria	Iceland	Portugal
Croatia	Ireland	Romania
Republic of Cyprus	Italy	Slovakia
Czech Republic (Czechia)	Latvia	Slovenia
Denmark	Liechtenstein	Spain
Estonia	Lithuania	Sweden
Finland	Luxembourg	United Kingdom
France	Malta	
Germany	Netherlands	

The United Kingdom voted in a referendum in 2016 to leave the EU. Once it has done that, it will no longer automatically meet the adequacy test for data transfers.

The additional conditions for transferring data to third countries also apply to transferring data to international organisations. Unlike third countries, international organisations are defined in the Regulation:

'international organisation' means an organisation and its subordinate bodies governed by public international law, or any other body which is set up by, or on the basis of, an agreement between two or more countries.

Public international law is the set of conditions under which nations interact with other nations, and with individuals, organisations and other entities internationally. As such, an international organisation would be one that operates internationally, under the auspices of a trade agreement or treaty.

The definition of international organisation comprises an extremely wide set of organisations. The designation even applies to organisations that are based within the EU/EEA but have operations outside it. For instance, a German company that has operations in the US is also an international organisation, even though its central operations are based within the EEA. You should always take care to ensure that you understand the full business nature of the organisations with which you interact.

Key requirements

Transferring personal data to a country outside the EU/EEA can only be done under two specific conditions:

1. The destination has been the subject of an adequacy decision.

2. The transfer is subject to appropriate safeguards to protect the personal data.

Simply meeting one of these conditions may not be adequate in itself, and it is possible that one of the appropriate authorities will ban all transfers of personal data to specific countries regardless of the security measures you put in place.

Any further transfers of the personal data – within the target country or beyond – are also subject to these same restrictions. If your organisation is based in the EEA and wants to transfer data to a third country or international organisation, you will need to ensure that all conditions are met, including that those third country or international organisations will abide by the requirements of the GDPR.

The exceptions under which the organisation can transfer personal data are:

1. With the data subject's consent, after having been informed of the risks for the data subject, in particular

the risks due to the absence of an adequacy decision and safeguards.

2. If the transfer is necessary to fulfil a contract between the data subject and the controller, or to implement pre-contract measures at the data subject's request.

3. If the transfer is necessary to fulfil a contract in the interests of the data subject.

4. If the transfer is necessary for important reasons of public interest.

5. If the transfer is necessary to establish, exercise or defend legal claims.

6. If the transfer is necessary to protect the vital interests of the data subject or other persons, and the data subject is unable to give consent.

7. If the transfer is made from a register intended to provide information to the public and is open to consultation, but only to the extent that the relevant laws permit consultation.

You will need to ensure that you clearly document your justification for the transfer, and that this documentation can be made available to the supervisory authority on request.

Adequacy decisions

Adequacy decisions are decisions made by the Commission that a given country or organisation is an acceptable destination to which to transfer personal data. This is usually because the destination country meets a set of criteria in law. The adequacy criteria require that the third country has at least the following:

• The rule of law.

- Access to justice.
- Respect for human rights and fundamental freedoms.
- Relevant legislation, both general and sectoral, with regard to:
  - Public security;
  - Defence;
  - National security;
  - Public order; and
  - Criminal law.[212]

There is already a short list of countries that meet the adequacy criteria, as shown in Table 3.

Table 3: Countries Meeting the Adequacy Criteria

Andorra	Guernsey	Jersey
Argentina	Israel	New Zealand
Canada	Isle of Man	Switzerland
Faroe Islands	Japan	Uruguay

A number of 'European' states are listed above because they are not actually members of the EEA. Switzerland is a member of the EFTA, for instance, while Jersey, Guernsey and the Isle of Man are part of the European Community (and thus have access to the single market without actually being members of the EU or EEA).

Note that the United States is not one of the countries on which an adequacy decision has been made. This is partly

---

[212] GDPR, Article 45.

because the United States has no national (federal-level) data protection law. Most member states of the USA have their own data protection or data breach laws, and these all provide varying levels of protection for consumers. Special arrangements exist to make data transfers between the USA and EU possible, and these are described later in this chapter.

Personal data can be transferred to any one of the above countries just as if the data was being transferred to a host within the EEA; there are no further requirements for doing so beyond those contained in the GDPR.

Adequacy decisions are reviewed every four years, so it is important to ensure that any country you transfer personal data to on this basis has retained its approval. It is worth checking to see if any countries are added to the list, as they may offer business opportunities for your organisation. The complete list of countries subject to an adequacy decision is published in the Official Journal of the European Union and on the Commission's website.

Safeguards

Transfers to third countries and international organisations are permissible if there are appropriate measures to protect the rights and freedoms of the data subject, and if the data subject will have enforceable rights and legal remedies. This means ensuring that the data will be secure, and that the personal data will only be transferred to an organisation within a legal system that will support the data subject's rights. If you cannot meet both of these requirements, the transfer will not be deemed legal under the Regulation.

The Regulation provides a set of acceptable safeguards, some of which require specific approval from the supervisory authority before they can be considered to comply with the Regulation:

- Legally binding and enforceable instrument between public authorities or bodies.
- Binding corporate rules.
- Standard data protection clauses adopted by the Commission.
- Standard data protection clauses adopted by a supervisory authority and approved by the Commission.
- An approved code of conduct together with binding and enforceable commitments of the controller/processor in the third country to apply appropriate safeguards and protect data subjects' rights.
- An approved certification mechanism with binding and enforceable commitments of the controller/processor in the third country to apply appropriate safeguards and protect data subjects' rights.
- Contractual clauses between the controller/processor and the controller/processor/recipient in the third country or international organisation.
- Provisions inserted into administrative arrangements between public authorities or bodies, including enforceable and effective data subject rights.[213]

---

[213] GDPR, Article 46.

The last two safeguards require approval from the supervisory authority. Many of the options for safeguarding personal data rely on structures that are either established in law or have been previously approved by the supervisory authority and/or the Commission.

It is important to recognise that the set of accepted safeguards is not a simple list of measures or controls. Rather, the safeguards as described could represent a broad range of solutions that are – crucially – backed up by legal measures.

If you choose to use one of these options in order to transfer personal data outside the EEA, you should consult the supervisory authority to see what your options are. You do not have to use one of the preapproved models, but they may prove enlightening if you want to develop your own solution to be agreed between yourself and the organisation you want to deal with, and will almost certainly make it simpler to get approval from the supervisory authority.

Binding corporate rules

Binding corporate rules were originally devised by the WP29 to allow large organisations or groups of organisations to securely transfer data internationally while reducing bureaucratic interference. They are defined in the GDPR as:

> 'binding corporate rules' means personal data protection policies which are adhered to by a controller or processor established on the territory of a Member State for transfers of a set of transfers of personal data to a controller or processor in one or more third countries within a group of undertakings, or group of enterprises engaged in a joint economic activity.

The GDPR establishes conditions for individual Member States to establish their own binding corporate rules to streamline international transfers.

The advantage of binding corporate rules is that the organisations involved can transfer personal data quickly and with a minimum of interference from a supervisory authority. However, they can **only** be used within an arrangement of organisations or a multinational, and the set of rules you elect to put in place will need to be approved by the supervisory authority.

Binding corporate rules do not provide a basis for making transfers outside of the approved group of organisations. If you want to expand the group of organisations to which the rules apply, you will need to get further approval from the supervisory authority.

Standard contractual clauses

Standard contractual clauses (SCC) are approved contractual terms that can be included in contracts between EU controllers and non-EU controllers, and between EU controllers and non-EU processors. They set out clearly and in legally enforceable terms how the requirements of the GDPR apply to the relationship. They are an effective method of securing the transfer (assuming both parties then abide by the clauses), but they cannot be modified and must be used exactly as they are provided by the Commission.

The EU-US Privacy Shield

As we have said previously, it is illegal for any EU organisation to transfer personal data to any country in respect of which there has not been an 'adequacy' determination by the EU Commission. This is a major issue for the EU-US trading relationship and led to the development of a 'Safe Harbor' framework by means of which US organisations could register with the US Department of Commerce, make a declaration as to their information security practices in respect of personal data and be given safe harbour from prosecution.

In October 2015, the European Court of Justice declared that the Safe Harbor framework was "invalid" and not an adequate mechanism for complying with existing EU data protection legislation. Work therefore started on creating a replacement mechanism: the EU-US Privacy Shield Framework.

The EU-US Privacy Shield was adopted by the EU Commission in July 2016 and became available on 1 August 2016. The EU Commission has deemed the protections provided by the Shield to EU residents in respect of their personal data to be "adequate" in terms of the GDPR requirements covering international transfers of personal data. These requirements are as applicable to the personal data of employees as they are to the personal data of customers collected by an organisation. In real terms, there are no categories of personal data that are outside the scope of the GDPR and, therefore, US organisations with operations within the EU that simply wish to process or store HR data relating to their EU staff have to comply with the GDPR and will need to join the EU-US Privacy Shield Framework. The alternatives are to limit all such processing to EU entities or to withdraw from doing business in the EU.

US organisations are able to sign up to the Privacy Shield, which is administered by the International Trade Administration (ITA) with the US Department of Commerce. The starting point is here:

www.privacyshield.gov/welcome. Once an organisation has voluntarily completed the application process and made a public commitment to comply with the Privacy Shield Framework, that commitment becomes enforceable under US law.

The Privacy Shield is subject to regular review, the last of which was completed in late 2018. This effectively confirmed that it is adequate for the purposes of the GDPR. Note that the Privacy Shield does nothing to help organisations comply with the requirement for extra-EU controllers and processors to nominate a representative organisation within the EU.

The first requirement of the Privacy Shield is that organisations must include their statement of commitment to compliance in their published privacy policies; the policy must also include a link to the website or other submission-starting point of the selected independent recourse, which the organisation must put in place to ensure that data subjects are easily able to make individual complaints. The "Key New Requirements" page (*www.privacyshield.gov/Key-New-Requirements*) of the Privacy Shield website sets out clearly what organisations have to do in addition to what they should have been doing under the now rejected Safe Harbor arrangements. These requirements are all contained in the formal EU-US Privacy Shield Framework and should be seen as extensions to those contained in the GDPR, rather than as an alternative. The starting assumption should be that, when EU residents raise a complaint, it will be because they believe their rights as set out in the GDPR have been transgressed. Privacy Shield members are required to resolve all complaints expeditiously and to submit, where necessary, to binding arbitration where a complaint has not been resolved through normal processes.

Even once an organisation leaves the Privacy Shield, it must continue to maintain its compliance with the requirements in respect of EU residents' data it collected while a member, and must recertify annually to demonstrate that it is doing so.

Privacy Shield membership is a self-certification process. The certification is enforceable by both the US Federal Trade Commission (FTC) and the US Department of Transportation (DOT). The full test and requirements are available here: *www.privacyshield.gov/Program-Overview*.

Privacy Shield Principles

To comply with the scheme, organisations must implement measures to meet the seven Privacy Shield Principles:

1. **Notice** – organisations are required to inform data subjects of a range of things, including about the Privacy Shield scheme and the data subject's rights.

2. **Choice** – data subjects must be free to choose to opt out of having their data disclosed to a third party or used for any purposes beyond those for which it was collected. Data subjects must have a clear and simple way to exercise this choice.

3. **Accountability for onward transfer** – the organisation is responsible for the personal data, and must ensure that it is transferred only to organisations that will also provide the same level of protection as the organisation under the Privacy Shield.

4. **Security** – the organisation must take "reasonable and appropriate measures" to protect personal data from loss, misuse, and unauthorised access, disclosure, alteration and destruction.

5. **Data integrity and purpose limitation** – the organisation must take reasonable steps to ensure personal data is "reliable for its intended use, accurate, complete, and current". It must also ensure that personal information is limited to what is relevant for the purposes of the processing.

6. **Access** – data subjects must have access to personal information about them held by the organisation, and must be able to correct, amend or delete the information if it is inaccurate or has been processed in violation of the Principles.

7. **Recourse, enforcement and liability** – data subjects must be able to seek independent recourse to resolve any complaints at no cost to themselves. Furthermore, the organisation is responsible for the processing of personal information it receives under the Privacy Shield and transfers to a third party.

There are 16 supplemental principles, which cover topics such as journalism, sensitive data, exceptions, dispute resolution, enforcement, access requests, data protection authorities, human resources data, and pharmaceutical and medical products. All of the principles generally align with the requirements of the GDPR.

Certification to the Privacy Shield is relatively simple for US-based organisations. An organisation should ensure that it conforms to the Privacy Shield Principles, which may involve developing specific measures and documented processes to do so. The organisation's privacy policy should reflect its adherence to the Principles and make specific reference to its compliance with the Principles. As described earlier, the privacy policy also needs to identify the organisation's independent recourse mechanism to inform data subjects of the process to lodge a complaint or seek other forms of recourse. The privacy policy should then be made publicly available, potentially as a physical copy if your organisation doesn't have a public website.

Limited transfers

It is possible to make transfers of personal data on a limited basis without having to establish more formal or permanent measures. Under Article 49 of the Regulation, such transfers are permissible if:

> the transfer is not repetitive, concerns only a limited number of data subjects, is necessary for the purposes of compelling legitimate interests pursued by the controller which are not overridden by the interests or rights and freedoms of the data subject, and the controller has assessed all the circumstances surrounding the data transfer and has on the basis of that assessment provided suitable safeguards with regard to the protection of personal data.

You will need to inform both the supervisory authority and the data subject of the transfer in question and of the "compelling legitimate interests". It is important to provide this notice with sufficient time to allow either of those parties to object.

Cloud services

If your organisation uses a Cloud provider to store or process personal data, you will need to confirm the location of the data centres where personal data is kept. It is easy to overlook Cloud providers, especially if they deliver software as a service (SaaS), infrastructure as a service (IaaS) or platform as a service (PaaS). In these instances, the user is often unaware that they are using a tool that is hosted remotely and, in many cases, is actually based in another country.

Because Cloud providers often take advantage of vast server farms located in disparate countries around the world, many of them will qualify as international organisations and, as such, you will need to ensure that you establish appropriate safeguards to protect personal data. In instances where Cloud providers have little control over the circumstances in which the data is actually stored and little power to secure appropriate assurances from the other parties involved, it would be advisable to change providers or develop an in-house capacity to replace the Cloud services.

Furthermore, because Cloud services may store data in a third country, controllers will have to meet the usual requirements of the Regulation with regard to international data transfer. This includes having a legitimate reason for the transfer, asserting the data protection principles, applying appropriate controls or measures to protect the personal data (such as standard contractual clauses approved by the Commission) and informing the data subject of the transfer of their personal data.

ISO/IEC 27018:2014, part of the ISO 27000 family of standards, presents a good starting point for protecting personal data hosted in the Cloud. The Standard proposes a set of controls that can be applied in order to protect this information, and provides guidance on implementing those controls.

CHAPTER 14: INCIDENT RESPONSE MANAGEMENT AND REPORTING

It is critical that organisations are prepared to respond to security breaches in respect of personal data. It has become a truism to say that, sooner or later, every single organisation suffers a data breach. Multiple surveys and reports demonstrate that most organisations are subject to multiple breaches in a year of varying sizes and impacts. The issue is not 'if' but 'when'. When there is a data breach, you need to have in place a mechanism that enables you to respond quickly and effectively.

Under the Regulation, a personal data breach is not merely marked by the loss of the data to an outside party, but is more broadly defined:

> 'personal data breach' means a breach of security leading to the accidental or unlawful destruction, loss, alteration, unauthorised disclosure of, or access to, personal data transmitted, stored or otherwise processed.[214]

Incident management is the process by which the ongoing impacts of such breaches are minimised. It entails recognising that an incident has occurred, responding to the immediate and long-term concerns and tracking the incident to ensure that the steps taken are effective.

---

[214] GDPR, Article 4(12).

Notification

The GDPR has specific rules regarding when and how an incident must be reported to the supervisory authority and to the affected data subjects. The data controller is required to notify the supervisory authority of a personal data breach "as soon at the controller becomes aware that a personal data breach has occurred [...] without undue delay and, where feasible, not later than 72 hours after having become aware of it".[215]

Although the organisation can avoid this requirement if "the personal data breach is unlikely to result in a risk to the rights and freedoms of natural persons",[216] the incident management process may be unable to identify the risks with the immediacy necessary under the notification rules. As such, it is good practice to make notifications by default in order to avoid accidentally breaking the law.

The notification needs to include several specific pieces of information, which can be submitted in stages where necessary:[217]

1. The nature of the personal data breach, including the categories and approximate number of data subjects affected, and the categories and approximate number of personal data records concerned.

---

[215] GDPR, Recital 85.

[216] GDPR, Article 33(1).

[217] GDPR, Article 33(3) and (4).

2. The name and contact details of the DPO or other contact for further information.
3. The likely consequences of the personal data breach.
4. The measures taken or proposed in order to address the personal data breach, including measures to mitigate possible adverse effects.

It is advisable to include these elements in a reporting template to ensure that your reports to the supervisory authority are comprehensive and meet the requirements.

Note that many supervisory authorities now provide standardised forms for reporting personal data breaches and other incidents, which may also highlight the actions that you are expected to take following the incident. By familiarising yourself with what the supervisory authority expects as a minimum response, you can develop a best-practice approach to incident response that will appease your regulators.

The Regulation also requires you to notify data subjects if "the personal data breach is likely to result in a high risk to the rights and freedoms of natural persons".[218] It should be noted that this is different from the requirements for notifying the supervisory authority, which only requires there to be a risk, not a "high" risk. The exceptions to the requirement for notifying data subjects of breach are[219]:

---

[218] GDPR, Article 34(1).

[219] GDPR, Article 34(3).

1. If the controller has implemented measures such as encryption, that mean the data cannot be read by unauthorised persons;
2. If the controller has taken steps to ensure the high risk is no longer likely to materialise; or
3. If notifying the affected persons would involve disproportionate effort. In this instance, the data controller will need to make a public communication to inform the data subjects in an "equally effective manner".

The breach notifications must be provided to data subjects "in clear and plain language"[220] and "in close cooperation with the supervisory authority",[221] and should include:

1. The name and contact details of the DPO or other contact for further information;
2. The likely consequences of the personal data breach; and
3. The measures taken or proposed in order to address the personal data breach, including measures to mitigate possible adverse effects.

Unlike notifications to the supervisory authority, using a standard notification is undesirable. A clear statement of what has happened and what you intend to do about it, along with the appropriate contact details, is much less likely to

---

[220] GDPR, Article 34(2).

[221] GDPR, Recital 86.

receive a negative response if it appears to have been composed specifically for the recipient rather than as a form letter.

Data processors must assist data controllers in meeting the breach notification requirements, as noted in Article 28, which requires that the processor "assists the controller in ensuring compliance with the obligations pursuant to Articles 32 to 36 taking into account the nature of processing and information available to the processor",[222] and in Article 33, which states that "the processor shall notify the controller without undue delay after becoming aware of a personal data breach".[223]

Events vs incidents

In the parlance of information security, an information security event is an occurrence that indicates a *possible* breach of information security policy or failure of controls,[224] while an information security incident is an occurrence that indicates a *probable* breach of information security.[225] An information security incident is a subset of an information security event.

For example, getting an alert from an intrusion prevention system (IPS) is an information security event. If the alert says that the intrusion was stopped as intended, then it is not even

---

[222] GDPR, Article 28(3)(f).

[223] GDPR, Article 33(2).

[224] ISO/IEC 27000:2018, Clause 3.30.

[225] ISO/IEC 27000:2018, Clause 3.31.

an event because the control worked as intended. However, if the alert says that the IPS failed to stop the intrusion, it is definitely an event but, because this is an expected possibility, an organisation typically has additional fall-back controls in place that are automatically triggered. If one or more of those controls are bypassed, the event might be upgraded to an incident. Incidents need to be investigated.

An incident management programme should make it clear how to distinguish between an event and an incident, and should also ensure that events are appropriately assessed to confirm whether or not they constitute an incident. Events will often be reported based on automated systems, emails from concerned employees, and so on. Each event might then be reviewed manually or with automated systems (depending on the nature of the event) to determine whether the event constitutes a threat to information security.

Types of incident

Information security incidents can come in a vast array of forms, ranging from physical disruptions to electronic intrusions. It is easy to fall into the trap of thinking that you only need to worry about computer-based incidents if your data is stored electronically. If the dripping water of a leaking roof shorts out a server and the information cannot be recovered, then it would be an information security incident that has resulted in data loss. An incident that prevents access to personal data means that you cannot support the data subject's rights to accessibility or to have their data corrected.

Incidents are the result of a threat successfully exploiting a vulnerability, so your risk assessment should provide a good idea of the variety of incidents possible within your organisation. Not all incidents can be predicted. Some incidents will occur that are, or appear to be, unrelated to any identified risk. This doesn't mean that the incident is harmless; it simply means that you have an additional data point to take into account at your next risk assessment.

Cyber security incident response plans

Incident response is mandated in a number of standards and frameworks, several of which will be excellent tools for maintaining GDPR compliance. ISO 27001, ISO 22301 and the Payment Card Industry Data Security Standard (PCI DSS) all require a systematic incident management regime.

These standards lay out a set of core requirements and record-keeping measures to ensure that incidents are appropriately managed, but they give organisations the scope to develop a programme appropriate to their needs.

CREST, a non-profit organisation for information security penetration testing, has developed a three-phase cyber incident management process that is generally applicable to any organisation.[226] In its simplest terms, the process is:

1. Prepare
   a. Conduct a criticality assessment for your organisation.
   b. Carry out a cyber security threat analysis, supported by realistic scenarios and rehearsals.

---

[226] CREST, "Cyber Security Incident Response Guide", 2013, *www.crest-approved.org/wp-content/uploads/2014/11/CSIR-Procurement-Guide.pdf*.

    c. Consider the implications of people, process, technology and information.

    d. Create an appropriate control framework.

    e. Review your state of readiness in cyber security incident response.

2. Respond

    a. Identify the cyber security incident.

    b. Define objectives and investigate the situation.

    c. Take appropriate action.

    d. Recover your systems, data and connectivity.

3. Follow up

    a. Investigate the incident more thoroughly.

    b. Report the incident to relevant stakeholders.

    c. Carry out a post-incident review.

    d. Communicate and build on lessons learned.

    e. Update key information, controls and processes.

    f. Perform a trend analysis.

Developing your incident management based on this best-practice structure would ensure that incidents are treated both before and after they occur, and that any incident results in a better understanding of the incident and how to deal with it.

Many of the points covered in the CREST framework are also contained in ISO 27001. The "Prepare" phase, for instance, aligns with the risk management practices that ISO 27001 describes, and the "Follow up" phase can be incorporated into the review and continual improvement processes.

Incident management processes should be built into wider business continuity management systems to ensure that there is continuity and integrity of processes, and clarity around roles and responsibilities when cyber incidents escalate to affect business continuity generally. The international standard for best practice in business continuity management systems is ISO 22301. There are two other standards in the ISO 27001 family that may be useful in structuring incident response processes: ISO/IEC 27031, for ICT business continuity and ISO/IEC 27035, for incident management.

Where CREST's scheme is focused on cyber incidents, your organisation needs to be prepared for incidents of all kinds that could harm personal data. This includes incidents caused without human intervention (natural disasters, etc.), those caused by failure to act (such as oversights or poor processes), and not just incidents with a clear attacker or malicious intent. Despite this, the overall approach of the three CREST phases supports managing incidents of all types.

Key roles in incident management

Incident management should be supported by a range of individuals across the organisation. First, it needs to be supported from the top to ensure it is given the resources it needs and that people understand that the processes involved in preparing for incidents (including preventive measures) are not pointless or useless tasks. It should be clearly communicated that incidents can threaten the organisation as a whole and put everyone's jobs at risk.

The people who will be implementing any preventive measures need to be on board, as do those who work with those measures. For instance, if an employee needs to lock a door each time they go through it, they should understand why and the consequences of failing to do so. The employee might not have implemented this measure, but they have to follow it consistently every day, even when it may initially appear to be onerous or wasteful.

Everyone within an organisation needs to understand their reporting obligations. If someone sees something odd, they need to know a) that it should be reported, and b) who they should report it to, even if that's as simple as reporting it to their line manager. There should be a clear reporting structure in place so that events can be reported, escalated, investigated and responded to appropriately.

Critically – and hopefully self-evidently – an individual should be assigned to the incident management process. This should be an identified person who has the authority and responsibility to investigate events (or have them investigated), to report to senior management if an incident occurs and to manage the organisation's notification process.

Prepare

Preparation is almost certainly the more important part of the whole process. Only sufficiently prepared organisations can mitigate the impact of incidents, recover quickly and potentially even come out of an incident looking better than before.

The preparation phase of incident management is analogous to your risk management and DPIA processes. Given that incidents can arise suddenly and that a failure to respond almost always worsens the situation, your preparation should ensure that incidents can be identified quickly and responded to almost as quickly.

Your incident response plans should be tested and rehearsed to ensure that they are effective and that they can be activated swiftly. If testing shows that the plan is ineffective or slow, you have time to amend the plan that you wouldn't have in the midst of dealing with an actual incident.

Respond

Getting the response phase right at the moment of activation is critical, and it is also when you are under the most pressure. Timescales are enormously important in incident management, so you will need to activate your responses as soon as possible to minimise damage. Just like in medical care, treating an incident promptly minimises the risk of long-term damage.

To identify incidents, you should have methods for reporting events and suspected incidents, and for performing 'triage' to establish which of these reports need to invoke the incident response process. Many incidents will only be evident to a small number of people – the person who updates the website, for instance, might be the first to discover that the website has been knocked offline by a denial-of-service (DoS) attack. This person must understand how to report the occurrence and there must be a clear method to determine whether the reported occurrence qualifies as an information security event or an information security incident.

When an incident has been identified, the situation should be investigated to determine the cause and define objectives for the response. In the event of a DoS attack, a response objective might be to get the website back online within four hours. You might even have a number of simpler objectives to make sure that all steps in the response are carried out before moving on to the recovery.

With defined response objectives based on an understanding of the incident, you can take the first direct action against the incident: containment. This might involve blocking an attacker from their point of access into your network, stabilising disrupted systems or otherwise preventing further immediate damage.

You also need to make an early decision as to whether or not the incident is one that needs to be reported to your supervisory authority. Pre-determined severity levels, combined with clarity about roles and responsibilities and a rehearsed and tested reporting procedure, are essential components for ensuring that the right decisions about breach reporting are made within the timeframes permitted by the GDPR.

Once the incident has been contained, you can take steps to eradicate the cause. These steps should include measures to ensure that the incident does not happen again and to eliminate the incident's capacity to cause harm, e.g. removing a weakness in a web application so that it cannot be exploited. In some cases, the costs of this stage will exceed the costs of the incident, so other solutions to reduce the impact of future incidents should be considered.

Throughout the incident response process, you should be gathering and preserving evidence to provide a clear picture of what happened and why your organisation was unable to prevent the incident. Part of your incident management programme should involve making sure you understand your legal obligations with regards to forensic evidence. In the UK, for instance, the Computer Misuse Act and the Regulation of Investigatory Powers Act – among others – have various requirements relating to the preservation of evidence.

The final step in response to an incident is to recover your systems, data, connectivity and any other process or resource that has been disrupted by the incident. Your incident response plans should include appropriate contact details for major infrastructure and resources, lists of preferred suppliers, and so on. You should also establish a set of processes for recovering data from backups, isolating and scrubbing malware infections, and any other pertinent actions.

Follow up

The follow up phase of incident management ensures that your organisation applies the lessons it has learned and that the response is appropriately reviewed for effectiveness. Although there are fewer time constraints than the response phase, it is important to ensure that the follow up is conducted while the incident is still fresh in people's minds and while the gathered evidence is still valid.

The first stage of following up is a thorough investigation of the incident. Without the pressures and time-sensitive operations necessary in the response phase, you can spend more time determining the precise details of the incident, and can apply more rigorous methods of analysis. CREST recommends:

- Problem cause analysis, using:
  - Failure mode and effects analysis (FMEA); or
  - Current reality tree (CRT) methods.
- Root cause identification, using:
  - The five-whys approach;
  - Why-because analysis (WBA); or
  - Cause-and-effect (fishbone) diagrams.

- Quantifying the business impact of the incident.

Whatever method you use, your aim is to positively identify the perpetrator or primary cause of the incident.

After you have concluded investigations, the incident should be reported to the appropriate stakeholders. In many cases, this will include customers and partners, but may extend to official authorities, law enforcement, suppliers, industry bodies, or other organisations in the same industry, sector or geographical region. You will need to establish how much detail it is necessary to include in the report, what information should be protected or redacted and whether you need to provide assurance of the security of personal data or the effectiveness of controls.

The organisation should conduct a thorough post-incident review to establish the effectiveness of the incident management programme with regards to the incident, its cause, impact and the success of the response. Much like a management review under ISO 27001, the post-incident review should have a number of defined inputs and outputs to support improving the incident management programme.

The organisation will also need to document, incorporate and clearly communicate the lessons learned. If a process is changed because of something learned in the incident, but the occurrence and purpose of the change is not made clear, there is a risk that it won't be correctly followed the next time the process is invoked. If this process is part of a preventive measure, then the efforts to examine and learn from the previous incident are effectively wasted.

Following an incident, all of your key information on incident management, the controls you have in place and your various other documentation will need to be updated.

For instance, if you found that one of your suppliers responded too slowly while you were trying to recover, you will need to find a better supplier. If you have identified a more effective configuration for your intrusion prevention mechanisms, that will also need to be documented so that it can be maintained.

The conclusion to following up an incident should be performing a trend analysis of the incident, including trends across your market and sector. If, for instance, cyber criminals gain access to new technologies that provide greater attack capabilities, you need to know about it so that you can predict what the developments will be in six months, a year, and so on. This part of the follow up phase shouldn't be a one-off event: you should continue examining incident trends so that you can update and amend your controls and responses accordingly.

Part 5: Enforcement and transitioning to compliance

CHAPTER 15: GDPR ENFORCEMENT

Although the scale of fines that can be levied for breaches of the GDPR is usually the primary focus of news stories and headlines, enforcement of the Regulation is more complex than this might suggest. Understanding how the Regulation is enforced is critical to all organisations seeking to stay on the right side of the law.

The hierarchy of authorities

The Regulation refers to a number of organisations and groups with varying levels of authority. Understanding how these different groups can influence how you implement compliance will be critical to staying on the right side of the law.

The supervisory authority in your country will be your primary source of information about the state of the law where you are based, and will be primarily responsible for investigating and prosecuting breaches of the Regulation. They have probably released a number of pieces of guidance explaining what they expect to see from GDPR-compliant organisations.

For some countries, this may be complicated by federalised structures, in which a central government authority asserts varying levels of control over regional departments. The GDPR allows for these circumstances by providing for each Member State to have one lead supervisory authority that has responsibility for ensuring coherence of regulatory activity.

Regardless of the situation, you should be able to identify your most immediate supervisory authority, which should be able to advise you on the applicability of other local laws and regulations, approved guidance, codes of conduct, and so on. If you have a DPO, you will need to identify them to the supervisory authority, as noted in chapter 8.

Member States have some leeway in terms of how the Regulation is implemented. Although the Regulation is a law in itself, Member States are specifically called on to set standards and further restrict conditions in a number of situations. In many cases, the Member State's case law may influence how the Regulation is applied, or the context in which the Regulation is managed.

The EDPB is established in Article 68 of the Regulation as a central body composed of representatives from each Member State's supervisory authority. The Board's duty is to ensure that the Regulation is applied consistently across the Union, and to advise the Commission on issues relating to the Regulation. The Board will coordinate the selection and development of codes of conduct and certification mechanisms, guidelines, recommendations and best practices.

The highest authority of the GDPR is the European Commission itself. The Commission is the executive body of the EU, and is responsible for a great deal of the day-to-day rule of the EU, much like the cabinet in an 'ordinary' democracy. The Commission may make executive decisions on topics such as awarding third countries an adequacy decision. In the course of complying with the GDPR, it is extraordinarily unlikely that any organisation will need to deal directly with the Commission.

One-stop-shop mechanism

The "one-stop-shop mechanism" referred to by the Regulation denotes a mechanism that ensures an organisation under investigation is only examined once. The Regulation states that

> the lead supervisory authority should decide, whether it will handle the case pursuant to the provision on cooperation between the lead supervisory authority and the other supervisory authorities concerned ('one-stop-shop mechanism'), or whether the supervisory authority which informed it should handle the case at local level.[227]

By limiting investigations to a single supervisory authority, the Regulation achieves the following objectives:

1. Organisations do not have to submit to multiple investigations for the same case.
2. Because this applies when organisations exist in multiple jurisdictions, it may remove the potential difficulties of being investigated in each country individually.

This mechanism does not apply in the case of processing carried out by public authorities or private bodies in the public interest. In such cases, the investigation should always be by the supervisory authority of the Member State where a public authority or private body is established.

---

[227] GDPR, Recital 127.

Duties of supervisory authorities

Supervisory authorities have a wide range of duties that are supported by a number of powers. In addition to monitoring and enforcing compliance, supervisory authorities are required to take the role of public educator. In particular, the GDPR requires them to "promote public awareness and understanding of the risks, rules, safeguards and rights in relation to processing".[228] This is an important duty because an educated public will be more likely to spot abuses or poor practices, and pass on their suspicions or concerns to the supervisory authority.

This role as an educator is not limited to the public. Supervisory authorities are also required to promote awareness of the Regulation among controllers, processors and governments to ensure that the business and regulatory environment supports a best-practice approach to privacy and data protection.

The supervisory authority must also provide all relevant information an organisation might need in order to comply with the Regulation. This will include guidance relating to binding corporate rules, standard contractual clauses, codes of conduct, the selection and accreditation of certification bodies, and so on. The supervisory authority should be your first consideration for obtaining guidance or ascertaining whether there is an approved methodology in existence.

---

[228] GDPR, Article 57(1)(b).

Powers of supervisory authorities

The supervisory authority's powers fall into three categories:

1. Investigative;
2. Corrective; and
3. Authorisation and advisory.

1. Investigative

Investigative powers enable the supervisory authority to gather appropriate information or evidence, including extensive rights to access personal data, and to gain access to controllers' and processors' premises.

2. Corrective

Corrective powers allow the supervisory authority to escalate the level of interaction with a controller or processor if the supervisory authority finds them to be in breach of the Regulation. These corrective powers range from issuing warnings that "intended processing operations are likely to infringe provisions of [the] Regulation" to imposing administrative fines and ordering the suspension of data flows to a recipient in a third country or international organisation.[229]

3. Authorisation and advisory

Authorisation and advisory powers enable the supervisory authority to develop and promote standards, codes of practice, certification mechanisms, and so on. This

---

[229] GDPR, Article 58(2).

essentially ensures that all Member States have an authority that can establish standards that are consistent with the other powers.

Duties and powers of the European Data Protection Board

The EDPB also has a number of duties and associated powers, and is generally responsible for making sure that the Regulation is applied consistently across the EU. Because the Board comprises one member from each of the EU's Member States, as well as a representative appointed by the Commission, it is an excellent venue for discussing how the Regulation is applied across differing legal jurisdictions.

Like supervisory authorities, the Board is also able to develop and promote codes of practice and certification mechanisms. Unlike those developed and promoted by the supervisory authorities, these will be more universally applicable, as the Board is responsible for the Regulation across the whole EU and not just in a single country.

Furthermore, because the Board reports directly to the Commission and its decisions are based on experiences from across the Union, they will have greater impact on data protection and how the Regulation evolves. Keeping track of the Board reports can provide insights into future requirements and changes. The Board produces an annual, public report on "the protection of natural persons with regard to processing in the Union and, where relevant, in third countries and international organisation".[230] This report

---

[230] GDPR, Article 71(1).

will be a good source of information if your organisation is heavily reliant on processing that may be risky under the Regulation.

Data subjects' rights to redress

Data subjects have a number of rights that relate specifically to how they can seek remedy and/or judicial redress for breaches of the Regulation[231]:

- **Right to lodge a complaint with a supervisory authority** – Data subjects have the right to complain to a relevant supervisory authority if they believe that processing of their personal data infringes the Regulation.

- **Right to an effective judicial remedy against a supervisory authority** – Data subjects are permitted to seek a judicial review of any decisions about them that have been made by a supervisory authority.

- **Right to an effective judicial remedy against a controller or processor** – Data subjects have the right to seek judicial remedy against a controller or processor if they consider their rights to have been infringed as a result of processing of their personal data in non-compliance with the Regulation.

---

[231] GDPR, Articles 77–82.

- **Right to representation** – Data subjects can be represented by a non-profit organisation to lodge complaints and seek compensation on their behalf.
- **Right to compensation and liability** – Anyone who has suffered damage as a result of an infringement of the Regulation has the right to seek compensation from the controller or processor. Note that this person does not need to be the data subject in order to suffer damage and seek compensation.

These rights are in addition to the supervisory authorities' rights to investigate controllers and processors, and in some cases may result in different judgements. For instance, the supervisory authority may find a controller to have operated in compliance with the Regulation, but when the data subject seeks a review, the court may find against the controller and award compensation. This would only be possible if the supervisory authority had elected not to take the matter to trial, as the Regulation does abide by the principle of *ne bis in idem*,[232] which means that a controller or processor cannot be tried in court for the same offence twice.

Administrative fines

Administrative fines regularly feature in headlines about the GDPR. It is true that they are much larger than previously permitted under law, which is to be expected as part of

---

[232] GDPR, Recital 149.

making the punishment effective. As the Regulation states, these fines "shall in each individual case be effective, proportionate and dissuasive".[233]

For many organisations, administrative fines will be significant enough to make compliance economically sensible. That is, the return on investment will suddenly seem quite reasonable. If it costs €20,000 to mitigate a severe vulnerability that could lead to infringements of the GDPR, the potential annualised fines of €100,000 for not mitigating said vulnerability make a one-off cost of €20,000 positively enticing.

Furthermore, administrative fines can be imposed on top of other measures permitted as part of the supervisory authorities' corrective powers.

The Regulation states that certain conditions should be taken into account when deciding the amount of each administrative fine.[234] These conditions highlight the importance of specific factors in complying with the GDPR:

(a) The nature, gravity and duration of the infringement, including consideration of the processing concerned, the number of data subjects affected and the level of damage they have suffered.

(b) If the infringement was due to negligence.

(c) Actions the controller or processor takes to mitigate damage to data subjects.

---

[233] GDPR, Article 83(1).

[234] GDPR, Article 83(2).

(d) Responsibility of the controller or processor, considering any technical and organisational measures that had been implemented.

(e) Previous infringements by the controller or processor.

(f) How well the controller or processor cooperates with the supervisory authority to remedy the infringement and mitigate negative effects.

(g) Categories of data affected.

(h) How the supervisory authority became aware of the infringement.

(i) Whether the supervisory authority had already ordered corrective measures against the controller or processor for the same subject matter.

(j) Whether the controller or processor adheres to approved codes of conduct or certification mechanisms.

(k) Other aggravating or mitigating factors relevant to the case.

There are really two categories of conditions for imposing administrative fines: those that reflect your willingness to abide by the Regulation, and those that reflect either negligence or a desire to circumvent, avoid or breach the requirements. To minimise any administrative fines that you might be subject to, as soon as you identify a personal data breach or significant infringement of the Regulation, you should[235]:

- Take immediate action to mitigate damage;
- Notify the supervisory authority at the earliest opportunity where relevant;
- Cooperate with the supervisory authority in managing the incident and minimising damage to data subjects; and
- Prepare evidence to demonstrate that you comply with the Regulation, including approved codes of conduct and/or certification mechanisms.

There are two levels of administrative fine that can be levied against organisations that breach the Regulation. The lower level of fine can be up to €10 million or, in the case of an undertaking, up to 2% of the total worldwide annual turnover (not profits) of the preceding financial year, whichever is the greater. The higher level can be up to €20 million or, in the case of an undertaking, up to 4% of the total worldwide annual turnover (not profits) of the preceding financial year, whichever is the greater.

The fines themselves are based on the specific articles of the Regulation that the controller or processor has breached.[236] In simple terms, breaches of the controller's or processor's

---

[235] Minor infringements should be managed relatively simply through corrective action and continual improvement processes as part of your privacy compliance framework.

[236] GDPR, Article 83(4) and (5).

obligations will be subject to the lower level, while breaches of the data subject's rights and freedoms, including consent and international transfer of personal data, will be subject to the higher level.

Some supervisory authorities have issued rulings on what they consider to be an "undertaking" and how they will calculate fines. In Germany, the Bavarian Data Protection Authority (Bayerisches Landesamt für Datenschutzaufsicht – BayLDA) has clarified that "when administering fines, it is the whole entity, not just an individual company in a group that is being penalised. Therefore, the fine is calculated as a percentage of the annual turnover of the entire group".[237]

The Regulation's impact on other laws

The most obvious impact on prior legislation is that it has repealed the 1995 DPD. Since coming into force, "references to the repealed Directive shall be construed as references to this Regulation".[238]

This also means that the Regulation has superseded all of the laws that were enacted across the EU in order to comply with the DPD. It should be noted that some Member States elected to update a broader law in order to comply with the DPD, and those sections of the law that are unrelated to data protection and privacy should remain unaffected.

---

[237] *www.privacylaws.com/news/bavaria-issues-gdpr-guidance-on-sanctions/.*

[238] GDPR, Article 94(2).

In relation to the ePrivacy Directive (also called the "Cookies Law"), the Regulation specifies that it does not "impose additional obligations on natural or legal persons in relation to processing in connection with the provision of publicly available electronic communications services".[239] That is, the Regulation should not make the process of agreeing to cookies even more onerous. The Cookies Law has been contentious throughout the EU, with many organisations claiming that it unnecessarily bothers both the users and the organisations forced to comply with it. As such, many enforcement bodies – including the UK's ICO – refuse to enforce that aspect of the Directive.

The Regulation does, however, require organisations to treat cookies as if they were personal data if, "when combined with unique identifiers and other information received by the servers, [the cookies] may be used to create profiles of the natural persons and identify them".[240] Although you shouldn't need to gather additional approval for the use of cookies, some cookies and associated data will need to be covered by appropriate consent or used under exemption, and you will need to ensure that they are appropriately protected.

---

[239] GDPR, Article 95.

[240] GDPR, Recital 30.

CHAPTER 16: TRANSITIONING AND DEMONSTRATING COMPLIANCE

Organisations that already had processes in place to manage compliance with previous data protection and privacy laws will need to make adjustments to ensure they are complying with the new requirements.

Assuming your current compliance programme is aligned with the DPD, it should be relatively straightforward to compare your established requirements against those of the GDPR. You should seek legal advice to ensure that you get a clear overview of what changes are appropriate to your specific circumstances.

If you already have a privacy compliance framework, transition may be somewhat simpler than it will be for organisations that are managing DPD compliance on a more ad hoc basis. However, you should still define a process for transition and prepare to demonstrate your compliance with the Regulation.

Transition frameworks

Existing transition frameworks can be leveraged to manage the transition from meeting the requirements of the DPD to meeting those of the GDPR. The COBIT implementation lifecycle, as shown in Figure 14, is a particularly straightforward model for planning the transition.

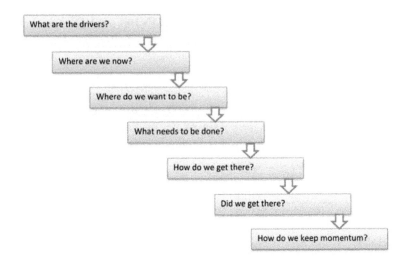

Figure 14: The COBIT implementation lifecycle

In this model, each phase is represented by a question that can be answered incrementally. This enables the organisation to adjust its approach as it progresses through the change lifecycle and encounters new challenges or is presented with new information.

Although the COBIT model is normally cyclical and iterative, your transition does not need to be. If you have an existing privacy compliance framework, a single iteration of a change process, like COBIT, to make a broad change to the framework and its requirements should suffice. The updated framework should then be capable of managing compliance on an ongoing basis.

Every phase and iteration of the transition process above should generate reports of some kind. These outputs provide the basis for the following stages. If you use the process iteratively, each complete cycle provides a report that can be reviewed separately or independently, as well as informing the next iteration.

Each iteration needn't take long; how long will depend on the scale and complexity of the organisation. As in any large or important process, maintaining momentum and keeping people interested is critical, and taking too long to get from phase to phase can jeopardise the entire process. Given the potential severity of administrative fines associated with the GDPR, it is especially important that the transition from DPD compliance to GDPR compliance is managed effectively; the Regulation did, after all, come into effect on 25 May 2018.

Transition – understanding the changes from DPD to GDPR

Although the DPD and its supporting case law and findings is a complex area of law, the GDPR as an instrument is itself large and complex, so a comprehensive, detailed statement of the differences between the two is more likely to emerge as a series of legal documents than from anywhere else. The key areas of change, though, are clear.

The GDPR introduces a number of new concepts beyond those contained in the DPD, as follows:

- **Scope** – the geographic scope of data protection is extended to include controllers and processors outside the EU but who are providing services that involve collecting the data of EU residents.
- **Accountability** – the GDPR clarifies who is responsible for data protection and privacy at each stage of data processing. Processors now have a legally defined role in data processing.

- **Transparency** – the GDPR introduces a set of requirements to ensure that processing is conducted in accordance with this principle.
- **Children's data** – the GDPR clarifies what constitutes children's data and sets minimum standards for its processing. There is a stronger emphasis on protecting children's data, and many organisations will need to change how they operate in order to comply with the Regulation.
- **Definition of personal data** – the GDPR provides a clear definition of personal data – including biometric and genetic data – that did not previously exist. Furthermore, the range of "special categories of personal data" contained within the GDPR is clearer and broader than that within the DPD.
- **Pseudonymisation** – the GDPR presents pseudonymisation as a method of securing personal data.
- **Data breach reporting** – the GDPR makes reporting requirements consistent across the EU, including much more specific requirements regarding who must be told what and by when.
- **Enhanced rights** – the GDPR strengthens and broadens the rights of data subjects. The data subject now has considerable control over how their personal data is to be used.
- **EDPB** – the GDPR establishes the Board as a central authority on data protection to oversee the application of the Regulation, ensure that it remains effective in protecting data subjects' rights and enforce consistency across the Member States.

The eight privacy principles of the DPD have been reduced to seven data processing principles in the GDPR. The principles that have been removed relate to "data subjects' rights" and "international transfers", which are both topics that are covered by separate chapters in the Regulation but should be considered as separate matters for compliance. For instance, complying with all of the data processing principles should be designed, checked and enforced in one way, while ensuring that data subjects' rights have not been infringed is managed by a second process, and the manner in which personal data is transferred is managed by a third.

The GDPR also gives data subjects two new rights:

1. The right to data portability; and
2. The right to be forgotten.

The right to data portability provides a mechanism for the free movement of data that is arguably in the best interests of the market.

The right to be forgotten had already been granted in some jurisdictions, and some interpretations of the DPD had already moved towards this, but the GDPR makes clear what controllers must do in response to requests for erasure of personal data, and the conditions under which they can refuse to do so.

Using policies to demonstrate compliance

The Regulation identifies a number of specific practices and documents that any organisation should be able to provide. Several of these refer specifically to "policies", which can be used to demonstrate that your organisation has at least established its fundamental approach to privacy.

In order to be able to demonstrate compliance with this Regulation, the controller should adopt internal policies and implement measures which meet in particular the principles of data protection by design and data protection by default.[241]

The "internal policies" here indicates that the organisation should have stated and consistent views on how to meet the Regulation's requirements. Although this recital is talking primarily about the principles of data protection by design and by default, the GDPR also describes a number of other policy positions that organisations need to establish.

For instance, in Article 4, the definition of binding corporate rules states that it "means personal data protection policies which are adhered to by a controller or processor".[242] The Regulation also mentions policies in the following contexts:

Where proportionate in relation to processing activities, measures [...] shall include the implementation of appropriate data protection policies by the controller.[243]

[The DPO will] monitor compliance with this Regulation, with other Union or Member State data protection provisions and with the policies of the controller or processor in relation to the protection of personal data.[244]

---

[241] GDPR, Recital 78.

[242] GDPR, Article 4(20).

[243] GDPR, Article 24(2).

[244] GDPR, Article 39(1)(b).

The controller should develop an explicit (therefore documented) policy on the protection of personal data, which will be closely associated with the organisation's compliance with the GDPR. Because of the relationship between policy and compliance, the DPO (or equivalent) should monitor the organisation's compliance with the policy as part of ensuring compliance with all appropriate laws and regulations.

It should be no surprise that an auditable, formal data protection and privacy policy will also be of interest to potential partners and clients.

A privacy policy that is available to the public should be a primary consideration for ensuring that processing abides by the principles of the Regulation. A publicly-available policy supports transparency, allows customers and partners to assess it, and provides a clear statement that supervisory authorities and other regulators can assess the organisation against.

Article 13 of the Regulation lists the information that should be provided within a privacy policy. This includes those details that should be provided whenever personal data is collected, such as the identity and contact details for the controller, any relevant DPO, whether the controller intends to transfer the personal data to a third country or international organisation, and so on.[245]

Your privacy policy should also provide additional information relating to fair and transparent processing, such

---

[245] GDPR, Article 13(1).

as the retention period, the data subject's rights (e.g. the rights to access, erasure and restriction of processing), the right to withdraw consent (where applicable), the right to lodge a complaint with a supervisory authority, and so on.[246]

Information about fair and transparent processing is supplemental and could vary considerably in detail depending on the specifics. You might need to refer to other documentation or, if the cases are simple enough, could be stated in general terms. For instance, the storage period for personal data could be described as "for the length of the contract with the data subject".

Your privacy policy should be readily accessible from the same place that you collect personal data. If you collect personal data via a website, for instance, your privacy policy should be available to be viewed there. If you collect personal data from a physical location, that location should have a copy of your privacy policy. If you collect data from a number of sites, such as by going door-to-door, you should ensure that data subjects will have no difficulty finding a copy of your privacy policy. This might be via your physical offices, a website or some other mechanism.

In addition to the privacy policy, you should determine what other policies will be necessary to your organisation. An information security policy in particular would be valuable. This could comprise a single policy document or a collection of different policies, not all of which will need to be as readily accessible to data subjects as the privacy policy.

---

[246] GDPR, Article 13(2).

The topics you might consider for information security policies include the following:

- Access control.
- Information classification.
- Backup.
- Information transfer.
- Antivirus and anti-malware.
- Vulnerability management.
- Cryptography.
- Communications.
- Supplier relationships.

In order to be effective, these policies will need to meet certain conditions. A good policy both reflects an organisation's aims and directs its actions, so these conditions are really symptoms of good policies.

- Policies must:
  - Be capable of being implemented;
  - Be enforceable;
  - Be concise and easy to understand; and
  - Balance protection with productivity.
- Policies should:
  - Explain the need for the policy;
  - Describe what is covered by the policy (the scope);
  - Define contacts and responsibilities;
  - Include at least one objective; and
  - Explain how violations will be handled.

These conditions should tie into the organisation's other operations. For instance, the objectives should link to the organisation's broader business objectives – if the organisation is aiming to increase profitability by a given percentage, then the information security policy might have an objective to reduce losses by eliminating fines for non-compliance.

Establishing good policies is only part of the battle. In order for a policy to work, it needs to be supported by processes and procedures that fall within the defined parameters set by the policy. Processes and procedures should be created with a view to producing evidence that they are being correctly deployed and thereby demonstrating that the policy they support is effective.

The ability to prove compliance is critical, and a comprehensive and effective privacy compliance framework will develop evidence to support your claims of compliance.

Documentation toolkits can be a practical and cost-effective starting point for developing appropriate GDPR compliance documentation; these toolkits (and there is one published by IT Governance Publishing[247]) provide pre-written templates for all key GDPR documents, and you can then adapt these templates as appropriate to meet your own compliance and privacy framework requirements.

---

[247] *www.itgovernancepublishing.co.uk/product/eu-general-data-protection-regulation-gdpr-documentation-toolkit-v2-0*.

Codes of conduct and certification mechanisms

One of the more prominent methods of demonstrating compliance will be through implementing approved codes of conduct and participating in approved certification mechanisms. You will need to identify those approved codes of conduct and certifications, but this should be made clear by your supervisory authority. It is safe to assume that frameworks such as ISO 27001 will be at least looked on favourably as evidence of good practice, alongside regional variations of personal information management systems such as BS 10012.

These codes of conduct should be taken into account in your privacy compliance framework from the start because they could have a significant bearing on how your organisation manages its compliance or protects personal data. You should be aware of sector-specific codes of conduct and certifications, as well as model contract clauses, binding corporate rules, and so on.

Codes of conduct and certification mechanisms do not prove compliance with the Regulation, but they do support claims of compliance. If you have a current valid certification to ISO 27001, for instance, it doesn't necessarily mean that your organisation is actually compliant with the Standard. What it does mean is that your organisation had all of the measures in place to support effective information security at a specific point in time. As these measures necessarily include mechanisms for keeping that system working, it is a good bet that your organisation still conforms to the requirements of the Standard. The same is true in relation to GDPR compliance.

Complying with approved codes of conduct and/or certification mechanisms has some impact on how the supervisory authorities are required to assess the organisation in the event of a personal data breach. Given the potential scale of fines and other penalties, as well as the potential intrusiveness of an investigation, it would be wise to put your organisation in a position whereby it can provide auditable evidence that best practice has been applied.

APPENDIX 1: INDEX OF THE REGULATION

Chapter I – General provisions

Chapter II – Principles

Chapter III – Rights of the data subject

Section 1 – Transparency and modalities

Section 2 – Information and access to personal data

Chapter V – Transfer of personal data to third countries or international organisations

Chapter VI – Independent supervisory authorities

Section 1 – Independent status

Section 2 – Competence, tasks and powers

Chapter VII – Cooperation and consistency

Section 1 – Cooperation

Section 2 – Consistency

Section 3 – European Data Protection Board

Chapter VIII – Remedies, liabilities and penalties

Chapter XI – Final provisions

APPENDIX 2: EU/EEA NATIONAL SUPERVISORY AUTHORITIES

	Country	National Data Protection Authority	Website
1	United Kingdom	The Information Commissioner's Office	*https://ico.org.uk*
2	Austria	Österreichische Datenschutzbehörde	*www.dsb.gv.at*
3	Belgium	Commission de la protection de la vie privée	*www.privacycommission.be*
4	Bulgaria	Commission for Personal Data Protection	*www.cpdp.bg*
5	Croatia	Croatian Personal Data Protection Agency	*www.azop.hr*
6	Cyprus	Commissioner for Personal Data Protection	*www.dataprotection.gov.cy*
7	Czech Republic	The Office for Personal Data Protection	*www.uoou.cz*
8	Denmark	Datatilsynet	*www.datatilsynet.dk*
9	Estonia	Estonian Data Protection Inspectorate (Andmekaitse Inspektsioon)	*www.aki.ee/en*
10	Finland	Office of the Data Protection Ombudsman	*www.tietosuoja.fi/en*

Appendix 2: EU/EEA national supervisory authorities

	Country	National Data Protection Authority	Website
11	France	Commission Nationale de l'Informatique et des Libertés - CNIL	*www.cnil.fr*
12	Germany	Der Bundesbeauftragte für den Datenschutz und die Informationsfreiheit	*www.bfdi.bund.de*
13	Greece	Hellenic Data Protection Authority	*www.dpa.gr*
14	Hungary	Data Protection Commissioner of Hungary	*www.naih.hu*
15	Iceland	Icelandic Data Protection Agency	*http://personuvernd.is*
16	Ireland	Data Protection Commissioner	*http://www.dataprotection.ie*
17	Italy	Garante per la protezione dei dati personali	*www.garanteprivacy.it*
18	Latvia	Data State Inspectorate	*www.dvi.gov.lv*
19	Liechtenstein	Data Protection Office	*www.dss.llv.li*
20	Lithuania	State Data Protection	*www.ada.lt*

Appendix 2: EU/EEA national supervisory authorities

	Country	National Data Protection Authority	Website
21	Luxembourg	Commission Nationale pour la Protection des Données	*www.cnpd.lu*
22	Malta	Office of the Information and Data Protection Commissioner	*www.dataprotection.gov.mt*
23	Netherlands	Autoriteit Persoonsgegevens	*https://autoriteitpersoonsgegevens.nl*
24	Norway	Datatilsynet	*www.datatilsynet.no*
25	Poland	The Bureau of the Inspector General for the Protection of Personal Data - GIODO	*www.giodo.gov.pl*
26	Portugal	Comissão Nacional de Protecção de Dados - CNPD	*www.cnpd.pt*
27	Romania	The National Supervisory Authority for Personal Data Processing	*www.dataprotection.ro*
28	Slovakia	Office for Personal Data Protection of the Slovak Republic	*www.dataprotection.gov.sk*

Appendix 2: EU/EEA national supervisory authorities

	Country	National Data Protection Authority	Website
29	Slovenia	Information Commissioner	*www.ip-rs.si*
30	Spain	Agencia Española de Protección de Datos	*www.agpd.es*
31	Sweden	Datainspektionen	*www.datainspektionen.se*
32	Switzerland	Data Protection and Information Commissioner of Switzerland	*www.edoeb.admin.ch*
33	European Union	European Data Protection Supervisor	*www.edps.europa.eu/EDPSWEB*

APPENDIX 3: IMPLEMENTATION FAQ

The following answers some of the most common questions regarding the interpretation and implementation of the GDPR.

Material scope and legal implications

Does the GDPR apply to all media and all personal data?

The GDPR applies to all personal data that is collected in the EU, regardless of where in the world it is processed. Any database containing personal or sensitive data collected within the EU is in scope, as is any media containing personal or sensitive data. Any organisation that has such data in its systems, regardless of business size or sector, must comply with the GDPR.

Personal data is any information relating to an identifiable 'natural person' – a living human – and can include information such as a name, a photo, an email address (including work email address), bank details, posts on social networking websites, medical information or a computer's IP address. Even if the data cannot identify someone by itself, it might still be personal data if it is linked to or can be combined with other data to identify someone. For instance, blood type by itself is not personal data, but it is personal data if it is linked to a person's name or other identifying information.

Relevant GDPR references

- Article 2
- Article 4

Previously, some EU countries had different definitions of personal data. Is this still the case?

The GDPR standardises data protection regimes across the EU. The DPD gave Member States the flexibility to implement their own laws to give effect to the provisions of the Directive, which also allowed them to establish different definitions for 'personal data', and so on.

The GDPR eliminates this situation because it is a regulation. EU regulations have direct effect in all EU Member States and the EEA, so the definition of 'personal data' will be consistent across all of them.

The GDPR also created a "consistency mechanism" to ensure consistent definitions and approaches across Member States and, thus, a level playing field for data controllers and processors, and for data subjects.

The GDPR does, however, permit Member States to vary the special categories of data (sensitive data). In this case, global companies may need to process sensitive data in accordance with the law of the Member State where the data subject resides. Keep alert to the changing data protection environment!

Relevant GDPR references

- Article 4
- Article 9

Is the GDPR focused more on B2C rather than B2B or business-to-employee organisations?

Any processing of personal data within territorial scope is within the remit of the GDPR. In that respect, B2B, B2C and business-to-employee organisations will all have the same obligations to fulfil under the legislation.

Relevant GDPR references

- Article 2
- Article 3

Is there an industry-standard definition of personal data or PII?

'PII' is originally a US term, defined in NIST SP 800-122 as:

> any information about an individual maintained by an agency, including (1) any information that can be used to distinguish or trace an individual's identity, such as name, social security number, date and place of birth, mother's maiden name, or biometric records; and (2) any other information that is linked or linkable to an individual, such as medical, educational, financial, and employment information.

This definition of PII and its use in the USA does not precisely match the GDPR definition of personal data. The preferred term in the GDPR is 'personal data', which is defined as "any information relating to an identified or identifiable natural person", whether it relates to his or her private, professional or public life. As a general rule, any information that can be used to identify an individual – either on its own or when combined with another piece of information – is classified as personal data. This can include biometric, genetic and location data; it is worth noting that IP addresses and email addresses fall within this definition.

Relevant GDPR reference

- Article 4

What is an online identifier?

An online identifier is a form of personal identifier (PID). PIDs are a subset of personal data that identify a unique individual and can permit another person to assume that individual's identity without their knowledge or consent. This can occur when PID data elements are used either alone, combined with a person's name, combined with other PID data elements or combined with other personal data. PIDs include account numbers, PINs, passwords, voice scans, credit card numbers, etc.

Relevant GDPR reference

- Recital 30

Do utility bills, driving licence and passport details qualify as special categories of personal data?

No. Special categories of personal data under the GDPR are personal data that reveal racial or ethnic origin, political opinions, religious or philosophical beliefs, or trade union membership, and genetic data, biometric data, data concerning health, or data concerning a natural person's sex life or sexual orientation.

Relevant GDPR reference

- Article 9

Does the GDPR apply to biometric information?

Yes. Biometric data is classified as a special category of data and falls strictly within the scope of the GDPR. This requires the data subjects' explicit permission.

Relevant GDPR reference

- Article 9

How does the GDPR apply to health data?

Health information is treated as special category data under the GDPR. Organisations processing health data must have lawful grounds to do so and must have the explicit permission of the data subject, unless there is a basis for processing that does not require explicit consent.

Health data controllers/processors will often rely on consent. They can, however, collect and use health data without consent if the processing is necessary for the purposes of preventive or occupational medicine, medical diagnosis, provision of health or social care or treatment, management of health or social care systems and services, under a contract with a health professional or another person subject to professional secrecy under law. Consent is also not required if the processing is necessary for public health reasons, or if the organisation can argue that the processing is necessary for scientific research.

If you think any of these grounds might apply to your organisation, ensure you discuss with your legal advisors how you will approach consent.

Relevant GDPR reference

- Article 9

Does the GDPR mean that equal opportunities forms cannot be collected?

No, but equal opportunities forms should in any case be optional to fill in. Under the GDPR, special category data can be processed if the data subject has consented. However, you must ensure that the consent you obtain for collecting the equal opportunities form is explicit, informed, specific and freely given. If you think that you have a contractual, statutory or other basis for collecting this information without explicit consent, you should discuss with your legal advisors how you will address the issue.

Relevant GDPR reference

- Article 9

Does the GDPR apply to universities and schools?

The GDPR applies irrespective of sector or activity. As long as personal data is being processed, and the processor/controller is established in the EU/EEA or the processing affects EU/EEA data subjects, the GDPR applies. Universities and schools are no more exempt than any other institution. In addition, schools may have to deal with the issue of consent to processing the personal data of children.

Relevant GDPR reference

- Article 2

Do you have to comply if you have access to information but do not store it yourself?

If the information you access is able to identify a natural person, then it is within the scope of the GDPR. Whether or not you store the information yourself is irrelevant; some controllers will use data processors to collect and store data for remote access, for instance, or will give processors remote access to data.

Relevant GDPR reference

- Article 2

If personal data is encrypted throughout its lifecycle using strong/approved algorithms, is it out of scope for GDPR compliance?

Encryption can take personal data out of scope of the GDPR. Article 32(1)(a) sanctions it as an appropriate security technique. However, there is still uncertainty around this point, particularly regarding the interpretation of anonymisation. It is possible that some encryption techniques may not be sufficient to put the personal data out of scope of the GDPR.

Controllers should review their encrypted data and assess the reasonable likelihood of that data being decrypted, taking into account future technologies.

Relevant GDPR reference

- Article 32

Is publicly available personal data covered by the GDPR, such as contact information gathered for business opportunities?

Although you do not have to obtain consent to process personal information that someone has deliberately made public, you will be required to inform the data subject of your intention to process their data and provide them with an opt-out route. Article 14 sets out the requirements for handling this sort of information.

For personal data being processed for direct marketing, you should also confirm that you are complying with the Privacy and Electronic Communications Regulations 2003 (PECR) in the UK, or the local implementation of the EU's Privacy and Electronic Communications Directive 2002 (ePrivacy Directive).

Relevant GDPR reference

* Article 14

Does the GDPR apply to hobby organisations? For instance, hobby groups with membership.

The scope of the GDPR excludes data processed by natural persons for purely personal reasons. It is not yet clear the extent to which this applies to hobby organisations, but will most likely depend on the scale of the organisation, what data is being collected and whether or not the organisation has grown beyond what can be classed as personal activity.

Relevant GDPR reference

* Article 2

How does the GDPR affect mobile phones and email data held on them while travelling?

Personal data is personal data wherever it is held. If a mobile device that contains personal data is breached while travelling, it is as much a data breach under the GDPR as one that occurs to a database within the EU.

If the device is taken outside the EU, it is possible that this might also constitute a transfer of personal data that must be accounted for in accordance with Chapter V of the GDPR.

Relevant GDPR reference

* Chapter V

Is an IP address personal data?

If the IP address can, on its own or with other information, be used to identify a natural person, then yes; if not, no.

Relevant GDPR reference

* Article 2

GDPR enforcement timeline

How will Brexit change the landscape for the GDPR in the UK?

The UK has implemented much of the GDPR into law through the DPA, and there are plans to implement the remaining provisions through a 'UK GDPR', which the UK government will bring into law following departure from the EU.

From a practical perspective, many of the changes for UK organisations will relate to the fact that the UK will no longer be an EU Member State, so organisations in the EU will have to treat the UK as a third country. Because of these changes, the UK will also no longer be able to approve binding corporate rules, so organisations that operate in both the UK and the EU may not be able to rely on them to continue transferring personal data between the EU and the UK.

There have been very few prosecutions or fines under the GDPR. Are supervisory authorities not enforcing the law?

Data protection cases often take a long time to investigate and prosecute. The UK's ICO, for instance, is still working through a backlog of cases that occurred under the DPA 1998, which had much lower potential fines. Once supervisory authorities are able to pursue cases under the GDPR, we expect that there will be a number of headlines about very large fines.

Territorial scope, international transfers and adequacy (including Brexit and EU-US Privacy Shield considerations)

Do processors based outside the EEA that process personal data for EU/EEA controllers have to comply in the same way as processors inside the EEA?

Article 3 of the GDPR sets the territorial scope of the Regulation:

1. This Regulation applies to the processing of personal data in the context of the activities of an establishment of a controller or processor in the Union, regardless of whether the processing itself takes place in the Union or not.

2. This Regulation applies to the processing of personal data of data subjects who are within the Union by a controller or processor established outside the Union, where the processing activities are related to:

   a) the offering of goods or services, irrespective of whether a payment of the data subject is required, to such data subjects in the Union; or

b) the monitoring of their behaviour as far as their behaviour takes place within the Union.

This means that organisations that are not established in the EU must comply with the GDPR whether they are controllers or processors. Data processors acting on behalf of controllers within the EU will usually find that their obligations with regard to the GDPR are written into contracts.

Relevant GDPR reference

- Article 3

Does the GDPR apply to EU-based companies processing the personal data (either as a controller or a processor) of non-EU residents?

Yes. The GDPR applies to all processing of personal data within the EU/EEA. It does not matter whose personal data that is or where the data subject is based.

Relevant GDPR reference

- Article 3

If somebody is living in the EU but is not actually an EU citizen (e.g. an expat), does the GDPR still apply?

Yes. When you travel abroad, you are subject to the laws of the country you travel to. Similarly, when you are living in the EU, your personal data is subject to its laws and regulations.

Furthermore, the GDPR makes it very clear that this is the intent in Recital 14: "The protection afforded by this Regulation should apply to natural persons, whatever their nationality or place of residence, in relation to the processing of their personal data."

Relevant GDPR references

- Article 3
- Recital 14

Is signing up to the EU-US Privacy Shield sufficient to satisfy the GDPR's processing clauses?

No – the EU-US Privacy Shield simply attests that your organisation meets a certain minimum standard. It is not proof that you actually meet all of the requirements of the GDPR, especially as different processing activities will demand different measures in order to comply.

Although Privacy Shield certification will provide a framework for receiving personal data from EU/EEA controllers, those arrangements should be accompanied by contractual requirements to ensure that your organisation meets the GDPR's standards for processing personal data.

Moreover, the EU-US Privacy Shield is subject to annual review and is therefore likely to change. This provides limited certainty regarding data protection. This, combined with the drastically different data protection culture in America, and in light of the GDPR principle of adequacy, means it is highly unlikely that current EU-US Privacy Shield conformance alone will suffice for GDPR compliance.

US organisations that are within the scope of the GDPR should proceed on the basis that they will have to comply fully with the requirements of the GDPR.

Relevant GDPR reference

- Article 46

Must all EU countries implement the Regulation exactly as written, or is there some flexibility?

There is very little flexibility. The GDPR is an EU regulation, which means that the legislation is directly applicable in every EU Member State. No further legislation is required to implement the GDPR, and one of the drivers of the GDPR is to ensure standardisation of data protection regimes across the Union.

However, there are some articles that permit Member States a degree of flexibility. Member States can, for instance, vary the definition of special categories of data and the age they deem to be the threshold for a minor in relation to information society services.

What is the procedure for making international transfers?

There are several options for transferring data from the EU/EEA to an organisation elsewhere in the world:

- On the basis of an adequacy decision from the European Commission.
- Using standard contractual clauses.
- Using binding corporate rules governing intra-group data transfers.
- Relying on an exemption.

Adequacy decisions are subject to a periodic review, in which the Commission consults with the entity and considers relevant developments in the entity and information from other relevant sources. Adequacy decisions therefore may involve some type of audit of the international organisation.

Standard contractual clauses and binding corporate rules are discussed in some depth in this manual.

Exemptions for other transfers include certification mechanisms such as the EU-US Privacy Shield.

Relevant GDPR reference

* Chapter V (NB Article 45)

How will Brexit affect the choice of supervisory authority?

The ICO will remain the supervisory authority of the UK, but this may not be adequate following Brexit as the UK may be a third country. In that instance, organisations based in the UK may need to identify a supervisory authority and appoint a representative in an EU Member State.

Relevant GDPR reference

* Article 27

In the case of US-based companies, do the NIST 800 controls cover the GDPR's requirements? If so, how much: fully, partially?

There is no reason they wouldn't; the NIST 800 publications include a good set of controls that are likely to offer coverage of all the relevant data risks. The critical factor will be ensuring that all the requirements of the GDPR are met, not just those relating to information security – that is, you will need to make sure that these controls guarantee data subjects' rights, uphold the data processing principles, etc.

What is a "third country"?

A country that is not a Member State of the European Union or European Economic Area.

How can the GDPR be enforced against third-country organisations?

Non-EEA controllers have to appoint an EU representative – that is the first step for a regulator in an enforcement action. Furthermore, trade between countries is governed on the basis of a number of international agreements that permit organisations and governments to take actions against other organisations and governments. This means that even organisations that have no representative within the EU can be held to account.

Furthermore, it is very likely that any organisation that shows no interest in meeting the GDPR's requirements will find it very difficult to win business with organisations that handle personal data that is subject to the GDPR. In this case, it is simply good business for such organisations to make sure that they comply.

Relevant GDPR reference

- Article 27

Is a server in the EU that is shared with a company in the US classed as transferring data internationally? What about Cloud environments based within the EU but logically supported by technical support staff based outside the EEA?

If a third country, company or person can access data on the UK/EU server, then you are giving access to someone outside the EEA – you are allowing processing by someone outside the EEA. 'Consultation' and 'use' of data are explicitly included in the definition of 'processing'.

Relevant GDPR references

- Article 4
- Article 44

What would happen if an organisation outside the EU refused to pay the fine, believing it to be outside the EU's jurisdiction?

Enforcement action under international treaties.

Would GDPR compliance be better led by information assurance professionals or legal/policy teams?

Implementing a compliance programme is usually better if led by practitioners with a lot of legal input and advice. What matters is how you implement the legal requirements, rather than how well you reflect them in your documentation.

How should companies and internal DPOs proceed in multinational companies that do business with countries that currently do not have data protection regulations or have regulations that conflict with the GDPR?

International companies will be able to deal with this through the use of binding corporate rules.

Controller or processor?

What is the difference between a data controller and a data processor?

Article 4 of the GDPR sets out separate definitions for the roles of processor and controller. The key issue to consider in determining the processor or controller under the GDPR is to establish who determines the means and purpose of the processing. Whoever determines the means and purpose will be deemed a controller under the legislation, and they will need to instruct the processor and agree the processor's obligations in a contract.

Fundamentally, compliance with the data processing principles is the controller's duty, and they must pass on those requirements to any data processors operating under their instructions. Furthermore, they are required to only use data processors that provide "sufficient guarantees to implement appropriate technical and organisational measures in such a manner that processing will meet the requirements of [the GDPR] and ensure the protection of the rights of the data subject." Data processors will normally only be held liable for GDPR breaches if they either act without instruction (or contrary to instructions) from the controller, or if they knowingly agree to act in contravention of the GDPR.

Relevant GDPR references

- Article 4
- Article 24
- Article 28

Is it the responsibility of the controller or the processor to notify data subjects in the event of a breach?

Typically, the processor is responsible for notifying the controller of a breach without undue delay, while the controller is responsible for notifying the data subjects if the breach is likely to pose a high risk to the rights and freedoms of the data subjects.

The data controller is also responsible for notifying the supervisory authority of data breaches.

Relevant GDPR reference

- Article 33

Is the data processor obliged to seek advice on DPIAs as well as the data controller?

The controller is typically responsible for DPIAs, so they will normally be responsible for seeking advice. The associated controls and safeguards identified by the assessment should subsequently be agreed in the processing agreement.

Relevant GDPR reference

- Article 35

If you pass data to a third party, do you become the data controller?

Whoever determines the means and purposes of processing is the controller; a processor may not pass data on to any third party without the agreement of the data controller.

Relevant GDPR reference

- Article 4

What obligations will suppliers have as data processors? Should we add GDPR compliance to our supplier due diligence?

Data processors face direct legal obligations under the GDPR in areas such as security, record-keeping and international transfers.

Under the GDPR, controllers can only use processors "providing sufficient guarantees to implement appropriate technical and organisational measures in such a manner that processing will meet the requirements of [the GDPR] and ensure the protection of the rights of the data subject." This means that controllers are likely to need to carry out a broader due diligence exercise when selecting a processor than they might have previously undertaken.

Processors must act within the remit of the contract agreed with the controller. A detailed list of provisions must be included in any processing agreement. This allows controllers to limit some of their risk in relation to their processors.

It is also important to note the restrictions that the GDPR puts in place around sub-processing, namely:

- It prevents the processor from sub-contracting without the controller's prior written consent.
- Where general rather than specific consent has been obtained, the processor must inform the controller of any changes.

- Sub-contracts must contain the same data protection obligations as set out in the main processing agreement.

Relevant GDPR reference

- Article 28

Legitimate interests

Processing of personal data relating to convictions and offences is covered in Article 10. Do we also need to identify a relevant condition for processing from Article 5 or 6 in order to process this?

Data in relation to criminal convictions and offences may only be processed under official authority or when authorised by Union or Member State law. This means that controllers/processors will need to ensure that they have one or more legal justifications to process the personal data for each purpose.

Relevant GDPR reference

- Article 10

Can organisations rely on legitimate interests to use data collected using a "soft opt-in" before the GDPR without having to reconfirm consent?

Not necessarily – take professional legal advice.

Data subjects' rights

How does the right to be forgotten work in relation to credit agencies that need to collect data to advise and inform banks and other clients of credit worthiness?

The right to be forgotten is not an absolute right – data subjects only have the right under certain conditions. In this case, credit agencies could rely on the "legitimate interests" condition as a lawful basis for the processing. As long as the data was lawfully collected and processed, it would be difficult for a data subject to assert the right to be forgotten.

Relevant GDPR references

- Article 6
- Article 17

The right to be forgotten says organisations need to erase any personal data they have on the data subject. Do they need to keep a record of the procedure?

Yes, you need to keep records of processing. Erasure is a form of processing. In this instance, the record might need to retain some information about the data subject (such as their name) to be able to prove that you have processed their request for erasure. This is acceptable under Article 17.

Relevant GDPR reference

- Article 17

Is the right to erasure overridden by other legislation such as mandated record retention periods?

Yes, as with all legal issues, GDPR requirements have to be considered within their legal context.

Relevant GDPR reference

- Article 17

Consent

Is contacting historical clients/customers for consent after May 2018 a breach in itself?

If you use personal data that does not meet GDPR requirements (e.g. if explicit consent has not been given/if you are using the data for a purpose other than what it was collected for, etc.), you are infringing the Regulation.

If you have not already done so, we recommend that you make it a priority to identify what personal data you currently hold and confirm whether or not it is legally held under the terms of the GDPR. It is possible that consent gathered before 25 May 2018 is still valid, but you need to be able to demonstrate this.

Relevant GDPR reference

- Article 6

Do previous contracts override the GDPR? For example, if a customer provided their data before 25 May 2018, is it lawful to continue using that data?

There are two aspects to this.

1. If you are only using the data for the purposes for which you collected it, and you are in compliance with all other aspects of the legislation, then you may continue to use the data. Recital 171 also states that consent remains valid if the basis on which you collected data meets the GDPR's requirements.

2. It is important to remember that consent can always be withdrawn, and the GDPR mandates that consent must be as easy to withdraw as it is to give. If the customer no longer consents to you using the data for the purposes you collected it, then you must respect the customer's wishes. This applies unless you have a different lawful basis for processing the personal data, such as based on compelling legitimate grounds that override the interests, rights and freedoms of the individual, or if the processing is for the establishment, exercise or defence of legal claims.

Relevant GDPR references

- Recital 67
- Article 18
- Article 19

If a user can withdraw consent, does that mean the company can fire an employee that does so?

Consent is very rarely an appropriate lawful basis for processing the personal data of employees because of the inherent difference in power between the employee and the organisation. Personal data processing in this instance should probably be on other lawful grounds, such as for the purposes of fulfilling a contract or for the business's legitimate interests.

Relevant GDPR references

- Recital 43
- Article 6
- Article 7

Is it acceptable to have a checkbox that says "May we contact you in the future for other items you might be interested in?"

This is probably acceptable as long as the box is not pre-ticked. As with all such issues, however, you should obtain and follow the specific advice of your legal advisors.

Relevant GDPR reference

- Article 7

If historical data subjects don't respond to contact about consent, should it be taken that their consent is withheld?

Yes – tacit or implicit consent (consent assumed from inactivity) is prohibited under the GDPR.

Relevant GDPR references

- Recital 32
- Article 6
- Article 7

For screening purposes (e.g. economic sanctions), can you process personal data without consent from the data subject?

Possibly – take professional legal advice. Such processing will almost certainly require a DPIA.

Relevant GDPR references

- Article 6
- Article 7

Are consent questions necessary on website contact forms where a person/company is simply requesting further info or a call back?

Probably not – this would likely be lawful on the basis that processing this information is necessary "in order to take steps at the request of the data subject prior to entering into a contract". However, you may need to include a request for their consent if you plan to use the personal data for more than simply contacting them.

Relevant GDPR reference

- Article 6

Can organisations collect personal data from social media profiles?

Organisations that collect data from social media platforms, for whatever purpose, are almost certainly data processors and need to have a contract with the data controller. The data controller must ensure that this processing is lawful, which may or may not require them to seek consent from the data subjects.

Relevant GDPR references

- Article 6
- Article 7

For employees, how and what do we need to get new consent?

Consent in an employment context is not generally considered to be freely given owing to the employer-employee relationship. This means that employers need to review the legal grounds on which they process employee data.

If relying on consent, employers will need to ensure that it can be withdrawn at any time. For this reason, most organisations will need to adopt another legal basis for processing data. Either contractual necessity (such as the processing of employee payment data), a legal obligation (e.g. for processing of employee data in relation to social security) or the legitimate interests of the employer (e.g. in the context of employee monitoring).

The legal grounds will need to be narrowly construed to ensure a balance with the rights of the employees as data subjects.

Where an employer is unable to rely on one of the legal grounds, they will need to restrict the range of data processed or stop processing altogether.

Relevant GDPR references

- Recital 43
- Article 88

When contacting data subjects, do you have to get consent before first contact or at the time of the first contact?

If your processing relies on consent, then you need to secure the data subject's consent before using that data.

Relevant GDPR references

- Article 6
- Article 7

Can children consent to processing?

Children cannot legally consent to the processing of their data in regard to information society services. These are services offered online. This means, however, that children may be able to consent to other forms of processing, although this might be limited by local laws, especially where special categories of data might be involved (such as health data).

Relevant GDPR reference

- Article 8

Can we require someone to consent to processing in order to access our products or services?

This is a complex topic that should be referred to your legal advisors. The UK's ICO, however, does say that "Consent should be separate from other terms and conditions and should not generally be a precondition of signing up to a service".

Relevant GDPR references

- Recital 32
- Article 6

- Article 7

Retention and disposal

The fifth data processing principle permits keeping personal data "for no longer than is necessary" – what is deemed as long as necessary?

The GDPR requires that personal data shall be kept for no longer than is necessary "for the purposes for which the personal data are processed". This means organisations need to identify what personal data they process and the purposes for so doing in order to determine appropriate retention periods for each record type.

Personal data may be stored for longer periods under the GDPR, provided that it is processed solely for archiving purposes in the public interest, scientific or historical research purposes or statistical purposes in accordance with Article 89(1). Personal data that is retained must be stored with appropriate technical and organisational measures in place to safeguard the rights and freedoms of the data subject, and due consideration must be given to the principle of data minimisation.

Relevant GDPR references

- Article 5
- Article 89

If personal data is contained in a SQL database system that is backed up for various IT best practices, how do you manage this data in relation to removing data?

You must take reasonable steps to remove data, including copies of it, when you no longer have consent to keep it, or when you are no longer processing it for the purposes for which it was collected.

SaaS providers often rely on various forms of caching techniques that store data around the world. What should the customer look for to avoid risking non-compliance?

Make sure the SaaS provider is offering – and you have selected – EU-compliant data storage. This should be clearly set out in terms and conditions and in contracts to ensure that your providers are bound by legally enforceable agreements.

These agreements should also allow you to guarantee that cached copies of data can be deleted, either by actively removing them or when updating the cache from the source.

Relevant GDPR references

- Article 19
- Article 28

What do you do if you don't have the required technical controls to delete data?

Implement them. Otherwise, you will be breaking the law because you will be retaining personal data in breach of the law. Remember that deletion of data is not an absolute right; you might be able to argue that deletion is neither practical nor possible for you. Take legal advice.

What proof is needed when data is deleted?

The GDPR is silent on this. You need to retain a record of the deletion because it is a form of processing. This record may need to include some elements of the personal data to demonstrate that it, in particular, has been deleted.

Does the GDPR set required retention periods for specific types of information?

No. Other laws and regulations may set minimum or maximum retention periods.

Compliance and certification

How detailed do policies, instructions for employees, etc. need to be to demonstrate GDPR compliance?

It is up to each organisation to determine the level of detail necessary to comply. We advocate following something such as ISO 27001 because it demonstrates that you are pursuing a widely recognised best-practice standard and provides a framework for establishing what appropriate documentation looks like.

Is there any certification designed to demonstrate compliance with GDPR issues?

Not yet, but it is likely that certifiable data protection standards – and certainly there is talk of a European data protection seal – will emerge across the EU.

Organisations with ISO 27001 certification are likely to meet many of the "appropriate technical and organisational" security requirements of the GDPR. Conducting a GDPR gap analysis in this context can be helpful to identify what is required to get an ISO 27001-compliant system up to scratch with the GDPR.

Additionally, organisations should also consider implementing a PIMS to account for the GDPR's data protection requirements.

BS 10012:2017 can help to provide a comprehensive PIMS.

Alternatively, the new ISO 27701 standard can be applied to extend ISO 27001 to account for data protection requirements in addition to information security.

There is currently no certification for ISO 27701, but implementing a PIMS according to ISO 27701 should help organisations demonstrate their conformance with the GDPR's requirements.

Relevant GDPR references

- Article 32
- Article 42

How much of the GDPR can be resolved with an ISMS?

The GDPR is a modernisation of data protection law for the 21st century. This means it recognises that data protection considerations must factor in information security if the confidentiality, integrity and availability of personal data is to be preserved. Additionally, the thrust of the GDPR is that data protection must become the cornerstone of an organisation. Organisational and technical measures are of equal importance to GDPR compliance. The balance of organisational and technical measures you implement will depend on the nature and purpose of the data you process.

It is therefore likely that companies that already have an ISMS will have a good foundation upon which to build a GDPR compliance framework, given the emphasis placed on information security within the GDPR.

Is there an official control framework or checklist for GDPR compliance?

No, there is no such framework or list. Appropriate controls will vary from organisation to organisation, but they are always likely to include encryption, penetration testing, access control and back up. Carry out a detailed risk assessment to determine where your risks are and what the appropriate mitigation might be.

We have ISO 27001 certification. Do we need to refer to the GDPR?

Yes. Although ISO 27001 will provide a good foundation for a GDPR compliance framework, it will not be sufficient in itself to ensure compliance with the Regulation.

Is there any guidance regarding the level to which data should be encrypted, and where it should be stored on your systems?

The ICO released a set of guidelines on encryption: *https://ico.org.uk/for-organisations/guide-to-data-protection/guide-to-the-general-data-protection-regulation-gdpr/security/encryption/*.

What is the first step for a small business?

Businesses of any size should start by identifying what data they hold or process, where that data was obtained, and whether they have the appropriate permissions and grounds for continuing to process that data. This can be done effectively through a data mapping exercise, which will allow you to identify which steps you need to take on your route to GDPR compliance.

For any suppliers, would new contracts need to include the GDPR?

Yes. Processors are within the scope of the GDPR. Although this means there are specific obligations on processors, it also means that controllers must ensure that there is a written processing agreement requiring the processor to meet the GDPR's requirements.

Practically speaking, this means that contracts with existing suppliers should also be reviewed and revised to ensure that they are GDPR-compliant.

Relevant GDPR reference

* Article 28

How should backups be governed?

Data storage solutions must be designed and built to protect data and maintain its privacy. The appropriate security measures need to be in place to protect data, including clear rules regarding data access and proper authentication mechanisms for access to sensitive data. Authorisations must be kept up to date to ensure appropriate access rights, and all data must be audited.

In order to meet these requirements, IT teams should:

* Automate data access processes, including those to grant, review and revoke access;
* Automatically inspect content to identify sensitive data; and
* Monitor and analyse access.

Because individuals can opt out of processing, organisations should be able to easily delete personal data. It is also important that solutions are built to ensure data portability where necessary.

Is GDPR compliance audited?

Audits are not routinely carried out for GDPR or DPA compliance. Some sectoral regulators already require organisations to prove DPA compliance. Under the GDPR, management must be satisfied that the GDPR is being properly applied, which they might do by, among other things, conducting internal audits and monitoring performance.

The Information Commissioner has enhanced powers under the GDPR, including the right to conduct audits.

Where does a small charity start with ensuring compliance?

Good first steps would be to inventory personal data, review processing and ensure you have necessary permissions, and protect the data.

How detailed should the record of processing activities be?

The GDPR sets out explicitly what these should be – see Article 30.

Relevant GDPR reference

• Article 30

We have hundreds of employment records that we have to keep for a number of years; how can we meet the requirements of the GDPR?

Inventory the records, determine the basis for continued processing, set retention periods accordingly and act on them.

Will there be any sector-specific guidance (e.g. healthcare) or has any already been published?

Yes. The ICO has already released some extra guidance and FAQs for specific sectors:

https://ico.org.uk/for-organisations/in-your-sector/

The PCI DSS suggests that we use background checks on potential new hires, but the GDPR states that we cannot use such data if it may have a negative impact on the individual. How will this contradiction work?

There is no contradiction: you can do background checks – you just have to inform data subjects of the possible outcome of automated processing. They can object, and you can refuse to take an application further.

Governance and the GDPR

How do we get senior managers to buy into the requirements?

Point them at the combination of administrative fines, data subject legal actions and the legal requirement for accountability. For organisations in the UK, you might also point out that the GDPR is closely related to the PECR, which now makes directors personally liable for fines. Given the overlap, it is quite likely that an organisation that doesn't comply with the GDPR doesn't comply with the PECR either.

If they still don't get it, find a job somewhere else.

Who within the controller is accountable if a breach occurs?

That is a governance issue for the data controller; the GDPR does not specify a role that is accountable.

Does every organisation need to assign a DPO?

DPOs are only mandatory under the conditions set out in Article 37.

Relevant GDPR reference

* Article 37

Is it acceptable to have one person (director) responsible for the GDPR even where a company is present in three other EU countries?

Yes.

Legacy data

Regarding email in general and specifically the right to be forgotten – do data controllers have to review systems and remove all mention of an individual where personal data is present?

Adhering strictly to the GDPR would mean that you need to review all the data, identify any personal data, and either securely destroy it or make sure that you have the appropriate grounds to process it.

Whatever data is retained must be properly protected with appropriate safeguards, such as encryption. Also bear in mind that the GDPR states that you must do what is possible and reasonable, and in practice this means that you may possibly never remove all data.

Relevant GDPR references

- Article 6
- Article 32

If I receive personal data (such as DOB and address) through email over a period of months, must I go through old emails (possibly thousands) to clean out personal data that is no longer needed?

Any personal data held by a processor or controller must be in accordance with the GDPR's requirements. It is therefore imperative that organisations complete a data audit to identify where consent is necessary and granted correctly, and delete records where consent was necessary but was not or cannot be obtained. If data can't be deleted (e.g. for reasons of financial or regulatory compliance), the GDPR recommends that organisations pseudonymise or anonymise the data.

Relevant GDPR references

- Recital 28
- Recital 32
- Article 4
- Article 5
- Article 6
- Article 7

- Article 32
- Article 89

DPOs

Does the DPO have to be located in the EU?

Although there seems to be no limitation on the territorial location of the DPO (provided that he/she is easily accessible), a DPO located outside Europe may struggle to build a strong relationship with the business if they are remotely located. DPO duties, such as monitoring an organisation's GDPR compliance, may be difficult to uphold from a remote location.

It will be difficult for an organisation to understand the role of the DPO, as well as to deploy him/her effectively, if the DPO is located outside the EU.

Relevant GDPR reference

- Article 39

Who does the DPO typically report to in a 100-200-person company that doesn't have a legal/compliance/risk department?

The CEO or CFO.

Is it acceptable to have the information security manager as the DPO?

Yes, as long as they are not also responsible for processing personal data or deciding how processing will be performed, or otherwise conflicted.

Relevant GDPR reference

- Article 38

Will the EDPB issue guidance on the role of the DPO?

The EDPB has adopted the WP29's guidelines on DPOs, which it may complement with further guidelines at a later date.

When must a DPO be appointed?

The ICO and GDPR state that you must appoint a DPO if you:

- Are a public authority (except for courts acting in their judicial capacity);
- Undertake large-scale systematic monitoring of individuals; or
- Carry out large-scale processing of special categories of data or data relating to criminal convictions and offences.

You may appoint a single DPO to act for a group of companies or for a group of public authorities, taking into consideration their size and structure.

Any organisation can appoint a DPO. Regardless of whether the GDPR obliges you to appoint one, you must ensure that your organisation has sufficient staff and expertise to discharge your duties.

Relevant GDPR references

- Recital 97
- Article 37

- Article 39

What minimum training is required for a DPO?

The WP29's guidelines on DPOs clarify the requirements around the DPO skillset. In particular, DPOs should have:

- Expertise in national and European data protection laws and practices, and an in-depth understanding of the GDPR;
- Knowledge of the business sector and of the organisation of the controller;
- Sufficient understanding of the controller's processing operations, as well as the information systems, data security and data protection needs of the controller, is recommended; and
- In the case of public bodies, sound knowledge of the administrative rules and procedures of the organisation.

Do you see the DPO needing the support of a team and what do you expect the team size to be?

The DPO must be properly supported by the organisation and have direct access to senior management, etc., as has been emphasised by the WP29 guidelines on DPOs. This guidance specifically lists adequate support in terms of financial resources, infrastructure and staff.

The size of the team that supports the DPO will vary depending on the nature and size of the organisation's processing activities and the complexity of their systems.

Relevant GDPR reference

- Article 38

What constitutes large-scale sensitive personal data?

The WP29 has provided some guidance in its DPO guidelines. It recommends that the following factors are considered when determining whether processing qualifies as 'large scale':

- The number of data subjects concerned.
- The volume of data and/or range of different data items processed.
- Duration or permanence of the processing.
- The geographical extent of the processing.

It also provides some examples of large-scale processing:

- Processing of patient data in the regular course of business by a hospital.
- Processing of travel data of individuals using a city's public transport system (e.g. travel cards).
- Processing of real-time geolocation data of customers of an international fast food chain for statistical purposes by a processor specialised in providing these services.
- Processing of customer data in the regular course of business by an insurance company or a bank.
- Processing of personal data for behavioural advertising by a search engine.
- Processing of data (content, traffic location) by telephone or Internet service providers.

Examples of non-large-scale processing:

- Processing of patient data by an individual physician.
- Processing of personal data relating to criminal convictions and offences by an individual lawyer.

Should an entity appoint a back-up DPO as well?

This depends entirely on how frequently you expect the DPO to be absent.

Should the DPO be a standalone role?

The DPO doesn't have to be standalone – the DPO does need sufficient time to perform their role, and must not be conflicted in performing the role by other requirements of the role or of their reporting line.

Relevant GDPR reference

- Article 38

Is the DPO a protected role in the UK?

The DPO must have direct reporting lines to the highest management level, must be able to perform their tasks and duties independently and cannot be dismissed or penalised for performing their tasks.

Relevant GDPR reference

- Article 38

Should organisations have a data breach investigator to support the DPO?

That depends on the number of breaches you plan to have.

Data breaches

Are there any guidelines for notifying data subjects of a data breach?

The ICO's data breach notification guidance is very clear:

https://ico.org.uk/for-organisations/guide-to-data-protection/guide-to-the-general-data-protection-regulation-gdpr/personal-data-breaches/

It is up to each individual organisation to develop its own internal policies governing how communications should be issued to data subjects in response to security breaches. However, when notifying data subjects of a breach, it is imperative to include the following information in clear and plain language:

- The nature of the personal data breach.
- Name and contact details of the relevant DPO.
- The likely consequences of the personal data breach.
- The measures taken/proposed to address the breach, including where possible, to mitigate any adverse effects.

Finally, it should be noted that in situations where the personal data of multiple data subjects has been breached, a public notice may be an appropriate means of notification.

Relevant GDPR references

- Recital 86
- Article 33
- Article 34

How can the 72-hour window to report a breach be enforced?

Failure to notify a breach that poses a high risk to the rights and freedoms of natural persons in the EU will result in fines of €10 million or 2% of annual global turnover, whichever is greater. Article 83(2)(h) provides that the manner in which the supervisory authority becomes aware of the breach will be a factor in any consideration of administrative fines imposed for any data breach. Organisations that do not notify the authorities of data breaches as appropriate are therefore likely to attract higher fines.

Although this does not answer the question of how authorities will ensure a breach is reported within 72 hours of its occurrence, the threat of significant fines facing any organisation found not to have complied with the notification obligation gives teeth to the requirement.

Relevant GDPR reference

- Article 31

Are we really expected to report every single breach, regardless of how minor they are?

Data breaches need only be reported to the supervisory authority when they are likely to pose a risk to the rights and freedoms of natural living persons.

Relevant GDPR references

- Article 33
- Article 34

Do you know if there will be a set of criteria to score incidents to decide what should be reported and what can be dealt with locally?

Any breach that could result in a risk to the rights and freedoms of natural persons will certainly have to be reported to the authorities and must be assessed on a case-by-case basis.

The ICO provides the following example: a supervisory authority would need to be notified about a loss of customer details where the breach leaves individuals open to identity theft. However, the loss or inappropriate alteration of a staff telephone list would not normally meet the threshold to trigger the notification requirement.

How long is an 'undue delay'?

According to the ICO website, "without undue delay" means 'as soon as possible' from the moment you become aware of the breach.

To whom do you report a breach?

A breach must be reported to your supervisory authority if there is a risk to the rights and freedoms of natural persons. When this risk is a high risk, you also need to notify the affected data subjects.

If you are a processor that experiences a breach, you will need to notify your controller without undue delay, who must notify the supervisory authority/data subjects as necessary.

Relevant GDPR references

- Article 33
- Article 34

Does a breach occur even if no data is taken, e.g. ransomware?

Yes. A data breach is not limited to the theft of data, but includes any unauthorised access that leads to the unlawful destruction, loss, alteration, disclosure of or access to the personal data.

Relevant GDPR reference

- Article 4

If we inadvertently give someone access to some data they shouldn't see, is that a breach, even if they have not seen or used the data?

Technically, this is a personal data breach, yes.

Is a breach of test data (randomised personal data) considered a breach that can be penalised?

If the test data includes data that would enable a natural person to be identified, then it is within the scope of the GDPR. If the security surrounding that data is breached, then it is a data breach. If the data is being used for testing without the data subject's permission, it is a data breach.

If the data is appropriately pseudonymised or encrypted, and the data necessary to link it to data subjects has not been breached, then it probably isn't a data breach.

DSARs

How long do we have to respond to a DSAR?

The timeframe for responding to DSARs under the GDPR is within one month of receipt, and two months in the case of complex requests, but the controller must still notify the data subject within one month of receipt if it intends to extend its response time to two months.

Relevant GDPR reference

* Article 12

Are there any exemptions for charging for DSARs?

You must provide a copy of the information free of charge.

However, you can charge a "reasonable fee" when a request is manifestly unfounded or excessive, particularly if it is repetitive.

You may also charge a reasonable fee to comply with requests for further copies of the same information. This does not mean that you can charge for all subsequent access requests.

The fee must be based on the administrative cost of providing the information.

Relevant GDPR reference

* Article 15

Should you redact third-party data that can identify that person or persons when responding to a DSAR?

In responding to a DSAR, you cannot provide information about persons who have not consented to their data being provided, so you would redact.

Relevant GDPR references

* Recital 63

- Article 12
- Article 13

Does the GDPR recognise "vexatious" subject access requests to control volumes?

Yes. The GDPR allows you to charge an administrative fee for unfounded, excessive or repetitive requests, as well as to refuse to respond to the request, but you must be able to demonstrate the vexatious nature of the request.

Relevant GDPR reference

- Article 12

Supervisory authorities and administrative fines

How do we register with the ICO?

You can easily register your organisation with the ICO via the ICO website. This will take you through the registration form and should take about 15 minutes to complete. Registration costs approximately £40–60 a year for most organisations.

How are the lower and higher fines defined?

There are two levels of GDPR fines:

1. 4% of global annual turnover for the preceding year or €20 million, whichever is greater, for violating the basic principles of data protection or for violating data subjects' rights.
   - To be imposed for infringement of GDPR Articles 5, 6, 7, 9, 12–22 and 44–49.

2. 2% of global annual turnover or €10 million, whichever is greater, for not properly filing and organising records, for not notifying the supervisory authority and data subject about a breach and for not conducting impact assessments.

   - To be imposed for infringement of GDPR Articles 8, 11, 25, 26, 27, 28, 29, 30, 31, 32, 33, 34, 35, 36, 37, 38, 39, 42 and 43.

GDPR Article 83(2) enumerates factors for consideration when determining fines for data breaches. These factors include but are not limited to:

- The nature, gravity and duration of the infringement;
- The number of data subjects affected and the level of damage suffered;
- Intentional or negligent character of the infringement;
- Mitigating action taken by controller/processor;
- Degree of responsibility of controller/processor, including technical and organisational measures implemented (including encryption) to safeguard the data;
- Relevant/previous infringements; and
- Categories of personal data affected by the breach, etc.

It is clear from the above that organisations that have taken appropriate measures to align their processes and procedures with the GDPR are likely to avoid the heavier fines. Precisely how the lower and higher fines will be determined will become clearer as the regulatory regime takes hold.

Relevant GDPR reference

- Article 83

What is involved in choosing the supervisory authority and what is the significance of doing so?

The GDPR identifies three 'types' of supervisory authorities:

1. Supervisory authority;
2. Supervisory authority concerned; and
3. Lead supervisory authority

The supervisory authority is an independent public authority designated by your Member State. Where more than one authority exists in a Member State, the Member State will designate which one is to act as the supervisory authority. The supervisory authority's powers are limited to the territory of its nation state.

A lead supervisory authority is required whenever cross-border processing is concerned. In most instances, the lead supervisory authority will be the supervisory authority for the main establishment of the controller/processor. (Main establishment is where purposes and means of processing are determined – typically this will be the controller/processor's HQ.)

In instances where cross-border processing involves both a controller and a processor, it is the supervisory authority of the controller's main establishment that acts as the lead supervisory authority. The processor's main supervisory authority then becomes the supervisory authority concerned.

It is important to understand who your supervisory authority and lead supervisory authority are as they play a significant role in enforcing and monitoring GDPR compliance.

Moreover, supervisory authorities are responsible for producing guidelines and codes of conduct, so they are a useful resource in achieving GDPR conformance.

Finally, given the 72-hour breach notification rules, having an awareness of and relationship with your supervisory authorities will be critical to ensuring all of your legal obligations under the GDPR are fulfilled.

Relevant GDPR references

* Recital 36
* Recitals 124–8
* Chapter VI
* Chapter VII

Who is the supervisory authority in the UK?

The ICO.

Do financial penalties also apply to charities or public-sector organisations?

Yes. Administrative fines apply to any controller or processor that processes personal or sensitive data and infringes the GDPR in relation to that data. Charities and public-sector organisations are no more exempt than any other (for one, it would undermine the consistency objective of the EU).

The ICO has historically had no qualms enforcing against charities, NHS trusts and public-sector organisations where it has found breaches of data protection law.

How should a multinational company determine which supervisory authority it falls under?

Supervisory authorities exist at the state level, so multinational organisations will have several associated supervisory authorities – one in each Member State. Multinational companies may choose a lead supervisory authority. In the event of a breach, investigation, etc., a lead supervisory authority will be nominated and the other supervisory authorities associated with the multinational organisation will become supervisory authorities concerned.

The lead supervisory authority is determined on the basis of where the main establishment of the controller/processor is located. (Main establishment is where the means and purposes of the processing are decided.) It is important to note, however, that the need for a lead supervisory authority is only triggered when the processing activity is cross-border.

Relevant GDPR reference

* Article 56

How is the GDPR enforced?

The regime is one of 'self-assure' with regulator intervention if something goes wrong.

Is the German court requirement that Facebook cannot gather data from WhatsApp an example of the sort of ruling that applies Europe-wide under the GDPR?

Indeed – that ruling was made on the basis that neither WhatsApp nor Facebook had established a legal basis for sharing the data. Under the GDPR, this would constitute an infringement of the first data processing principle.

Who assesses and certifies controllers and processors?

There is currently no certification framework for controllers or processors. ISO 27001 certification can provide evidence that appropriate technical and administrative controls are in place.

What is the appeals process against any judgement?

It depends on the legal process in the relevant Member State.

Does proof of compliance need to be submitted to any authority?

You don't ordinarily need to prove compliance to any authority. However, if you are breached, or a data subject brings an action against you, you will need to demonstrate that you were compliant as part of your defence.

Do GDPR fines apply to NHS organisations?

NHS organisations are just as much within the scope of the GDPR as any other organisation processing personal and health data. If an NHS organisation is found to violate the basic principles or data subjects' rights, and the supervisory authority judges it to be proportionate, dissuasive and effective, then yes, in theory, NHS organisations could see themselves susceptible to the higher fines.

The ICO has had no qualms handing out fines to NHS organisations and charities found to be in breach of previous data protection legislation. For example, Chelsea and Westminster Hospital NHS Foundation Trust received a fine of £180,000 for revealing the email addresses of more than 700 users of an HIV service.

Privacy policies and notices

Do you need to provide translations of privacy notices for speakers of other languages?

There are some cases – such as in Wales – where you are obliged by law to provide privacy notices in another language. However, the requirement for notices to be delivered in "in a concise, transparent, intelligible and easily accessible form, using clear and plain language" suggests that these notices should at least be provided in the language that your intended audience is most likely to understand.

Relevant GDPR reference

- Article 12

Do we need an individual privacy notice per processing activity, or per group of data subjects?

Per processing activity.

Privacy notices must be issued each time the purpose for which you are processing the data changes from the purpose for which it was originally collected. This ties in with the requirement that organisations may not use blanket consent for data subjects – their consent must be collected anew for each processing activity where the purpose, means or grounds for processing is different from the initial one, to ensure that processing remains transparent.

Relevant GDPR references

- Article 13

- Article 14

DPIAs and data mapping

In what scenarios do organisations need to conduct DPIAs?

A DPIA is not required in every circumstance, only where the data processing is likely to result in a high risk to the rights and freedoms of natural persons. Article 35(3)(a)–(c) specifies three circumstances in which a DPIA is specifically required, namely:

1. Where a systematic and extensive evaluation of personal aspects relating to natural persons based on automated processing takes place, and on which decisions are based that produce legal effects concerning or significantly affecting the natural person;
2. Where there is large-scale processing of special categories of data or personal data relating to criminal convictions and offences; or
3. Where processing involves a systematic monitoring of a publicly accessible area on a large scale.

Any processing that falls within the above scope must indeed be subject to a DPIA to ensure that appropriate measures are taken and controls implemented to safeguard any high-risk data. You are allowed to use a single assessment for similar processing operations that produce similarly high risks.

There are other conditions that may also require a DPIA. The EDPB and supervisory authorities maintain lists of the types of processing activity that should be subject to a DPIA. The

ICO also provides a code of practice that explains when DPIAs are required.

In determining the necessity of a DPIA, it is helpful to establish the volume, value and variety of data that your organisation processes. The higher the volume, value and variety of the personal data, the more likely that a DPIA is required.

Relevant GDPR references

- Article 9
- Article 10
- Article 35

Do you do a DPIA for the organisation, or for each 'pocket' of personal data, e.g. employee data, customer data?

You need to first conduct a data mapping exercise for the whole organisation in order to identify where and how you collect and process personal data. Once the mapping exercise is complete, you can then look at these activities to determine which might need a DPIA and, of those, which are similar enough to use the same DPIA.

Relevant GDPR reference

- Article 35

Are DPIAs the same as PIAs?

Yes, DPIAs are essentially the same.

Do you advise using a technology solution to build your data maps?

Yes. An effective tool will significantly streamline the project and help you keep track of GDPR compliance activities. We recommend Vigilant Software's Data Flow Mapping Tool:

www.vigilantsoftware.co.uk/topic/data-flow-mapping-tool

What constitutes "high risk to the rights and freedoms of natural persons"?

Activities that could lead to "discrimination, identity theft or fraud, financial loss" are given as clear examples of high risks (Recital 75 provides a more detailed list of the types of things that could be classified as high-risk activities). This means you need to identify what type of personal data you process and consider the ways in which its loss, corruption or theft could result in discrimination, identity theft, fraud or financial loss in order to determine where your high risks are.

Recital 76 recommends an objective risk assessment that takes into account the nature, scope, context and purpose of the processing.

The EDPB and supervisory authorities maintain publications that set out what constitutes high-risk processing.

Relevant GDPR references

- Recital 75
- Recital 76
- Recital 77
- Article 32
- Article 33

Who is responsible for the DPIA if we provide the processing based on a client's specification?

DPIAs and data flow mapping are the responsibility of the controller, who is identified on the basis of whether they control the means and purposes of the processing – unless otherwise agreed in the processing agreement.

Relevant GDPR references

- Article 24
- Article 26
- Article 27
- Article 35

Are DPIAs and data flow mapping required retrospectively for activities that pre-date the GDPR?

Your legacy data and systems need to comply just as much as any new data or systems that you acquire. A DPIA and a data flow mapping exercise are helpful ways to identify where your non-conformances lie. A retrospective DPIA will be mandatory if any of the existing systems pose a high risk to the rights and freedoms of natural persons.

Relevant GDPR references

- Recital 75
- Recital 76
- Recital 77
- Article 35

A DPIA is required whenever there are 'new systems'; what about changes to existing systems?

DPIAs are not only required when new systems are to be implemented, but rather whenever there is a high risk posed to the rights and freedoms of natural persons. This means you will need to assess whether a DPIA is necessary whenever there is a change to any of your personal data processing activities as well as when you develop new ones.

Relevant GDPR reference

*   Article 35

What is the difference between risk analysis and a DPIA?

A DPIA is one component of risk analysis. A risk is a combination of likelihood and impact. A DPIA deals with the impact aspect of that relationship and helps determine the required controls. It is also particularly focused on the impact to personal data and data subjects.

Cloud providers

If your personnel data for HR is in a Cloud provider's environment, who is responsible for declaring a breach?

The Cloud provider is responsible for reporting the breach to the controller without undue delay; the controller becomes responsible for reporting the breach to the supervisory authority and, if it poses a high risk to the rights and freedoms of natural persons, to the data subjects as well.

Relevant GDPR reference

*   Article 33

Is a Cloud provider classified as a data processor?

It depends entirely on the role of the Cloud provider. If a Cloud provider collects the data and determines the means and purposes of processing, then they will be treated as a controller under the GDPR.

How can Cloud SaaS providers comply with the GDPR?

Cloud SaaS providers are data processors under the GDPR and simply need to ensure that they meet all of the same requirements as other data processors.

The most notable requirements on processors concern accountability, engaging sub-processors, data security and data breach notification.

Relevant GDPR reference

- Article 28

Security

How do we need to approach pseudonymisation?

Pseudonymisation is the processing of personal data in such a way that the data can no longer be attributed to a specific data subject without the use of additional information.

To pseudonymise a data set, the additional information must be kept separately, and be subject to technical and organisational measures to ensure non-attribution to an identified or identifiable person.

You should start by identifying which data you want to pseudonymise, and, within that data set, determine which parts of the data qualify as directly identifying data. Hold this data separately and securely from the processed data in order to ensure non-attribution.

Organisations should keep an eye on their supervisory authorities for further guidance in this area.

Relevant GDPR references

- Article 25
- Article 32

Is it better to store personal data in the Cloud or on a local server/file share?

That's a decision for each individual organisation to make.

Third parties

If we used a payroll company that came onto our site and used our systems to run payroll and all data stayed on our systems, would this be classed as a third person?

The payroll company would be treated as a processor. It is possible to be both a third party and a processor.

What are your responsibilities for third-party data traversing your network?

You are processing personal data; you may only do this in accordance with a contract with the data controller. You have to secure the data and generally comply with your contractual terms.

Can we give personal data to auditors?

Personal data may only be shared with third parties under the provisions of the GDPR; this includes auditors.

Derogations

What is the latest position on national derogations?

Each Member State is permitted to restrict individual rights and transparency obligations with legislation, provided that the restriction respects fundamental rights and freedoms, is necessary and proportionate, and acts a safeguard to one of the conditions provided in Article 23(a)–(i). These restrictions must contain the provisions listed in Article 23(2)(a)–(h) in order to be valid.

Relevant GDPR reference

* Article 23

Public bodies

How does the GDPR apply to public-sector organisations?

The GDPR has a number of implications for public-sector bodies:

* They must appoint a DPO.
* The "legitimate interests" grounds for processing is not available to public bodies. An alternative basis for processing will need to be established (e.g. processing is necessary for performance of a task in the public interest).
* Public sector bodies no longer need to register details of data-processing activities, but detailed internal records will need to be kept instead.
* More information must be included in privacy notices than was required under the DPA 1998.

- DPIAs are likely to be necessary in many cases.

If I instruct the DVLA not to supply my personal data to companies such as parking companies, etc. do they have to comply?

No – they are a public body and the rules are different for them. They can and must share personal data in line with any statutory obligations imposed on them.

Relevant GDPR reference

- Article 6

Employment

Do we need to issue new contracts to staff or can we supply a letter amendment?

A letter amendment will probably suffice, but you should confirm with your legal advisors.

Relevant GDPR reference

- Article 88

What do we need to include in employees' contracts?

You will need to provide them with more detailed information about the purposes and means of the processing of their personal data, explained in clear and intelligible terms. This will most likely need to be included in all relevant employment contracts in order to demonstrate compliance, but you should confirm with your legal advisors.

Relevant GDPR reference

- Article 88

IT GOVERNANCE RESOURCES

ITGP is part of GRC International Group, which offers a comprehensive range of complementary products and services to help organisations meet their objectives.

IT Governance is at the forefront of helping organisations globally address the challenges of General Data Protection Regulation (GDPR) compliance. Our international websites are one-stop shops, providing information, advice, guidance, books, tools, training and consultancy.

For information on the GDPR and our compliance solutions, visit:

UK: *www.itgovernance.co.uk*

Europe: *www.itgovernance.eu*

Americas: *www.itgovernanceusa.com*

Asia-Pacific: *www.itgovernance.asia*

Publishing Services

With books and tools covering all IT governance, risk and compliance frameworks, we are the publisher of choice for authors and distributors alike, producing unique and practical publications of the highest quality, in the latest formats available, which readers will find invaluable.

www.itgovernancepublishing.co.uk is the website dedicated to ITGP. Other titles published by ITGP that may be of interest include:

- *Information Security Risk Management for ISO 27001 / ISO 27002, Third edition,* by Alan Calder and Steve G Watkins, *www.itgovernancepublishing.co.uk/product/informatio n-security-risk-management-for-iso-27001-iso-27002-third-edition*
- *ISO 27001 Controls – A guide to implementing and auditing* by Bridget Kenyon, *www.itgovernancepublishing.co.uk/product/iso-27001-controls-a-guide-to-implementing-and-auditing*
- *EU GDPR & EU-U.S. Privacy Shield – A pocket guide, Second edition* by Alan Calder, *www.itgovernancepublishing.co.uk/product/eu-gdpr-eu-u-s-privacy-shield-a-pocket-guide-second-edition*

We also offer a range of toolkits that provide organisations with comprehensive and customisable documents to help create the specific documentation required to properly implement management systems or standards. Written by experienced practitioners and based on the latest best practice, ITGP toolkits can save months of work for organisations working towards compliance with a given standard.

Designed and developed by expert GDPR practitioners, and used by hundreds of organisations worldwide, the bestselling GDPR Documentation Toolkit provides all the templates, worksheets and policies required to comply with documented aspects of the Regulation. The EU GDPR Documentation Toolkit provides all the critical documents any organisation needs to ensure compliance with the new Regulation, including professional guidance on GDPR compliance obligations and personal information best practices; you are able to put in place the necessary controls having adequately identified risks to personal data; Data Protection Impact

Assessments, Incident Response and Breach Reporting. You can see the full list of contents here: *www.itgovernance.co.uk/shop/product/gdpr-toolkit*.

Please visit *www.itgovernance.co.uk/shop/category/itgp-toolkits* to see our full range of toolkits.

Books and tools published by IT Governance Publishing (ITGP) are available from all business booksellers and the following websites:

www.itgovernance.eu   *www.itgovernanceusa.com*

www.itgovernance.co.uk   *www.itgovernance.asia*

Certified GDPR training and staff awareness

IT Governance is the leading global provider of GDPR training courses.

Our GDPR Foundation and Practitioner training courses offer a structured learning path to equip attendees with the specialist knowledge and skills needed to deliver GDPR compliance and fulfil the role of a data protection officer (DPO).

All courses are available in classroom, Live Online and distance learning formats, and offer successful attendees ISO 17024-accredited qualifications from IBITGQ.

- **Certified EU General Data Protection Regulation Foundation**
  This Foundation-level course provides a complete introduction to the GDPR, and an overview of the key implementation and compliance activities.
- **Certified EU General Data Protection Regulation Practitioner**

This advanced-level course gives attendees a practical understanding of the methods and tools for implementing and managing an effective compliance framework, and how to fulfil the role of a DPO.

- **Certified EU General Data Protection Regulation (GDPR) Foundation and Practitioner Combination**
  Save 15% when booking this combined training package.
- **GDPR Staff Awareness E-learning Course**
  Educate your staff on the key requirements of the GDPR with our simple-to-use interactive modular e-learning programme. Multi-user licences, customisation and hosting options are available.

To learn more about our GDPR training courses and to book, visit:

UK: *www.itgovernance.co.uk/shop/category/data-protection-eu-gdpr-training-courses*

Europe: *www.itgovernance.eu/shop/category/data-protection-eu-gdpr-training-courses*

Americas: *www.itgovernanceusa.com/shop/category/data-protection-eu-gdpr-training-courses*

Professional services and consultancy

As a compliance specialist, IT Governance has been helping organisations implement data protection programmes for more than ten years. Our specialist consultancy team has a wide range of data protection expertise and can support your GDPR project from start to finish. We offer a wide range of services to help you meet your GDPR compliance objectives, including support with:

- GDPR gap analysis
- Data flow audit
- Data protection impact assessment (DPIA)
- Incidence management and breach reporting
- Establishing a personal information management system (PIMS)
- Implementing an ISO 27001-compliant information security management system (ISMS)
- DPO as a service
- Cyber security health check
- Penetration testing

For more information, visit:

UK: *www.itgovernance.co.uk/dpa-compliance-consultancy*

Europe: *www.itgovernance.eu/eu-gdpr-consultancy*

Americas: *www.itgovernanceusa.com/gdpr-compliance-consultancy*

Asia-Pacific: *www.itgovernance.asia/gdpr-compliance-consultancy*

Newsletter

You can stay up to date with the latest developments across the whole spectrum of IT governance, including data protection and the GDPR, risk management, information security, ITIL® and IT service management, project governance, compliance and so much more, by subscribing to our newsletter.

Simply visit our subscription centre and select your preferences:

UK: *www.itgovernance.co.uk/weekly-round-up*

IT Governance resources

Europe: *www.itgovernance.eu/en-ie/daily-sentinel-ie*

Americas: *www.itgovernanceusa.com/weekly-round-up*

Asia-Pacific: *www.itgovernance.asia/daily-sentinel*